# Management for Professionals

The Springer series "Management for Professionals" comprises high-level business and management books for executives, MBA students, and practice-oriented business researchers. The topics cover all themes relevant to businesses and the business ecosystem. The authors are experienced business professionals and renowned professors who combine scientific backgrounds, best practices, and entrepreneurial vision to provide powerful insights into achieving business excellence.

The Series is SCOPUS-indexed.

Gerhard Köhler • Werner Roth •
Achim Schmidtmann

# Adaptive IT Service Tendering

## The Path to Agile and Effective IT Outsourcing

Springer

Gerhard Köhler
Fsas Technologies GmbH
Frankfurt, Hessen, Germany

Werner Roth
NTT DATA
Detmold, Nordrhein-Westfalen, Germany

Achim Schmidtmann
Fachbereich Wirtschaft
Hochschule Bielefeld
Bielefeld, Nordrhein-Westfalen, Germany

ISSN 2192-8096 ISSN 2192-810X (electronic)
Management for Professionals
ISBN 978-3-658-49725-5 ISBN 978-3-658-49726-2 (eBook)
https://doi.org/10.1007/978-3-658-49726-2

English Translation of the German language edition: “Adaptive IT-Service-Ausschreibung”, Köhler, G., Roth, W., Schmidtmann, A., Springer Fachmedien Wiesbaden, 2024, 978-3-658-45535-4



This Springer Gabler imprint is published by the registered company Springer Fachmedien Wiesbaden GmbH, part of Springer Nature.
The registered company address is: Abraham-Lincoln-Str. 46, 65189 Wiesbaden, Germany

# Foreword

Services are not products because, by their very nature, they are always delivered by (other) people and used for specific situations. The urge for standardisation and measurability is strong, resulting in extensive—but often rigid—contracts, IT service level agreements and penalties that get in the way of truly demand-driven services.

To some extent, this is logical. Stereotypically, sellers and buyers are initially sceptical or even suspicious of each other. One wants high performance at a low price. The other wants the exact opposite.

But when you zoom in on the situation, it becomes clear that they need each other.

Collaboration is therefore the way to create a long-term solution for both sides that does not overburden the supplier and provides the customer with exactly the services he needs today and in the future.

But how does it work?

Fortunately, the authors of this book have set out to do just that and to develop a new, comprehensive framework that does justice to the changed, highly complex conditions of the VUCA and BANI world. It was exciting to see how the pain of doing the same thing over and over again, with the same often unsatisfactory results and associated problems, gave rise to the desire to create something new. Something that would provide better answers than what was available.

The size of the search space that Werner and his team opened up at that time can be seen from the fact that viadee appeared in this search space. As an IT consultancy, we had little or no experience with managed services, but we had a lot of experience with agile methods and sales approaches in large tenders and negotiations with our customers.

Our contribution was limited to targeted workshops and impulses. But they have obviously led to a new basic idea in the customer–supplier relationship. Namely, that of continuous collaboration from the first contact to the end of a contractual relationship.

This paradigm shift, which has been standard in agile software development for many years, was and is groundbreaking for business development.

This book shows how to do it in a very practical way. A detailed guide that describes the paradigm shift in terms of attitude, communication and organisation and shows how the transition to a new, demand-driven collaboration can work while maintaining a high level of reliability. It is called Adaptive Managed Services.

Enjoy reading!

viadee IT-Unternehmensberatung AG
Münster, Germany
Volker Oshege

# Preface

In our search for efficiency, we have found cooperation and empowerment of people.

The authors' common interest in IT service management was the starting point. Our cooperation between university and practice began several years ago. We established a link between the university, the IT service provider and the customer in order to familiarise the students with the practice and to learn from each other. In particular, this connection through teaching has intensively promoted cooperation between customer representatives, students and us.

The foundations for this book were laid about eight years ago when we set out to find new methods to make our work more efficient. We started with the naive idea that not much would change at the core of our work. We thought that we would gain structure with new methods, eliminate superfluous work steps and thus take better account of our organisation's key figures. We quickly shed this initial naivety when we realised what a new culture we had created together.

In previous years, we had seen so many impressive examples of customers and organisations that had used their structured methods to achieve savings over many years that went far beyond a KPI such as minus 8% manufacturing costs per year. These organisations had also, after a systematic analysis of their processes and structures, and with a great deal of perseverance, removed obstacles that most organisations simply dismissed with phrases such as "this is deeply rooted, you can't do anything about it".

Over the years, we met with these impressive people again and again, asking them curiously about the latest developments. It quickly became clear that these were not just any old stories of questionable reality. These stories were instructive, they could be explained in detail, and the successes kept coming year after year. During this time we met many new fellow practitioners who gave us friendly information late in the evenings and subsequently helped us to develop the approach presented here.

However, it was still a long way from the enthusiasm to do the same to the development of an adaptive managed services approach. After all, these organisations had successfully transferred knowledge of Lean-Agile methods from production environments or software development methods to an IT operation. Transferring a set of methods that was developed in a completely different world to a new environment is a major task that is not always crowned with success. Some methods are very successful in their original environment, but have never really been transferred to other areas.

Lean originates primarily from automotive production, the "Toyota Production System". Lean is based on the principles of a lean organisation and has less of a technical or production automation origin. The transfer of lean methods from production to the processes of an IT organisation is a major achievement. Many agile methods, such as Scrum, are not native to the IT service world. IT services function in a fundamentally different way than the creation of software products. But here, too, there were approaches in the organisations mentioned above. Our project therefore seemed feasible; after all, we could ask our masterminds for advice if we got stuck with a transfer.

On the other hand, we have also seen numerous traditional tenders that try to regulate every detail and penalise every deviation. In the end, they led to a difficult relationship between customers and service providers. As a result, customers and end users did not get what they needed to do their jobs. And the service provider was also unhappy because it was providing a costly bespoke service and was constantly being asked for additional demands.

Some of these customers and service providers repeated this mistake or approach in subsequent tenders. Unfortunately with the very human idea of simply doubling the severity of their measures for a control system that does not work. This means even more details in the requirements, even more and stricter service level targets and usually also higher contractual penalties. It often takes three tendering cycles before such undesirable developments are recognised, and by the time this happens, more than nine years have usually passed.

The realisation that tenders can end in these extremes prompted us to investigate the reasons behind this. We researched the causes, obtained documentation of failed tenders and used a lean methodology to ask customers what was important to them in the pre-sales process. At this point, we would like to emphasise that the majority of tenders with subsequent delivery are entirely satisfactory. The problematic and very good tenders only make up a small proportion. This probably corresponds to a normal distribution with a few problematic tenders, a few perfect tenders and a large midfield of tenders that are okay but not particularly good (Fig. 1).

The search for the most promising methodology for a tender was given a second important stimulus. Namely, the ability to adapt to ever more rapidly changing business requirements, as this is problematic in many cases. While changes in purchasing volumes are often well regulated, most customers are not able to realise new opportunities for high efficiency gains by adapting the service in the current contract.

Changes in the core business and the need to respond to ever faster competition pose an increasing risk for many companies. The number of cases in which a customer turns to its IT service provider because the company has run into serious difficulties has increased in recent years. It is true that a solution has always been found in business relationships based on partnership. Nevertheless, we believe that, in addition to a good relationship of trust, it is important to have the necessary mechanisms in place to ensure that IT adds value to the business.

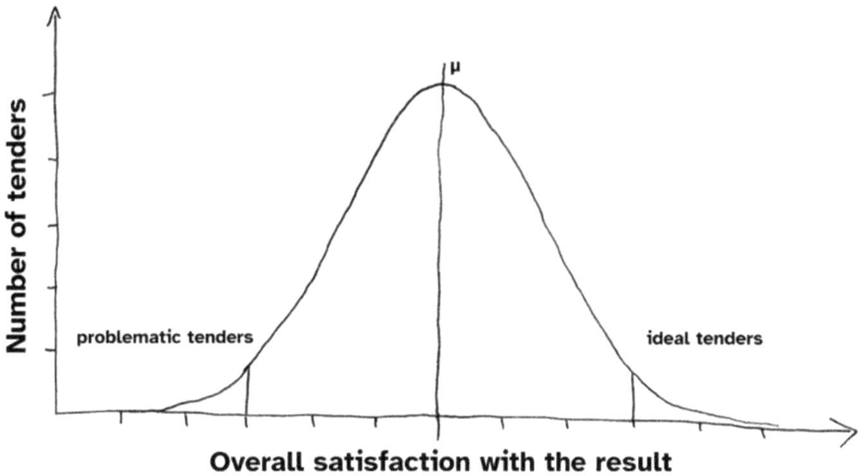


**Fig. 1** Normal distribution of the value of tenders

The collection of methods presented in this book is the result of a great collaboration with many dedicated colleagues, customers, partners, trainers and coaches. It was a demanding process that presented us with numerous challenges. We are all more grateful that we have always been supported and advised by these inspiring people. We got stranded again and again along the way, got up, knocked the sand out of our trouser legs and kept walking towards our goal. In addition to a strong stamina, good friends are part of such an endeavour, who helped us get back on our feet again and again.

This is also an initial piece of advice to you, the readers of this book. Don't expect your first ideas to take off immediately. Sometimes it takes a long time to develop ideas into working versions. Use existing knowledge in your company, seek advice from your network and consult specialists in critical phases.

We are delighted to be able to present these 8 years of development in the form of this book. We hope that you will be able to take many ideas back to your company and rely on Adaptive Managed Services in the future.

**Keywords** Adaptive Tendering, IT Service Management, Agile Methods, Outsourcing, Business Value

Hessen/Nordrhein-Westfalen, Germany

Gerhard Köhler
Werner Roth
Achim Schmidtmann

# Acknowledgements

Writing a book alongside your job, research and teaching is not a matter of course. It was important to us to present our experiences, findings and research work of recent years to a wide audience in a compact book. We hope that it will support you in your daily work and provide a basis for further developments and research.

Our first thanks therefore go to our families, who have always supported and encouraged this project. We would like to thank all our supporters, both on the customer side and in our organisations, for their commitment. It's great when people believe in ideas and are committed to them. When they share knowledge, talk about mistakes, give freedom and or simply do it. This book was written with this in mind.

**Competing Interests** The methods and guidance provided in this book have been developed by the authors in the course of their daily work. The authors have received no direct support from any organisation for the work presented, apart from permission to develop these concepts during, but mostly outside, working hours. Gerhard Köhler and Werner Roth currently work as consultants for IT services in the IT industry. Achim Schmidtmann is a university professor and teaches on the subject.

# About this Book

This book is a comprehensive work that addresses the tendering process for and management of IT services. It is divided into a number of parts, each of which contains didactic elements to make the subject accessible to people new to the field.

The book begins with an introduction and basics that explain the importance of IT services and the challenges involved in calling for tenders. This is followed by an introduction to the topic of tendering for IT services, which covers the basics of IT services and tendering in the IT sector.

The body of the book describes the classic methods and processes of IT tendering, including the different types of requests such as RFI, RFQ and RFP. Numerous figures and tables illustrate complex methods, processes and structures.

The next section is a comparative presentation of Adaptive Tendering. Here, a new model is presented that focuses on business value and emphasises flexibility and adaptability to changing business needs. Case studies and practical reports provide insights into real-life scenarios and show how the methods and frameworks described can be applied in practice.

Next is a chapter with practical examples of how the approach can be introduced and tested in typical organisations. Here, the authors share their experiences of how to avoid the first pitfalls.

The final part of the book summarises the most important findings and provides an outlook on future developments in the field of IT service tenders.

Especially for beginners, there are summaries at the end of each chapter that emphasise the most important points once again and help the reader to internalise what they have read. A detailed glossary at the end of the book explains important terms and concepts used in the text.

The teaching elements are designed to actively engage the reader in the learning process and promote understanding of complex topics. Illustrations and tables provide visual support, while case studies and practical reports link theory to practice. Summaries help to consolidate learning and the glossary serves as a reference for key terms.

This approach ensures that the book not only conveys theoretical knowledge, but also provides practical guidance and examples that can be applied in the real world. The combination of visual, textual and practical elements makes the book a valuable tool for students and practitioners in the field of IT service tendering.

# Contents

# About the Authors

**Gerhard Köhler** is Principal Consultant IT Service Management at Fsas Technologies GmbH with decades of experience in the areas of outsourcing and outtasking on the part of the transferring customer, on the part of the receiving provider, as well as from the perspective of an employee affected by outsourcing. As a Pre-Sales Specialist, he developed solutions and offers in the Managed Workplace area for his customers and also implemented these as a Transition Manager. As Service Delivery Manager, he was responsible for the operation of managed services in complex and international projects for his clients, and as a consultant in the private and public sector as well as for sector clients, he supported his clients in tenders, from preparation to publication and implementation.

**Werner Roth** is Senior Manager GTM Practice Solutions at NTT DATA with many years of experience in IT tenders. In the course of his career, he has worked both on the customer side and as a programme manager and pre-sales consultant for various IT service providers. As head of a pre-sales department, he and his team of consultants have developed a powerful New Work concept based on diversity, lean and agile approaches. Lean-agile methods for sales organisations, consulting teams and IT service providers are his passion.

**Achim Schmidtmann** has been Professor of Information Systems, in particular Business Information Systems/ERP Systems at the Faculty of Business at Bielefeld University of Applied Sciences since 2017. From 2006-2017, he was Professor of Information Systems at the Department of Computer Science at Dortmund University of Applied Sciences and Arts. His teaching and research activities focus on IT service management, information security management and business information systems. For over 15 years, he has successfully taught about IT services and IT sourcing in Bachelor's and Master's courses and regularly carries out practice-oriented projects in cooperation with companies.

# List of Figures

# List of Tables

# 1 Various Causes for Adaptive Tenders

What role does an IT organisation play in a company? Does it act as an internal service provider, delivering certain industry standards in the most cost-effective way possible? Does IT management have a say in strategic decisions for the company's core business? Or is IT even one of the most important drivers of innovation for the company's core business?

Many of our customers can look back on over a hundred years of company history. The first points of contact with IT were usually either in the 1970s with mainframe computers or, for smaller requirements, in the 1980s with the first personal computers in accounting. The beginnings of IT outsourcing also emerged around this time. As part of the division of labour and specialisation, external IT service providers began taking over certain IT tasks, such as hardware maintenance.

Therefore, it is not surprising that IT has had to evolve from a purely supportive role to becoming part of the core business at different speeds and stages of development. The trend remains unbroken. The role of IT is becoming increasingly important. Even if the core business involves a physical, high-tech product, IT now plays a key role in all processes and must help to increase efficiency.

This development is also reflected in IT outsourcing. Initially, it involved clearly defined divisions of labour, a high degree of industrialisation to save costs through economies of scale, and the full outsourcing of IT (full ITO). One of the main drivers was that it allowed companies to focus more effectively on their core business. In the area of applications and data, it also made data centre capacities more easily accessible and scalable.

In the context of advancing digitalisation, there is an increasing role for access to expertise and skilled workers, better support for business requirements and outsourcing as opportunities for change. There can be many reasons for a necessary transformation in our environment. For example, the current model may be based on outdated technologies, or there may be interdependencies within the organisation and cost centres that are almost impossible to resolve. Some customers solve this by



G. Köhler et al., *Adaptive IT Service Tendering*, Management for Professionals,
https://doi.org/10.1007/978-3-658-49726-2_1

outsourcing these areas completely, including a new cost structure for internal customers.

The primary focus here will be on the organisation's ongoing development. This could be a structural change, a shortage of skilled labour, or a management response to tough external competition. The focus will always be on a development that makes a substantial contribution to the organisation's future.

Outsourcing IT services is a proven method for companies to optimise their IT-related business processes and save resources and costs. However, tendering IT outsourcing projects is critical and time-consuming, as the aim is to select a provider that best fulfils the company's needs while offering an appropriate price–performance ratio. In many cases, the provider should also be able to deliver this service sustainably and on a long-term basis.

The search for a suitable IT service provider and, conversely, the search for a suitable customer for an IT service provider is a complex and complicated endeavour. There are tried-and-tested procedures, recommendations and tips for this in the traditional tendering processes, which we have trained and tested with our customers over the years. Although we have been on the customer side ourselves and have purchased IT services, we have gained most of our experience as technical pre-sales consultants.

There are good concepts and consulting services for a traditional tendering process, but we were always missing crucial elements for optimising value creation for the client. This was particularly evident in the discussions when it came to potential improvements compared to the previous service. These improvement approaches were often not even part of the tender, although they would have been valuable features for the client's business. This was rarely due to inadequate preparation of the tender, but mostly because these points were aimed at future collaborations whose specific requirements could only be formulated in a few years' time.

**Important** Some traditional tenders include chapters that set out specific requirements for future technologies. These requirements may relate to basic services or the provision of interfaces for future extensions. If these are possible future scenarios and not part of a known project that will be implemented in the following year, then, in our experience, this is a waste of budget. Unfortunately, in our professional lives, we have not yet seen a corresponding technical description of the future that actually materialises.

This does not refer to sections in the tender price sheet asking about the costs of specialists in various roles or possible additional services. Price enquiries are a useful tool. They are especially valuable for planning future projects more effectively. What is meant here, by contrast, is the creation or provision of services that are never utilised in this form. The worst-case scenario is when the IT service provider provides a service element that has no business value for the customer.

With traditional tenders, it is difficult to judge whether the customer's business is receiving optimal support. It is vital to grasp the needs and business of all the parties involved. This allows you to assess whether anything is missing, if anything inappropriate has been requested, or if there is any unused value potential. The customer should also have a clear understanding of the provider's business value. Which services can be provided particularly efficiently? Which gaps in the customer's IT can easily be closed? And how can development keep pace with the future of the business?

**Important** As a customer, you are under no obligation to understand your provider's business values, but doing so can give you an idea of the kind of relationship you can expect. A provider that focuses on maximum industrialisation, automation, AI integration and 100% shared services will deliver his type of service at the lowest price. Conversely, a provider that fosters innovation in the transformation of services might be a perfect fit for your current service setup and save costs in the long run. However, its current price is higher.

We suggest understanding a provider's value streams to a certain extent. Market intelligence and well-informed consultants can help you gain an insight that goes beyond marketing brochures. Use this information to speak with provider representatives and reference customers to get a full sense of the provider. A service that meets your needs and a low-maintenance operational relationship are highly desirable and should be the second selection criteria after price.

These and similar questions are dealt with in a traditional tendering process, but the corresponding options are limited. From the initial market enquiry (request for information) to the invitation to tender (request for proposal) and the various bidding rounds, communication is rather limited. On the one hand, it would be a challenge to organise large discussion rounds with all participants and providers; on the other hand, these procedures are sequential. In this waterfall process, it is not possible to integrate major changes without taking a step backwards and losing time. Changes in the scope of services, strengths, but also the specific needs of the various providers cannot be integrated to a satisfactory degree.

The procedure is usually limited to individual sequential communication points with the internal stakeholders and subsequently with the various IT service providers. From the perspective of such a tendering process, the control and associated limitation of communication and the restriction of alternatives is definitely a sensible measure. These procedures often lead to the selection of a competent future partner. However, the design of these traditional tendering procedures harbours a number of risks, which are discussed below.

**Warning** If communication is limited, errors will be detected later. In a tender, an error could mean that the organisation gains more insight by comparing two solution architectures. If this happens during a traditional tender process, it will be as if they have to start nearly from scratch. This is often complicated because of the timeline and sunk costs. In some cases, attempts will be made to conceal the error. According to the rule of ten, the cost of an undetected error increases by a factor of ten at each stage of the value creation process, so this is a very bad idea. Adaptive tendering offers an alternative approach to dealing with this issue.

Instead, we're going to show you a new adaptive model that approaches business value differently. We developed this model in recent years to address some of the issues with established tendering procedures. We would like to see this model used as an alternative to traditional tendering procedures. Adaptive models also work well in hybrid setups within existing organisations, policies, and procedures. The advantages and disadvantages of this model can thus be adapted to your individual needs.

Unless the supplier and customer have known each other for a long time and are able to assess each other, it is worth noting that the point at which trust is established is completely different in an adaptive model than in a traditional tender. In traditional tenders, this occurs during the tender presentation, i.e. when you first meet to discuss the solution. This is usually shortly after all bidders have responded to the tender in writing, providing a technical concept and an initial price.

The participating providers and customers meet at the offer presentation and conduct a kind of "speed dating". The term "speed dating" describes the situation quite well, at least for all IT service providers that are still unknown. Figures, data, and facts about the provider and its solution tailored to the tender are known in advance. Based on the written offers, the client now invites some of them to an exchange. Depending on the size of the tender, three or more candidates can be presented to the client per day.

The respective provider sits in front of the customer and presents slides showing the services offered and references from satisfied customers. The IT service provider usually has relevant experience of providing services. The presentation is elaborately designed to suit the occasion, usually based on the IT service provider's standards, which are more or less well adapted to the subject of the tender and the customer. At this point, specific questions and answers are used to determine whether the solution fits the tender or, more precisely, the customer's situation.

It is precisely at this stage that trust between the customer and the IT service provider is established, at least according to feedback from our customers and colleagues. From this point onwards, the final round of negotiations takes place with a small number of IT service providers, usually two. The solutions have been finalised, the prices have been refined and the contract negotiations can begin.

When tendering for services, a high level of trust must therefore be built up in the presentation of the offer. Even though many customers and providers refer to services as building blocks, such a concept does not exist. Services must be individually customised to the customer's situation. Customers have an evolved IT system that is customised to their needs. IT service management processes differ at the latest at the procedural or process level. The tool landscape used is different. The maturity level of customer organisations and their processes also varies widely.

We also worked with students on a master's course in Business Informatics at Hochschule Bielefeld—University of Applied Sciences on these industry-standard tendering procedures, the methods used and real customer examples. It was precisely at this point, when the customer and provider have established trust, that the students asked whether it would not be a good idea to start with a very small service so that both sides can check whether the collaboration, the level of maturity and the culture fit together. It is actually a good idea to start small with the services. However, as the majority of customers take the risk, we had to answer this question in the negative. In our experience, it is more common to tender for complete sets of services over 3 or 5 years.

**An Excursus on IT Tendering in the Master's Course**

It is always an exciting endeavour to bring the tendering process closer to the students, as in most cases they have an unbiased viewpoint that corresponds to their generation. Questions are regularly asked that do not come up in conversations and discussions with people who are familiar with the process or at least partially familiar with it.

It is clear that the students have gained initial experience of agile practices in both teaching and their practical work, and they are open to the topic. In most cases, they are more familiar with a prototypical approach (from software development) than with the strict separation of phases in line with development according to the waterfall model.

The aim of the course is to brief students to the various roles in the tendering process with their different requirements and objectives through close cooperation with experts from the field. This should make the divergent perspectives and their effects on the individual process steps clear and comprehensible. They learn to assess certain situations and correctly categorise the reactions of those involved. In this way, students gain important practical experience and can then adapt better and more quickly to the various stakeholders in the process.

The integration of lean principles into the master's course offers students additional benefits. By applying lean principles, students learn to recognise and eliminate waste, which is of great value in their future careers. They develop a deeper understanding of efficiency and process optimisation, both of which are in demand in almost all industries. In addition, the course enables students to better understand and apply agile practices, which further strengthens their adaptability and potential in the modern workplace.

Working closely with experts from the field provides students with a realistic insight into the world of work and helps them to translate their theoretical knowledge into practical skills. Ultimately, the course prepares students not only for the challenges of the tendering process, but also for the demands and dynamics of modern working life in general.

But now back to the practical side of the tender and the next steps after the tender presentation.

Very few customers organise a so-called proof of concept (PoC) of the services to be provided by the provider. This involves the IT service provider demonstrating in a kind of test environment that the service offered can fulfil the customer's requirements. However, such PoCs usually only cover certain technical sub-areas, have limited interfaces and are only tested by a few of the customer's users. We consider the informative value of a PoC to be limited, at least when it comes to predicting the success of a collaboration. After all, important technical aspects of a transformation can be clarified in a PoC and the customer and provider teams get to know each other before the contract is signed.

Proof-of-concepts are a tried-and- tested means of tendering for hardware and software. The subject of such tenders tends to have a product character. The necessary requirements for hardware or software, such as required computing power, network throughput or transactions per second, can certainly be tested in a PoC. Again, this is limited by restrictions regarding integration, interfaces, and real data. The differences between services and products are an important point that we will return to repeatedly. Services have significantly different characteristics to products. This is also evident when using agile methods, which cannot simply be transferred from the world of software development, i.e. the product world, to the world of managed services.

A common practice among customers when testing a managed service is to use a customer reference in advance from an existing customer of the provider who uses a similar service in order to reach a compromise. These references can range from documented marketing material and discussions with reference customers to visits to a provider's delivery centre. In our experience however, references have rather limited value in terms of providing information for the subsequent customer–provider relationship.

Often, customers require references from the same sector, of a similar size, and offering a comparable range of services. These are conditions that only very large IT service providers can fulfil. In some sectors, it is also not possible to provide references for reasons of confidentiality. But even in cases where a reference request can be fulfilled, the reference is a satisfied customer of the provider. Despite any difficult situations that may have arisen during the partnership being overcome, the overall impression is positive.

If the maturity level of the requesting customer and the maturity level of the reference customer differ greatly, the insights gained from the reference are more misleading than informative. Other components of the architecture, such as service level targets, are also often not comparable. In our view, a reference for managed services is meaningful if there are doubts as to whether the IT service provider already provides this type of service. For example, because they are very new or because the service provider has a different focus. Reference visits are a great way to get to know the people who'll be involved on both the customer and provider side.

Traditional tendering can also be problematic from other points of view. There is a saying in the industry that "you can't outsource problems". This means that the tendered service is currently not working well for the customer. The spectrum of such problems ranges from social challenges to procedural deficiencies or, in rarer cases, problematic technology. In the best-case scenario, this can mean that the problem must first be eliminated as part of a transformation process before the service can be taken over.

In the worst case, the problem is not communicated in advance. Here, too, there are a variety of reasons, and this does not always have to be for negative reasons. It may be that the customer's management is not sufficiently informed, or that the prevailing opinion is that such problems are typical in the market and that the provider will get them under control. Another possibility is that the cause lies with the current provider, although it is more complex than that.

In fact, it is often difficult for the customer organisation to assess which challenges will cause problems for the IT provider later on, and which can actually be solved during the transition and transformation phase. A clear sign is when a service does not function consistently, even before the tender is issued. The same applies if a service can only be maintained by deploying personnel who have not been designated for this purpose. In such cases, it is clear that the service must first be made operational. In practice, there is also the scenario where a service is only provided by one employee. In this case, it is not a service in the true sense of the word, but it can be developed into a managed service.

Providers often hear from their customers how smoothly everything works and how mature the documentation and processes are. They are often presented with particularly well-documented processes. Occasionally, these are even further optimised after internal weaknesses have been uncovered during the tendering process. In the case of large client organisations, it can also happen that special company functions present hundreds of pages of operating manuals that are described in great detail. However, hardly anyone in the company knows about or uses these manuals when asked during due diligence.

**Important** Due diligence is usually carried out before a binding offer is submitted. In this phase, the service provider assesses the subject matter of the order and the risks. The customer usually uses this phase to visit a delivery centre or a reference project. A brief explanation of this and other terms can be found in the glossary (Chap. 8).

In practice, providers often find that there is little or no documentation or processes in place at the start of the transition. If the documentation was created separately from the actual operation, there will be little usable documentation. Such situations leave a lot of room for interpretation and require customised procedures, often involving negotiation of expectations. In our experience, it is not possible to adequately include such surprises in contracts.

Such a challenge begins with the different expectations of the two parties, the customer and the service provider. Even if the contract attempts to use clauses to make the service provider responsible or liable for all defects and gaps, in extreme cases the service provider may pull out in the event of massive defects on the customer side. Conversely, if prices for the rectification of processes and documentation have been agreed in "Time and Material" (T&M) clauses, an exaggeration of this clause can massively annoy the customer. This is particularly the case if, from the customer's point of view, the order performance was not optimised.

Therefore, there is a further risk here for both sides. It hardly seems possible to contain these risks with absolute effectiveness. The assessment of experts on both sides and an intensive and open dialogue can certainly help here. However, there is usually not enough time to work out the opportunities and risks with feedback on the tender.

Certain risks only materialise in the transition phase if certain services of a customer have to be outsourced because there is simply a lack of personnel. For example, this may involve services that were set up as a pilot project by an already fully utilised team and are now in high demand. However, it may also be a service that has fallen into a crisis due to the leaving of employees, which has had a significant impact on its ability to function effectively. In transition projects to hand over the service to the provider, the necessary expertise is then lacking, or the existing employees are so busy with the remaining day-to-day business that meaningful collaboration is not possible. This results in delays, quality losses or even project failure.

**Important** Even if many pitfalls in the tendering of IT services can be mitigated by methods, in our experience there are still major gaps in securing the service. One effective means is the continuity of all parties involved. On both the customer and provider side, people should be successively involved at all levels who carry out and are responsible for the service transition and operation.

With a managed service, the continuity of specific individuals cannot be contractually agreed. This would also contradict the service concept. However, this brings us back to an important differentiator between managed services tenders and product-like tenders, such as hardware and software tenders. In our view, this is where open and transparent communication and trust are needed. If the future teams trust each other, continuity can be established.

In hardware and software tenders, the required properties can be checked physically and factually. A keyboard can be precisely described in the specifications. The customer knows what he is buying. In case of doubt, the customer knows what the keyboard will look like after a long period of use and what properties or quality criteria the keyboard will then have. The keyboards on the market can be compared on the basis of their characteristics and a selected keyboard can be purchased from various suppliers according to the most favourable price, the fastest delivery time or other criteria.

A product is a combination of sometimes physical components that create a certain added value in accordance with a requirement. Similar products from different manufacturers can be tested in a standardised way so that the required properties can also be tracked over production periods. In practice, however, more and more products also have service features, but this will not be discussed in detail here.

A service can be seen as a process of joint value creation that makes it possible to fulfil the customer's desired requirements and services. The service provider makes certain resources, costs, risks, etc. available in order to guarantee the benefit. To make services from different providers comparable, the value chains, such as the organisations and people involved, must also be comparable.

Furthermore, in practice, the required properties of a service change much more over time than with pure products. The scaling of a service alone can have an impact on its architecture. Imagine a company with an initial IT user base of 10,000. Due to the sale of a division, this number is reduced to 3000. The supply contract changes from 2500 keyboards per year (replacement of keyboards approx. every 4 years) to 750 keyboards. The price per keyboard will probably increase by a few percentage points. The characteristics of the keyboard will not change.

A service desk service for this customer was organised in such a way that a core team of three absolute experts was always available at peak times to quickly resolve even complicated cases. Thanks to these experts and the additional employees managing the service desk, the base amount for this service was still considerable, resulting in a reasonable price per ticket for 10,000 users. If the number of tickets is reduced by more than ⅔, the ticket price can easily double in this scenario. The reason for this is that the service must still be covered by the core team of three people, as they are subject to shift requirements including holiday, sickness, and training times. The lower ticket volume must continue to finance these three experts, so the price per ticket increases.

To cope with this massive change in purchase volume, the service provider and customer will certainly change the characteristics of the service. One of the design goals will be to reduce the base amount. This can be achieved by changing the subject matter experts and therefore the service requirements. If there are no subject matter experts available at peak times in future, the performance of the service desk for the end user calling in will be reduced. However, it is also conceivable that in future the customer will work with a shared service desk team that serves 3–4 customers, each with specialised experts. Ideally, the user experience would hardly be affected and the price per ticket would remain acceptable.

We are seeing companies' core business changing at ever shorter notice and more frequently. Traditional managed service contracts do not adequately reflect these changes. At the latest, this becomes clear when the underlying service architecture needs to be changed in order to become more cost-effective or to add an innovative new sub-service. Traditional tendering procedures are unable to cope with this. This can result in a customer's company being unable to realise its full value potential.

This means that customers find themselves in serious crisis situations. For example, they may face new competition in their core business, or they may have to reduce their workforce by a third, as described above. In situations like these, where customers find themselves in serious financial difficulty, we have experienced mutual cooperation between customers and service providers. In such exceptional situations, they support each other to get out of the crisis. In all cases that we are aware of, existing contracts were initially put on hold. The situation was brought under control as best as possible, after which the order situation was jointly regulated.

In most cases, smaller innovations can be realised and amortised in the short term by mutual agreement. Investment activity can be affected by cost pressure on both sides, potentially resulting in a lack of investment in certain cases. However, it should be noted that existing managed service contracts rarely take such innovations into account. Typically, they stipulate that the service provider must become more efficient by a certain percentage each year, but do not regulate positive changes to the service level. Both sides see these small changes in a positive light, meaning that the contract is overlooked in the best sense of the word.

In our experience, important innovation and efficiency potential that lies between these two extremes is only realised in very few customer–service provider relationships. Sometimes, specific market changes need to be responded to; at other times, value potential in the overall process has hardly been analysed. The classic approach to service tenders solves this by simply carrying these changes over into the next tender round. Compared to clients who take an adaptive approach, we believe that it is no longer appropriate to cycle important innovations over periods of 3–5 years.

In discussions with customers who have encountered an innovation gap, we explored their ideas for solutions, namely expanding the traditional tendering process to include an innovation engine. However, we could not find any suitable means of maintaining the protective function of a traditional tendering process while leaving enough room for manoeuvre. In our view, this is due to the methods used to select a service provider. As previously explained, today's service tenders are the result of procedures used for hardware or software tenders.

Many clients and consultants are tempted to treat services as though they were products. Despite the existence of a large number of specific customer requirements, it is not uncommon to act as if the service market has to provide these services in a product-like manner. In tenders, this often results in an extensive list of requirements, including detailed definitions of operational processes. On top of this, there are performance requirements in the form of demanding service level targets.

At the beginning of the 2000s, this tendency was widespread. The processes to be applied were broken down to the smallest activity and it was determined how the operations team had to perform an activity, and which role had which involvement. The tenders grew and grew to several thousand activities and requirements. Even for the tendering of individual services, several hundred pages were created.

The customer's challenges were not communicated in a way that would allow the provider to offer a better or more favourable solution. As with a product, the IT service provider was expected to deliver and accept thousands of features without any possibility of influencing them. In the evaluation process, comments on requirements were assessed with a deduction of points, comparable to a non-existent product feature in a product selection process.

In addition to the ever-increasing number of requirements, there was an expanding measurement system. Service provision was evaluated according to a range of factors, and corresponding corridors were defined in service level targets. If a service deviated from these targets, the service provider had to improve the service or pay corresponding contractual penalties. Over time, this tendering methodology became very rigid.

As a service is more than just its product features, and as there was no uniform catalogue of requirements across industries or similar among customers, there was no standardisation of any kind for managed services. Although the main components that made up a service were similar for many service providers, a list of requirements with thousands of entries in combination with over a hundred metrics could not realistically be fulfilled by anyone without customisation.

Moreover, a number of these service agreements did not fulfil the needs of the clients or the individuals who consumed the service. Important requirements for certain user groups were sometimes overlooked or contradicted the numerous requirements that needed to be met. What's more, the providers made sure the metrics were within the agreed limits. Otherwise, there might have been legal consequences. This resulted in the so-called watermelon SLAs, particularly for customers who purchased services from several providers. This means that, while all metrics were "green" as required, the service did not deliver the necessary business value and was therefore "red" from management's point of view.

In response to this unsatisfactory situation, the market introduced additional requirements to address all user groups, as well as more metrics with narrower bandwidths. We believe that this was a response that only works for complicated challenges. Nearly all managed service demands involve complicated environments, especially when any type of innovation is planned. Consequently, many service providers gradually withdrew from such tenders. The effort involved on the customer side has also fallen in relation to the benefits of the tendering process.

This was followed by a period of searching for the right approach. In particular, discussions between customers and service providers often centred on negative experiences with the definition of service level targets in many service environments. It had been learnt, on the one hand, that a large number of metrics with narrow bandwidths lead to high costs. However, it was also realised that this approach offered no satisfactory protection against "watermelon" SLAs.

Even back then, we had the impression that IT managers were searching for the Holy Grail. Ideally, there would be a single metric per service that would show each customer and each of their internal users whether their business value was being properly supported. As a result, it was discussed whether XLAs could fulfil this role. In this context, eXperience Level Agreements (XLAs) are more of a variant of

SLAs that focus on end-user oriented metrics and Key Performance Indicators (KPIs). This could be, for example, the perceived quality of IT services and support.

As expected, the one key figure per service could not be found, and XLAs did not triumph. Nevertheless, during this time, dedicated IT management teams researched which metrics truly reflected the necessary benefits and quality of a managed service. These discussions often led to the adoption of adaptive services, with eXperience Level Agreements finding their place among the service level targets. SLAs and XLAs are often combined, with XLAs typically measuring services requiring a high level of interaction with end users, such as processes operated by a service desk.

Currently, the field of traditional service tenders is highly diverse. On the one hand, there are still tenders that attempt to define services in great detail, while on the other hand, there are tenders that openly seek solutions. Between these two extremes, there is a wide range of tenders in terms of the scope of requirements. Naturally, there is also a certain degree of professionalism among the tenders, but ultimately, we always prefer professionally prepared tenders.

Procedures that openly search the market for solutions usually begin communication very early on in the tendering process. The clients describe in a few pages what their initial situation is, which technological or structural requirements take centre stage and which framework conditions they see for the service. In this way, the clients can get an idea of the various providers and incorporate their ideas about future, usually technological, developments into the tender.

Since customers rarely commit to a specific provider at this early stage, a more typical tender process usually follows. This often involves a combination of the customer's original requirements and ideas from the providers who were asked to tender. While this may sound problematic, as the various providers will not all have the same outstanding features, they will each have their own strengths and weaknesses. In practice, however, customers who have opted for this process continue to communicate openly. In most cases, all service providers contribute their strengths, and the customer selects the best overall package.

Even with these methods, which initially identify solutions on the market, the main risks are only mitigated. We believe that effective communication at the outset, where requirements and services are clearly defined, is of paramount importance. When many different ideas for the requested service are discussed, the probability increases that a service provider will focus on its core competencies. It remains to be seen whether the customer and service provider have a similar level of maturity and whether the services ultimately tendered support the customer's business.

In summary, after more than 20 years of developing traditional tendering procedures for services, certain fundamental conditions remain in place. In our view, the risks to customers and providers that result from this are inherent in the system and can hardly be minimised. We are convinced that these methodologies are applicable to particular customer environments. However, environments that require guaranteed business value or customers dependent on increased efficiency or continuous innovation are no longer well-suited to these methods.

What if a service was ready for the first user groups after only 10% of the implementation of functions? What would it be like to check these functions immediately to see whether they actually deliver the business value for the company? Could it not be that after implementing 80% of the originally planned functionalities, 98% of the business value has already been achieved and the resources and innovative strength would now be better invested in another area?

The answer to all these questions is Adaptive Managed Services. It is a concept that we have developed over the last 5 years together with customers and Hochschule Bielefeld—University of Applied Sciences and Arts. In doing so, we have learned from agile organisations' ability to innovate their services together with their providers on the basis of business value. This was an important building block for the development of a collection of methods that can also be applied to traditional forms of organisations.

In fact, the use of adaptive methods in managed IT services is not yet widespread enough to be an industry standard. Most customers have developed their own processes to overcome the difficulties of transferring methods from software development to managed services. The result is often a mixture of the traditional world of managed services and agile frameworks.

These mixed methods usually work very well for their creators. Above all, many of them were open to our questions and talked about the advantages and limitations. With the present work, we have developed a framework that clearly follows a Lean-Agile approach by design. However, our methods are very well suited to finding your own compromises between the old world and an adaptive managed service.

During development, it was important to us that each organisation can define its own mix of proven and new, adaptive methods. It is precisely these diverse combinations that have proved successful with customers and partners. The advantage of our model is that we do not prescribe any compromises, and each organisation can develop more or less in the direction of adaptive services over time and based on its own decisions.

Our aim is to provide you with valuable support that aligns with your business values. The speed and intensity with which your organisation needs to achieve this varies from company to company. Lean-Agile methods represent a different way of working, and there is a wide range of approaches here, too. This can be set up in a variety of ways, such as projects, programmes, or sub-areas, including IT. It can even be used as the basis for the whole organisation.

For this reason, we have structured this book to highlight the differences between typical traditional tendering processes and the changes brought about by an adaptive approach. In this way, we hope to give you some ideas for the introduction of adaptive services. Even if the individual phases, roles and circumstances in your organisation are different for your services, many individual aspects should be helpful for a transformation.

During the development of this framework, we realised that we had also learnt a lot about traditional tendering processes and methods compared to adaptive ones. For instance, adaptive managed services ideally require contracts that primarily protect the company's interests and allow for the creation of added value. This is essentially similar to traditional managed service contracts. The definition of output should be limited to what is required in this case. The way in which the service is provided should be allowed to evolve.

Surprisingly, in both worlds we are repeatedly confronted with contract proposals that do not fulfil these premises. When working in traditional tenders, this has repeatedly prompted us to point out that only elements worthy of protection and not obstructive elements should be included in the contract. Even if such contracts tend to disappear into virtual drawers for years in practice, it is only professional to keep them close to the delivery item even in good times.

With the structure we have chosen, we hope that this book will be suitable for both traditional and adaptive tendering procedures. For this reason, we have also decided to make the book suitable for beginners. As this is a book written by practitioners for practitioners, some passages are difficult to understand without first-hand experience of tendering. For this reason, it is probably best suited as reading for the first tender in which a newcomer to the profession is already taking on tasks.

Despite all the challenges we encountered when developing our methods, we learnt one thing. We faced many problems that seemed structurally almost impossible to solve. We had developed solutions that, to our disappointment, did not work in the first variants. The Lean-Agile way of thinking has helped us time and again to move closer in small steps. This approach also involved discarding an interim result. In the end, an overall structure emerged from many small contributions, which created wonderful added value.

*That's the reason why we want to get you moving: Get going! Dare to start! The direction is clear: create value, start small and achieve great things.*

# 2 Basics and Methods

This chapter lays the theoretical and conceptual foundations for a better understanding and comprehension of the following explanations. It can be worked through in full as preparation or used as a reference work and therefore only in parts. At the same time, however, it provides a brief introduction to the various subject areas. If you are more interested, please refer to the additional and more detailed sources listed.

We begin with an introduction to the topic of tendering for IT services, which forms the basis of this book. The basics of both IT services and tenders in the IT sector are explained. Furthermore, the differences between services and products are discussed, as these have a major influence on the way a tender is organised. In addition, some special terms, such as catch-all clauses and BAFO, are explained in more detail.

> **Important** To ensure that the contents of this book are accessible to a wide audience, we have developed a detailed glossary (Chap. 8). In an eBook you can easily jump back and forth, in a printed copy a sticky note or dog-ear should serve you well. The glossary focuses on IT tenders; however, if you search the internet for catch-all clauses, you are likely to come across results dealing with trade secrets.

Agile and agility are the core concepts of the second chapter. These must be understood in their basic features in order to be able to recognise and understand the difference between agile and Scrum, the special features of agile change management and agile tendering in comparison with traditional methods.

This chapter also contains a brief outline of artificial intelligence (AI), as this is currently fundamentally changing our lives in many areas and is therefore also having a significant impact on IT service management and therefore IT tenders in companies.



G. Köhler et al., *Adaptive IT Service Tendering*, Management for Professionals,
https://doi.org/10.1007/978-3-658-49726-2_2

Another section deals with the maturity level of companies. Here we also look at frameworks and methods for continuous improvement, such as Lean Management, Six Sigma or the Continuous Improvement Process (CIP).

After diving into these three areas, we explain further terms and their use, such as the difference between a framework and a method. We explain what distinguishes a vision from a mission and why it is so important. We will also look at the Cynefin methodology and explain what OKR (Objective and Key Results) is and what benefits can be derived from it for your own organisation.

The insights into the various frameworks and methodologies provided here serve to improve understanding of the further explanations.

## 2.1 Tenders

There is hardly a company, institution, or public authority whose IT department does not utilise the services of one or even several external IT service providers. The service content can vary greatly and include, for example, a managed WAN (wide area network) service, the development of specialised software, operational support or even complete responsibility for the operation of the LAN (local area network) and security infrastructure. In the maximum case, full IT outsourcing, the entire IT infrastructure, including the complete application portfolio such as operation, maintenance, support, and large parts of a company's service management, is put out to tender and awarded to an external service provider.

Deciding which IT services to put out to tender and to what extent is a strategic question that requires a strategic decision-making process. The aim of this process is to develop a sourcing strategy. The core question of this process is also referred to as the make-or-buy decision (make = provide service by yourself vs. buy = purchase the service), whereby the focus here is not on products but on services. As part of this decision, these two fundamental alternatives must be carefully weighed up against each other in terms of value creation and competitiveness. This is usually done by carrying out a make-or-buy analysis. In addition to a profitability analysis, this also includes a risk assessment and the consideration of various influencing factors such as costs, quality, specific objectives, liquidity of the company itself, but also of the future service provider, and image considerations (Johanning, 2022).

A potential analysis should also be carried out in order to assess the fundamental readiness of the company and its employees for outsourcing. This is because outsourcing a service entails many changes and possible disruptions for an organisation. This requires organisational change management (see Sect. 2.11), which deals with the human side of the service outsourcing project, i.e. the involvement, commitment, and willingness to accept the change. This is achieved through activities such as communicating the change, managing emotions and involving employees wherever and whenever possible. Last but not least, the decision as to whether outsourcing can be implemented favourably also depends on the search, pre-selection, and evaluation of suitable providers (Oshri et al., 2023b; O'Regan, 2025).

However, the different tenders for IT services described above have one thing in common: they should (ideally) be provided economically according to clearly defined "rules of the game". Typically, these service providers are not simply commissioned by private contract, but are selected as part of a tendering process according to specific criteria such as performance, cost-effectiveness, etc.

With an invitation to tender, an institution invites other institutions in writing to submit (contractual) offers for certain goods and services that fulfil the conditions specified in the invitation to tender. There are open and restricted invitations to tender. The conditions are sometimes very extensive and are structured and summarised, for example, in a specification sheet or catalogue of requirements. These then form the basis or a template for the requested tenders.

A call for tenders has a clear objective: to establish a contractual relationship with a contractor with a needs-based scope of services, a defined appropriate quality of service and an acceptable price–performance ratio. The offers of the most suitable contractors and the associated price offers should be obtained in a competitive process.

Contracting authorities are subject to special rules in procurement procedures that depend on the value of the contract. For example, the EU has defined threshold values (in euros). Above these thresholds, contracting authorities must comply with EU procurement law or the procurement law in the respective EU country then refers to the EU regulations. Below these thresholds, only the law of the respective EU country applies (Bovis, 2025).

In the purely private sector, the formal and legal requirements of public procurement law do not apply. However, industry-specific regulations or group guidelines may need to be observed. A distinction is made between the following enquiry variants, which can also be part of a tender in combination (Fig. 2.1).

### 2.1.1 RFI

RFI (Request for Information): This is a non-binding enquiry to potential suppliers as to whether they can basically fulfil an outlined requirement under specified conditions. The outline is still very rough. This enquiry can be used to sound out the

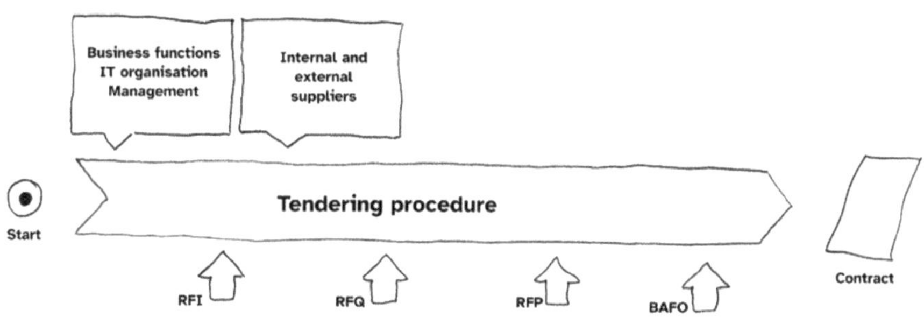


**Fig. 2.1** The tendering process

market. RFIs are often used when the client knows what they want but still needs more information from the suppliers. It can also be used to obtain basic information about a provider and their range of products and services. The RFI is usually followed by an RFQ or RFP (Nicoletti, 2018).

### 2.1.2 RFQ

RFQ (Request for Quotation): In this enquiry, a detailed description of requirements (specifications) is used to request a service description with a price that is as precise as possible but generally non-binding. These enquiries are addressed to suppliers whose basic capability the client is already convinced of, e.g. through the RFI. The client therefore knows what he wants but needs information on how the suppliers can fulfil his requirements or what this will cost. RFQs are therefore also suitable for the procurement of standardised goods and can be evaluated and priced by the potential supplier in a fairly general way (Nicoletti, 2018).

### 2.1.3 RFP

RFP (Request for Proposal): This request for proposal is an invitation to tender in the usual sense, i.e. the tenders submitted within the specified binding period are binding in such a way that a contract is concluded by a simple declaration of acceptance by the company issuing the invitation to tender. The tender documents contain a detailed description of services or specifications as well as all additional agreements required for the conclusion of the contract. There are often strict procurement regulations for the content, schedule and supplier responses.

The RFP also provides the client with an overview of all providers by asking specific questions to determine whether a provider can fulfil one or more of the most important business requirements. The process should be seen as an objective and systematic approach to procurement and purchasing (Nicoletti, 2018) (Fig. 2.2) (Table 2.1).

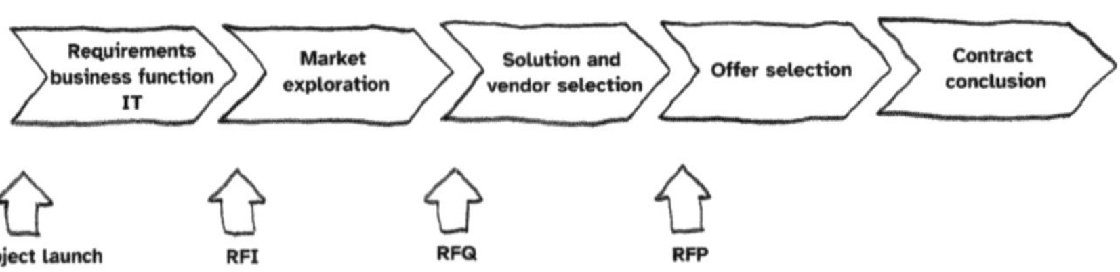


**Fig. 2.2** The tendering process

**Table 2.1** Tendering process

| Start | RFI | RFQ | RFP | Contract |
|---|---|---|---|---|
| Create a project vision<br>Collect requirements from the specialist departments<br>Compiling central requirements for a request | Analysing the feedback<br>Detailing the requirements<br>Compiling an enquiry.<br>Objective: To explore pre-selected providers and understand the solution options available on the market | Analysing the feedback<br>Integration of providers<br>Detailing of the requirements<br>Compiling an enquiry<br>Objective: Target prices for a more precise analysis of the business case | Analysing the offers<br>Further development with providers<br>Coordination of the requirements<br>Compilation of a draft contract<br>Objective: Binding offer from the providers that leads to the final contract | Contract negotiations<br>Conclusion<br>Objective: Contractual agreement and basis for the start of project implementation |

### 2.1.4 Other Types of Enquiries

In addition to the three most common request types listed above, there are also the following types that cover some special cases:

RFF (Request for Feature): This is a request to extend a system or offer. As the name suggests, it is a specific property or feature that is to be included in the offer.

RFS (Request for Solution): An RFS is a request to submit a solution offer or a request for a solution. This type of tender has emerged as a result of the trend towards outsourcing. The aim is to tackle complex requirements and problems together, i.e. between the client and the supplier. It is a collaborative process characterised by broad criteria, the evaluation of multiple options and an open dialogue, rather than specific checklists requiring precise answers. This makes the RFS much more open and leaves more room for innovation (ISG-ONE, 2013).

RFT (Request for Tender): An RFT is an open invitation to suppliers to submit bids, usually in the form of sealed bids, in a structured format. An RFT can be considered a document that sits between a comprehensive RFP and a very detailed request for proposal. RFTs tend to be more specific than RFPs, but less so than RFQs, when it comes to defining and describing the required work.

RFP (can also mean Request for Partner): An RFP is also known as a Request for Collaboration or a Request for a Mutual Value Solution. It is a highly interactive process that is used when a buyer is seeking a solution from a supplier, as well as compatibility between their culture, mindset, and the willingness of multiple suppliers to engage in a collaboration agreement. A key part of this process is the Request for Solution, which is often used when selecting a supplier for vested outsourcing. Vested outsourcing is a hybrid business model in which the parties enter into a formal contractual relationship based on shared values, goals, and a results-driven economy, with the aim of creating a mutually beneficial arrangement. A partner enquiry typically focuses on supply solutions involving joint investment or collaboration between the buyer and the selected supplier(s) over an extended period (Krause & Schnitzler, 2022; Mandl, 2023).

### 2.1.5 IT Service vs. Product

The tendering process for an IT service (see Sect. 2.2) differs little or not at all from the tendering process for the pure delivery of hardware or software, i.e. a product. However, IT services are usually much more complex, and the process is therefore more time-consuming.

The difference between an IT service or a service in general and a product becomes very clear in the course of use or service provision. A product can be described very precisely, as can its purpose and area of application. Everyone involved in the tendering process knows exactly what is to be delivered, as there are internationally standardised descriptions of physical characteristics, such as centimetres, weight, colours, or technical features, such as storage space, access speeds, etc.

The situation is different for services, i.e. the provision and measurability of services. Here, people often have their own ideas of what a perfect service should look like. These are generally not as detailed, precisely described and standardised as is the case with physical goods. As we will show below, it is also not possible to describe IT managed services in such detail that it would be helpful for their utilisation.

What's more, our world and the demands placed on us are changing so quickly that the provision of services would actually have to adapt in order to continue to meet the customer's requirements. But services are defined in contracts between at least two parties. Contracts can only be changed by mutual agreement. It may therefore be that a necessary change to the service requires a change to the contract.

This is precisely where the core problem lies! If one party feels disadvantaged when the contract is concluded, they will often do everything in their power to compensate for this when the contract is amended. This puts the other party in a worse position. The resulting conflict is obvious (Volker & Schotanus, 2023).

**Important** When I worked on a service desk in the 90s (American company) one of my bosses said, "we generate 20% of our costs with what the customer has tendered and the remaining 80% with what the customer has forgotten". Certainly the 90s were a different time than today, but it shows a fundamental problem with contracting services. Without mutual trust and a "live and let live" attitude on both sides, cooperation can be difficult.

### 2.1.6 Catch-All Clauses

The terms catch-all clause or sweep clause are terminology for sections in tenders or contracts that attempt to extend the required services or requirements very far. In extreme cases, such a clause contains the sentence: "Everything that is not described is included". In the area of outsourcing or the awarding of services, such clauses are often used by some clients if they cannot estimate what is to be covered by the service provider in the future. In IT, such clauses are usually only used for services or service guarantees and are generally only used by customers in relation to service providers (Keith et al., 2016).

The basic intention is to require the service provider to provide the service in full. A safeguard against additional claims by the service provider if a gap occurs in the future, that this must then be closed by the service provider free of charge. Especially with immature customers, this behaviour clearly shows the negative side of service tenders (see Sect. 2.7).

If this catch-all clause is accepted by both parties, two types of gaps may occur in the subsequent service. Variant A: A process step is missing from the requirements, a list is not complete, or an industry-typical delivery service is not well described. In these cases, the basic intention of the catch-all clause would have a positive effect, as closing the gap should not represent any additional effort for an industrialised or market-compliant service.

The second variant of a gap is that the requested service does not match the surrounding services, does not fit in with the customer's historically grown IT service management or does not contain certain components that were previously available in a self-produced service but were never requested. Especially if the provider can meet all requirements with an industrialised service and gaps are now to be closed that have arisen due to a grown, non-standard service cut, this sometimes cannot be realised within the framework of the provider's service factory.

In practice, such problems are frequently encountered by customers who are outsourcing an internal IT service for the first time. The profiles of potential IT service providers that can provide good support for such first-generation outsourcing are very diverse. Manufacturing-type service providers that allow a high degree of flexibility would be a solution here. Unfortunately, the low costs at which a highly industrialised provider can deliver services seem very tempting. Perhaps it is a mixture of inexperience and low price that produces too great a difference in maturity. However, professional service providers are very careful not to accept any catch-all clauses.

There is also the third option of including catch-all clauses in the contract. We would like to briefly discuss the variant of trying to plug loopholes at the expense of the provider with malicious intent. However, as elsewhere, we would like to refrain from giving grossly negative examples here. In principle, the assumption of the risk of unclear service descriptions by the contractor is legally permissible. However, there are limits here too. Especially if the client is experienced in the sector or has the necessary expertise through expert advice.

**Example** An example of a variant where a customer is unhappy, but the service is standard in the industry, would be a service desk for end users. This service desk should act as a single point of contact for all enquiries from end users and ensure a good initial resolution rate. Here we sometimes see lists of the software products to be supported as product names including version numbers. If the browser version changes from 11.0 to 12.0 during the contract term, a good IT service provider will of course also support this.

An example of a variant in which the customer has a less industrialised in-house IT operation but has purchased a standardised service would be a managed network service in which the customer subsequently requests a separate network service telephone number for the end users. Such second line support services are usually managed in an IT service management tool. The service desk or other IT employees of the customer can access the telephone numbers of the provider, but not the end users. Setting up such a hotline for end users would involve very high costs for the service provider.

The name of a catch-all clause is to catch everything, and a sweep clause is to sweep everything up. What is swept up are additional services that are to be provided as a general clause at a fixed price. With such a provision, the contractor is supposed to take on services, functions, processes, and responsibilities that are not explicitly addressed or regulated in the service description.

Such clauses require the provision of services that are usually provided in connection with the requested services, that are necessary for the complete provision of the service or that are provided as part of the existing service without describing it in detail. In the case of variants of these clauses, the contractor shall confirm that it shall at all times organise its work processes in accordance with the client's guidelines, operating manuals or other documents. However, the contractor has no influence on the design of these documents.

Other variants of catch-all clauses require the contractor to point out any gaps or contradictions in the requirements during the tendering process and to confirm that all calculation parameters are available and that all risks have been named and included in the calculation. The provider thus confirms that there are no unclear service descriptions. Should gaps nevertheless occur in the transition or operation, the provider bears the financial risk.

In our experience, a clear separation between the requirements of the service and the operational processes of how that service is to be provided is sufficient to ensure adequate protection for an inexperienced client. To achieve this, clients and potential providers should work together as closely as possible during the tendering phase. During due diligence, a mutual analysis and review, the client should be open about the actual operational processes and not rely on embellishing documents.

The client should take the time to discuss the typical operating procedures of the services in detail with the customer. In addition to the delineation of requirements or needs and operations, financial provisions can also be included in the contract to make certain types of gaps and inconsistencies calculable. A mutual right of cancellation with staggered terms to cushion investment and remanence costs can also have a confidence-building effect here. Retention costs are costs that continue to be incurred for a product, even though the product for which they were incurred is no longer manufactured or is only manufactured to a lesser extent.

Catch-all clauses do not appear to us to be suitable for a successful customer–service provider relationship. Professional service providers will try to remove these clauses or render them ineffective during the tendering phase anyway. Asymmetries in the customer–provider relationship are stressful for both sides and often lead to disputes.

**Important** As Adaptive Managed Services are developed via values and only the outcome counts, catch-all clauses are not needed anyway.

### 2.1.7 BAFO

This established term is an acronym for "Best and Final Offer". In a tendering process, the technical and commercial bids are refined or sharpened in several stages. The final phase is usually referred to as BAFO, where the technical offer is no longer changed and the providers submit their final best and binding commercial offer (Mandl, 2023).

The client can then select the most competitive tender. The best and final offer is usually submitted in response to a competitive tender. A contracting authority that has received multiple bids will invite all eligible bidders to submit their best and final offer at a specified time, rather than attempting to negotiate with each bidder individually.

As tendering procedures are not standardised, it can happen, as described above, that a client goes to the final round with the two most promising IT service providers, for example. Contracts are drawn up with both providers and finally both providers are asked to submit their best offer. However, such a procedure can also be structured differently, so that the two most favourable service providers are selected in the BAFO phase and only then are the contracts negotiated. In this case, it is not unusual for minor changes to the scope and prices to be possible even after the best and final offer.

### 2.1.8 Due Diligence

Due diligence is an investigation, examination or review conducted to confirm facts or details of a matter under consideration. It is a systematic method for analysing and mitigating risks arising from a business or investment decision and can therefore relate to both the customer and the service provider. In the context of a tender, this term is used in particular by providers, for whom the information in the Request for Proposal (RFP) is often not sufficient and who require further details from the customer before a contract can be concluded.

A due diligence checklist is an aid to this systematic method of analysing a service provider with whom a collaboration is planned. The checklist should enquire about the liabilities, benefits, and potential problems of the service provider and consider six key areas:

- General company information
- Review of finances
- Reputational risk
- Insurance
- Technical review of information security
- Policy review

The questions are based on your own requirements or the company, sector, size or region. More knowledge about potential providers enables a better assessment of the risk.

With regard to tenders, due diligence is usually carried out before a BAFO. The finalists among the bidders for a tender are given a deeper insight into the customer's documents and processes in order to be able to make a valid calculation of the BAFO (Oshri et al., 2023a).

## 2.2 IT Services Provision

ITIL defines a service as:

> "A service is a means of delivering value to customers by facilitating outcomes customers want to achieve without the ownership of specific costs and risks."

A service provides a benefit to customers by making it easier for them to achieve their desired results without bearing specific costs or risks. Therefore, a service is a means of providing customer benefits and supporting their business processes. A service always exists when an economically independent decision-maker—for example, a private household or a company—carries out a paid activity for others that is oriented towards its own business purpose. (Krishna Kaiser, 2023; Liedtke, 2024).

### 2.2.1 IT Service

However, this book is about specialised services, namely IT services. They play a central role in supporting business processes and functions.

IT services refer to the application of business and technical expertise to support organisations in the creation, management and optimisation of, or access to, information and business processes.

The market for IT services can be categorised according to the type of skills used to provide the service (design, development, operation). In addition, there are the different categories of services listed above, which can also be divided into business product services, business process services, application services and infrastructure services. If these services are outsourced, we speak of business process outsourcing (BPO), application outsourcing (AO) and infrastructure outsourcing (IO) (Willcocks et al., 2024).

### 2.2.2 IT Service Management

IT service management is a sub-area of IT management. The increasing importance of IT for the implementation of business processes requires process-oriented IT that provides its services in a customer-oriented, efficient, and effective manner. IT service management has the task of monitoring and controlling the quality and quantity of IT services in a targeted, business process-oriented, user-friendly, and cost-optimised manner. This also includes the adaptation and further development of IT services to meet the current and future requirements of customers. Customer orientation and customer satisfaction should take centre stage.

According to Tiemeyer (2020), IT service management is defined as follows:

> "A process to plan, monitor and control the quality and quantity of IT services delivered. At the same time, the goals of business process and customer orientation as well as cost optimisation must be maintained."

Accordingly, the introduction of IT service management pursues the following objectives:

- Improve the alignment of IT services with current and future business needs
- Reduce costs in the long term
- Increase service quality
- Optimise performance and efficiency
- Improve customer satisfaction
- Create transparency
- Fulfil legal requirements
- Identify and reduce risks
- Manage complexity effectively

These aspects are also reflected in the following, more comprehensive definition of IT service management.

The term "IT service management" (ITSM) refers to the entirety of all measures and methods that are necessary to achieve the best possible support of business processes (BP) by the IT organisation. In this respect, ITSM describes the transformation of information technology towards customer and service-orientation. This involves ensuring and monitoring business services, i.e. the IT services visible to the customer. In this way, the efficiency, quality, and profitability of the respective IT organisation can be continuously improved and joint added value can be generated with the customer (AXELOS Limited, 2019).

**Norms, Frameworks, and Standards**

ISO/IEC 20000 is a standard for defining minimum requirements for IT service management processes. An organisation can have its service management system (SMS) certified on the basis of ISO/IEC 20000. There are also other frameworks and standards. Some of these are company-specific specifications or industry-orientated solutions. Examples include

- ITIL as a de facto standard
- COBIT
- Business Process Framework (eTOM)
- FitSM
- Microsoft Operations Framework (MOF)

## 2.3 TOGAF

TOGAF (The Open Group Architecture Framework) is one of the most widely used frameworks for enterprise architectures (The Open Group, 2024). TOGAF is an overarching design approach and addresses the business, application, data and technology levels. As an enterprise architecture framework, it offers an approach for the design, planning, implementation, and management of an IT architecture, particularly for the further development of existing technologies and products.

TOGAF is an extremely useful method that is ideal for IT systems and can also be successfully applied in the areas of business architecture, application architecture, data architecture and technology architecture. The division into these four levels is an excellent starting point, as they must be present in every organisation. With the help of TOGAF, a direct derivation of business requirements into IT requirements can be achieved. Although this is usually based on requirements that manage output, it is still a classic way to optimise an organisation's IT systems.

TOGAF's central process model, the Architecture Development Method (ADM), describes a method for developing and managing the lifecycle of enterprise architectures that meet the business and IT requirements of an organisation. The ADM process is iterative and cyclical, but more aligned with traditional project and implementation methods. Once the architecture vision has been created, the four domains are addressed.

- The *business architecture* comprises the business strategy, corporate management, organisation, and central business processes.
- The *data architecture* contains the structure of an organisation's logical and physical databases.

- The *application architecture* covers the landscape of the application systems in relation to the core business processes, including the interfaces.
- The *technology architecture* defines the hardware, software, and network infrastructure of the core applications.

The TOGAF framework also contains concepts for an enterprise continuum, which is intended to ensure the reuse of architectural elements. It is a directory of architecture descriptions, models, building blocks, patterns, viewpoints, and other artefacts. These can be organisation-specific, but also external, e.g. industry-specific reference architectures. The repository describes the development of architectures at various levels, from foundation to organisation-specific architectures (Fig. 2.3).

In Sect. 5.3.2 we will introduce a method called "Alternative Horizon" in which architecture alternatives and ideas are collected. The framework that TOGAF proposes for an enterprise continuum can be used here as additional structuring (The Open Group, 2022).

## 2.4 Agile

Agile stands for a way of working that makes it possible to adapt and react quickly and flexibly to changing conditions and requirements. As our environment is changing faster and faster, this ability is becoming increasingly important. The working method is based on an iterative "philosophy", which describes the process worked on incrementally. The focus is on the rapid and repeated delivery of interim results in order to generate trust with customer benefits. Extensive and early planning efforts are reduced, as many things are only planned directly before

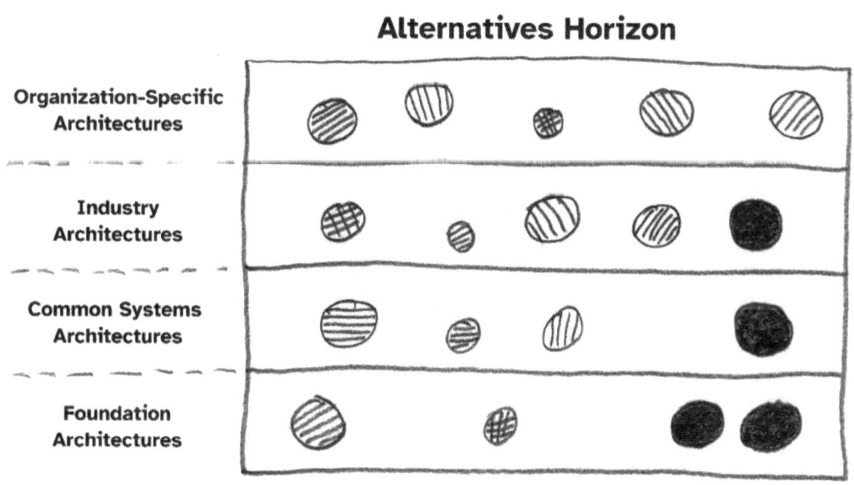


**Fig. 2.3** Classification of alternative architectures according to abstraction level

implementation. Changes can be introduced into the process at any time. Transparency, communication, and team spirit are key elements between those involved.

The term agility encompasses values as well as methods, principles, and practices that build on each other. At the same time, agility is also a generic term that encompasses the following methods and frameworks, among others: Scrum, Extreme Programming (XP), Adaptive System Development (ASD), Feature-Driven Development (FDD), Dynamic Systems Development Method (DSDM), and Crystal Clear. These methods, which were published before the Agile Manifesto (see Sect. 2.4.5) in order to find a solution to the failing traditional methods, are briefly presented below (McKinsey, 2020).

**Important** Agile working methods have the disadvantage that they may have an existing meaning in other languages, such as German. Some managers use it to more or less deliberately mislead people. For example, by claiming that their organisation has always been agile. A regime of constant chaotic course corrections has absolutely nothing to do with agile methods such as Scrum.

### 2.4.1 Extreme Programming

Extreme Programming (XP) was introduced by Kent Beck in 1996. The methods used by XP, such as pair programming, unit testing and customer acceptance tests, already existed before, but XP took these proven practices to a new "extreme" level. XP emphasises collaboration between customers and developers and pair programming. XP also has short development cycles and focuses on the needs of today rather than the future. The aim is to deliver software that is needed when it is needed. XP is best suited to small teams working on projects with dynamic requirements or high risk and working closely with managers and customers (Beck & Andres, 2004).

### 2.4.2 Feature-Driven Development

Feature-Driven Development (FDD) was introduced by Jeff De Luca in 1997. The foundations of FDD are proven software development practices, such as modelling domain objects, development by features and code responsibility. In FDD, these practices are merged to create a coherent whole. This consists of five basic activities, namely the development of an overall model, the creation of a feature list, the planning per feature, the design per feature and the programming per feature. Each project has its own unique model that leads to a feature list. The last three activities are short, iterative processes, with the creation of a feature taking no longer than 2 weeks. If it takes more than 2 weeks, it must be split into smaller features. The goal of FDD is to consistently deliver tangible, working software in a timely manner. FDD is also scalable for large teams (Palmer & Felsing, 2002).

### 2.4.3 Dynamic Systems Development Method

The Dynamic Systems Development Method (DSDM) was published in 1995 by the DSDM Consortium, a consortium of vendors and experts in software engineering, to provide a structure for the rapid application development techniques brought about by object-oriented programming. The consortium jointly developed and promoted a tool- and technology-independent development framework based on the best-practice experiences of employees of large companies. It has since evolved into a project delivery framework that is fully compatible with ISO 9001 and PRINCE2.

DSDM consists of eight principles that guide the team and create a mindset that enables delivery on time and within budget. The principles include focusing on business requirements, delivering on time through timeboxing and collaborating with end users, team members, company representatives and other stakeholders (Al-Saqqa et al., 2020).

### 2.4.4 Crystal Methods

The Crystal Methods are a family of software development methods developed by Alistair Cockburn based on his studies and interviews with teams. The methods are colour coded to indicate the risk to human life. For example, Crystal Sapphire is used for projects where there is a risk to human life, while Crystal Clear is used for projects where there is no such risk. Crystal focuses on six primary aspects: People, Interaction, Community, Communication, Skills, and Talent. Process is considered secondary. There are also seven common characteristics of Crystal that indicate a higher likelihood of success: frequent delivery, reflective improvement, osmotic communication, personal safety, focus, easy access to expert users and technical environment with automated tests, configuration management, and frequent integration. The method is very flexible and avoids rigid processes as it is people-centred.

Crystal methods are people-centred, so processes should be designed to meet the needs of the team. It is adaptable and lightweight, without a set of prescribed tools and techniques and too much documentation, management, or reporting. The weighting of the methodology depends on the project environment and team size (Al-Saqqa et al., 2020).

### 2.4.5 Agile Manifesto

Based on these methods and with some of the named developers as signatories, the Agile Manifesto was formulated in February 2001. Since then, the agile way of thinking and working has been based on this so-called Manifesto for Agile Software Development. At the centre of the Agile Manifesto are four guiding principles or values (Beck et al., 2001):

1. Individuals and interactions are more important than processes and tools,
2. Functioning software takes precedence over comprehensive documentation,

3. Cooperation with customers is more important than contract negotiations and
4. Reacting to change comes before following a plan.

The signatories of the manifesto also propose a total of 12 principles to operationalise these four core values. These include, among others

- early and continuous delivery of software,
- close cooperation between business functions and software developers,
- motivational measures,
- focus on technical excellence and
- self-organising teams.

And the first principle hovers over everything:

"Customer benefit is at the centre of everything we do and sets the priorities."

When applying agile working methods and the associated incremental delivery of products and services, it must be accepted that a predefined end product or a service described in detail does not exist. As a product or service evolves with each increment in order to deliver the best result for the customer, the end product or service may deviate from the initial expectations. However, the framework conditions defined for a product or service at the start of the project are adhered to, unless the stakeholders discover and decide during the project that these need to be changed.

### 2.4.6 Agile Practices

The aim of agile practices is a flat effort curve, which means that new or changed requirements can be taken into account during the course of the project with as little effort as possible. Some of these practices have already been mentioned in the presentation of the methods and frameworks. The following list completes the presentation but does not go into the individual practices in more detail. Various of these practices are also used in the context of agile tenders (Block, 2023).

- Continuous integration—the process of continuously combining components into an application with particular attention to quality
- Continuous refactoring—ongoing manual or automated structural improvement of source code while retaining the observable programme behaviour
- Continuous Delivery—collection of techniques, processes and tools that improve and automate the software delivery process
- Continuous Deployment—a more advanced form of Continuous Delivery, in which the software is also delivered automatically to the productive infrastructure

- Pair programming—two programmers create source code together and control each other
- Test-Driven Development—the programmer consistently creates software tests before the components to be tested
- Behaviour-Driven Development—during the requirements analysis, the tasks, goals, and results of the software are recorded in a specific text form, which can later be executed as automated tests
- Story cards—means of communication between requesters and implementers, contains the description of the story and the result of an estimate
- Rapid code reviews—each work result can be subjected to a review by another person (analytical quality assurance measure)
- Agile testing—the goals of agile software development are optimally supported—basic principles: High degree of automation, low overhead, dissolution of test roles, dissolution of test levels, close team collaboration
- Rapid application development—a prototypical procedure in which software requirements are collected and converted into executable code as quickly as possible based on the spiral model

### 2.4.7 Agile Contracts

An agile approach as part of a customer project also requires agile contracts, as traditional contracts are particularly at odds with the fourth guiding principle of the Agile Manifesto: "Responding to change comes before following a plan". Contracts generally pursue the intention of risk protection for both sides. On the one hand, the aim is to avoid the risk of a higher production price and the selection of a provider based on the tender price and, on the other hand, to prevent the risk of incomplete, insufficiently detailed or ambiguous service descriptions and IT technical requirements. This approach is based on the assumption that all requirements are fully described in terms of type and scope during the contract negotiations and that they will not change until the contract is concluded and, if possible, thereafter. In this way, the service is artificially fixed, and adjustments based on new information from the market do not materialise or lead to cost-intensive contract adjustments (Sabharwal et al., 2022).

An agile contract tries to avoid this dilemma. According to (Sutherland, 2008),

> "A good agile contract creates incentives to intelligently combine the client's intention of capping costs with the supplier's goal of capping performance."

The aim is therefore to limit the risks for both contracting parties while at the same time allowing both parties a certain degree of freedom so that they can react to changes in the company or in the environment.

## 2.4.8 Scrum

Scrum is one of the best-known agile frameworks and forms the basis for many methods derived from it. Its inventors describe it as a lightweight framework that supports people, teams, and organisations in creating value through agile solutions to complex problems. In just a few pages, Scrum defines a framework for collaboration within a Scrum team.

Ken Schwaber and Jeff Sutherland first presented Scrum together at the OOPSLA conference in 1995. The resulting Scrum Guide (Schwaber & Sutherland, 2020) documents Scrum as it has been developed and maintained by Jeff Sutherland and Ken Schwaber since the first version (Fig. 2.4).

**Roles: Scrum Team**

The Scrum team consists of a Scrum Master, a product owner and the developers. The Scrum team rarely works independently but is usually embedded in an organisation. This creates interfaces with other parties within and possibly also outside the organisation. The product owner is in close contact with the stakeholders. He collects their requirements and refines them together with them. By communicating closely with all stakeholders, he ensures that he fulfils his responsibility—maximising the value of the product—in the best possible way. The Scrum Master, on the other hand, is responsible for the process. He therefore maintains contact with the organisation's management and expands their understanding of agile techniques and Scrum. In this way, they ensure that the self-organisation of the Scrum team is accepted throughout the organisation and that disruptive factors for the team can be avoided. The developers are jointly responsible for the quality of the product. They therefore consciously create points of contact with the users who will later use their

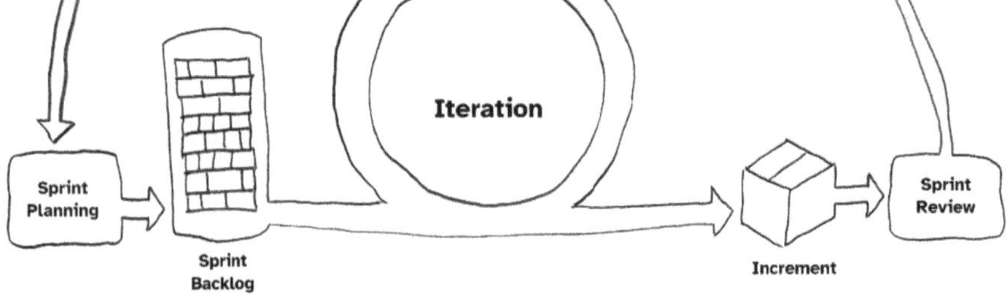


**Fig. 2.4** The Scrum cycle based on Scrum.org (2024b)

product. This gives them valuable insights into the required quality and other details. Users often also carry out user tests to increase the quality of the product.

**Roles: Product Owner**

Each product has a single product owner. The Product Owner in the Scrum team is responsible for maximising the value of the product. This is why he is also referred to as the value maximiser. He is responsible for the range of functions that the product contains. At the same time, they are responsible for the product as a whole. How the Product Owner achieves this varies in practice depending on the organisation and Scrum team. The product owner is always a single person, not a committee of several people. In order to carry out their work, they need either technical knowledge or an understanding of the market—whereby the exact requirements usually depend on the type of product to be developed.

The Product Owner is not a project manager:

In Scrum, we don't talk about projects and he therefore there is no project manager, as the Scrum team organises itself.

**Roles: The Scrum Master**

The Scrum Master is responsible for the functioning of Scrum and thus for the processes and effectiveness of the Scrum team. Each Scrum team has exactly one Scrum Master. The Scrum Master is a servant leader. In the agile sense, this term can be taken literally. His priority is to serve his team. Leading comes second after supporting the self-management of the developers. "Serve" refers to several functions.

For example, serving the Product Owner includes the Scrum Master teaching them best practices for maintaining the Product Backlog. It also gives them the right understanding of agility and the advantages of the empirical approach. It also makes both the product owner and the developers understand the importance of clearly formulated backlog entries.

At the service of the entire Scrum team, he removes obstacles so that each individual and the team as a whole can work in a focussed manner. For example, if the developers are disturbed in their work by stakeholders with new requirements, the Scrum Master refers them to the Product Owner. The Scrum Master also helps with the implementation of the events.

**Roles: The developers**

All developers are jointly responsible for the quality of the product and the plan they use to achieve this quality (quality-orientated). Ideally, a Scrum team consists of up to eight developers. They are the developers or creators of the resulting product. In order for them to be effective, there should be neither too few nor too many developers in a Scrum team. Their composition as a group should remain stable over the entire product development period. This is important for team dynamics and efficient collaboration. If one member is replaced by another, the team must accept a drop in productivity as the focus of the Scrum team shifts from development to the newly forming team dynamic. Together, the developers have all the skills required to create a valuable product. To do this, they work as a feature team. Developers who work in feature teams are characterised by interdisciplinary knowledge. Their profile is based on the letter T, also known as the T-shape: The horizontal line stands for the broad basic knowledge of a developer—such as knowledge of software development in general or knowing what a website looks like and what functionalities it must have. If everyone in the team has these basic skills, the team members can help and replace each other. The vertical line describes deeper expertise in a specific subject area. For example, one developer might be a proven C++ expert, another developer might be more familiar with front-end development. This diverse expertise ensures that every requirement in the product backlog can be fulfilled by the team.

Developers do not have to be programmers, although the name Developer might suggest this. They are the developers of the product. The development team is a cross-functional team and should include all the skills needed to develop the product.

**Artefacts: Product backlog**

The product backlog is an organised list of all requirements and is the only source of requirements for all changes and work on the product. The purpose of this artefact is to make the requirements visible to all stakeholders throughout the life of the product. The product backlog contains all features, functionalities, improvements, and bug fixes. This means that as soon as something needs to be changed in the product or new market requirements arise, this change is added to the product backlog in the form of a requirement. What may initially be a short list becomes a long, detailed list over time. For this reason, the product backlog should never be regarded as exhaustive. It is a highly dynamic artefact, which is why it is also referred to as a "living artefact". The requirements in the product backlog are prioritised. Prioritisation is carried out by the product owner. This means that they decide the order in which the requirements are to be processed. In doing so, they take into account criteria such as value for the customer, dependencies, and risks. The product owner chooses the order of the entries as they see fit. They seek advice from the developers and stakeholders. He alone is authorised to make changes to the product backlog or have them made. A requirement usually includes a description, the rank in the order, the developer's effort estimate, the value for the customer and acceptance criteria. The Scrum team itself decides what additional information it wants to add.

**Artefacts: Sprint backlog**

The Sprint Backlog is created as a result of Sprint Planning. It consists of the Sprint goal, the set of product backlog items selected for the Sprint and a plan for implementing the increment. The Sprint Backlog as a whole answers the three questions from Sprint Planning:

- The Sprint goal shows why the Sprint is valuable
- The team recognises what is being implemented based on the selected product backlog entries
- The plan for creating the increment shows how the implementation is carried out

The Sprint goal is created at the start of planning in order to develop a common understanding of what is to be achieved in the Sprint. The Scrum team then specifies exactly how the goal is to be achieved. To do this, the developers transfer the Sprint goal and the product backlog entries to the Sprint backlog. They adopt the order of the requirements so that the resulting Sprint backlog is also prioritised.

**Artefacts: Increment**

The product increment is an artefact and the result of all completed product backlog items in a Sprint. In addition, each increment is more extensive in terms of features and functions than the previous one, as the increments of all Sprints are cumulated. The result of the current Sprint therefore builds on the product increments of previous Sprints. The current increment is therefore the sum of all increments. At the end of a Sprint, the new product increment must be "completed". This means that it must be in a usable state and fulfil the team's Definition of Done. It does not matter whether the product owner currently wants to deliver the increment to users or not. The Definition of Done must be fulfilled in any case. In other words, the product increment must be potentially deliverable.

**Definition of Done**

The Definition of Done is a commitment of the development team and formally describes the state that each increment should have after a Sprint. You can think of this commitment as a list of quality criteria that are reviewed after each Sprint. It helps developers to decide how many entries they can plan for a Sprint. It also makes a decisive contribution to increasing transparency and quality. The Definition of Done is determined by the respective Scrum team, unless the associated development organisation has established a generally applicable convention for the Definition of Done. The criteria therefore vary considerably from team to team and from organisation to organisation. Normally, a Definition of Done contains components such as guidelines and standards of the development organisation as well as the quality requirements of the Scrum team.

**Event: The Sprint**

The Sprint is a central event that determines the work rhythm and structure of the development process. A Sprint is a fixed period of time during which a Scrum team works on the development of an incremental part of the end product. During this period, the team concentrates on completing the tasks defined in the Sprint backlog and creating a potentially deliverable product increment.

A Sprint typically has the following characteristics:

- *Fixed duration:* A Sprint has a fixed duration, which is usually between 1 and 4 weeks. The length of the Sprint is determined at the start of the project and remains constant throughout the entire duration of the project.
- *Clear goals:* Before the start of a Sprint, the objectives are defined and recorded in the Sprint backlog. These goals can be prioritised based on the requirements from the product backlog and should be achieved during the Sprint.

- *Commitment of the team:* During a Sprint, the Scrum team commits to completing the tasks defined in the Sprint backlog. The team works together to realise the tasks and strives to deliver a finished product increment at the end of the Sprint.
- *Regular events:* Regular events take place during a Sprint, including the Sprint Planning at the beginning, the Daily Scrum Meeting every day, the Sprint Review at the end and the Sprint Retrospective after the review. These events are used to review progress, identify problems and make adjustments.
- *Continuous improvement:* A Sprint offers the opportunity for continuous improvement. By conducting regular reviews and retrospectives, the team can reflect on its approach, share experiences and optimise the development process.

Overall, the Sprint serves as a recurring work period that enables the Scrum team to work in short, focussed iterations and continuously deliver high-quality product increments.

**Event: Sprint Planning**

During Sprint planning, the team lays the foundation for the subsequent Sprint. The entire Scrum team must be present. The overall aim of the event is to plan the necessary key data and activities in order to start implementing the upcoming Sprint. To this end, all team members work together to find answers to the following questions:

- Why is the Sprint valuable?
- What can be done?
- How is the work implemented?

Based on this, the developers decide how they want to achieve the Sprint goal. To do this, they transfer the selected items from the product backlog to their Sprint backlog. For the requirements, the items are formulated that need to be processed to fulfil the individual requirements in order to produce the new product increment. The amount of functionality that was created in the last Sprint is always referred to as an increment. In other words, the functional sub-product at the end of a Sprint.

The Sprint backlog does not have to be fully completed at the end of Sprint planning. Optionally, part of the organisation of the work can be completed in the Sprint itself. This is because during the implementation one or two tasks may be added or even omitted. However, the product backlog entries should be as detailed and comprehensible as possible at the start of Sprint planning. Otherwise, problems may arise during the event when the team tries to estimate how much work it can complete. However, the more developers have learnt about their skills over the course of development and the better they understand the requirements, the easier it becomes to plan the work. Therefore, the product backlog, the estimated capacity of the developers, their previous performance and the last product increment serve as helpful input variables in Sprint planning.

**Event: Daily Scrum**

The Daily Scrum is a crucial event for transparency, review, and adaptation. It ensures coordination between the developers. Only they need to be present at the Daily Scrum. If the Scrum Master or Product Owner also acts as a developer, they are also there to actively participate in the Daily Scrum. Otherwise, the Scrum Master can be present in their role as a facilitator. In this role, he supports the developers in adhering to the short timebox. He also allows anyone who wants to contribute something relevant to have their say. The Daily Scrum takes place every day at the same time and in the same place. Its timebox is 15 min, regardless of team size and Sprint length. The aim of the event is to encourage an exchange of information between the developers so that progress towards the Sprint goal is always clear. New experiences and insights are gained between each Daily Scrum so that the Sprint backlog can be adjusted as a result of the event. This increases the likelihood that the developers will achieve their goal.

**Event: Sprint Review**

The Sprint review takes place after implementation by the developers and is the penultimate event in a Sprint. Not only the entire Scrum Team takes part in this event, but also the stakeholders invited by the Product Owner. The main aim of the Sprint review is to review the increment, i.e. the sub-product created during the Sprint, and make any necessary adjustments. At the end, there should be an updated product backlog that reflects the feedback from the stakeholders and the new prioritisation of the entries. New details can also be added and requirements that have become obsolete can be eliminated. The Sprint review is considered a working session. It is more of an informal meeting than a status report. The focus should not be on presenting the results, but on working together on the product: it is about a shared understanding of progress, collaboration and added value, not justification. Firstly, the entire Scrum team shows the results of the Sprint, i.e. the finished increment. This is a way of checking what has been achieved and what progress has been made towards the product goal. It is therefore important that all members of the Scrum team take part in this event, as it is about respect and appreciation for the work done as well as constructive criticism from stakeholders.

**Event: Sprint Retrospective**

The Sprint retrospective is the last event in a Sprint. It gives the team the opportunity to review itself, adapt processes and improve collaboration. The Sprint retrospective requires the presence of the entire Scrum team and lasts a maximum of 3 h for a 4-week Sprint. For a 2-week Sprint, the timebox corresponds to 1½ h. The aim of the Sprint retrospective is to develop measures to become more efficient and ensure higher product quality. The exact procedure depends on the respective team and its area of work. There are many different ways to conduct a Sprint retrospective. Ideally, a different one should be chosen for each Sprint. This way, the team always generates new and different feedback and can improve step by step in different areas.

We have only provided an overview of Scrum and its roles and artefacts. To gain a more in-depth understanding of Scrum, we recommend: "The Art of Scrum" by Dave McKenna (2016).

### 2.4.9 SAFe

The Scaled Agile Framework (SAFe) is a framework that helps organisations scale Lean, Agile and DevOps practices (Scaled Agile, Inc., 2024). It extends methods to allow multiple teams to work on a project in parallel and offers a comprehensive collection of organisational and work organisation concepts.

SAFe has evolved from a concept of taking a holistic view of processes from the product portfolio, governance, programme management and software development through to the customer. The current version 6.0 (at the time this book went to press) is publicly available. In addition to the documentation, Scaled Agile, Inc. also offers an academy and an extensive training programme with personal certifications.

SAFe 6.0 is based on the seven key competences of business agility

1. Lean-Agile leadership—promoting organisational
2. Team and Technical Agility—Creating high-performance agile teams
3. Agile Product Delivery—Building high-performance product development through DevOps teams
4. Enterprise Solution Delivery—building and maintaining the world's largest applications and solutions
5. Lean portfolio management—realisation from portfolio vision to road mapping
6. Organisational agility—harmonisation of strategy and implementation in the organisation
7. Continuous Learning Culture—Establishing a culture of continuous learning, i.e. creating a learning organisation

SAFe is very widespread. It is basically a hybrid model that attempts to establish and manage agile methods in a hierarchical organisation. A good example of this are traditionally managed software development companies whose development departments have been working with agile methods such as Scrum for years and now have to scale up by increasing the number of developers. In our view, SAFe is a good framework for these types of organisations. The SAFe framework impresses with its completeness and topicality. It is definitely worth a look, as you will always find suitable components and further literature (Block, 2023; Meissner et al., 2024).

### 2.4.10 NEXUS

As a second framework, we would also like to mention Nexus for scaling agile methods (Scrum.org, 2024a). The Nexus framework was developed by one of the co-founders of Scrum, Ken Schwaber. It is hosted by Scrum.org, where the Nexus Guide can also be found.

Nexus has the advantage that it is minimalistic and only coordinates the collaboration of up to nine Scrum teams in the spirit of Scrum. After organisations have started with adaptive managed services and have successfully improved some services, they reach the threshold of working on a roadmap with more than two cross-functional teams. Here, Nexus can serve as a reference example to get an idea of how Scrum can be scaled.

Nexus describes how to work with a central product backlog in order to create a Nexus Sprint backlog together with the Sprint goals. An important point here is to resolve the dependencies of the individual backlog elements in such a way that the individual teams can work with them.

The development work is managed by a Nexus Integration Team consisting of the Product Owner, Scrum Master and other members who coordinate the integration work centrally. The main task of the Nexus Integration Team is to ensure a standardised understanding and use of the necessary practices and tools in the Scrum teams.

Events such as Sprint Planning, Cross-Team-Refinement, Daily Scrum, Review and Retrospective are either extended across the teams or split into Nexus and the individual teams. The interim result of the review, the Integrated Increment, is the current overall solution of all teams that was created in the Sprint. A nexus generates an increment or a service with minimal value (Bittner et al., 2018).

## 2.5 Artificial Intelligence

The term artificial intelligence (AI) refers to the ability of computers and machines to simulate human-like intelligence. This is achieved by performing tasks such as learning, problem solving, language comprehension and decision-making.

The use of AI is helpful in many areas as it automates processes, increases efficiency and creates a better basis for decision-making. It enables precise data analysis, improves the personalisation of services, supports the prediction and prevention of problems and optimises the use of resources and workflows.

As part of an adaptive IT tendering process for managed services, AI can provide support in various ways.

- For example, it can optimise the process by accelerating analysis and decision-making. AI can be used to carry out automated analyses and gain quick insights into large volumes of data. This enables decision-makers to make informed decisions in a timely manner.
- Furthermore, AI can provide real-time feedback on the tendering process and help to dynamically adjust criteria and weightings to better support the objectives of the adaptive approach.

- Another advantage is that AI continuously learns from the data and can improve the tendering process over time by recognising patterns and trends and making recommendations for optimisation.
- AI-supported tools also enable automated communication and collaboration between the parties involved by providing automated notifications, chatbots, or collaboration platforms that speed up the exchange of information and thus increase efficiency.
- AI also helps to react quickly to unforeseen changes in the tendering process by analysing data and making recommendations for adjustments to achieve the goals of the adaptive approach.
- Finally, by applying predictive analytics, AI enables the prediction of resource requirements for the tendering process as well as ensuring the availability of the required resources at the right time. As a result, potential bottlenecks can be avoided, and efficiency maximised.

Overall, AI can support the adaptive IT tendering process for managed services by improving the speed, flexibility, and efficiency of the process, thus helping to achieve the goals of the adaptive approach.

However, the use of AI is associated with certain risks. One of the most serious disadvantages is the potential incompleteness and associated lack of quality of the data sets used. If the data basis on which AI systems make their decisions is incomplete or incorrect, this can lead to incorrect decisions with all the associated consequences for the respective area of application. In addition, the regulatory risks associated with its use (in particular compliance with data protection laws and copyrights) and reputational risks must be taken into account. The latter include, for example, incorrect decisions due to AI bias or distortions. Organisational risks must also be considered, which may be caused by inadequately trained employees or an inadequate infrastructure, for example to secure the stored data (Myklebust et al., 2025; Roth-Dietrich, 2024; Sarferaz, 2024).

**Important** In many organisations today, there are considerable gaps in the exchange of information between the functions or roles involved in tendering processes. This is due to various factors. On the one hand, it is assumed that there is no general knowledge about certain aspects; on the other hand, information is not exchanged, the effort is shied away from, or the complexity is misjudged. The use of AI in such an environment cannot utilise the potential of AI but even harbours the risk of generating falsified information or instructions.

## 2.6 Methodology vs. Framework

It is important to point out that, again, there is no official legislation or standards governing these terms. In general, a framework is a description of what needs to be done but leaves the way of doing it up to the actor. In contrast, a method is a predefined procedure (more like a process) that tells us when to do something in a certain way.

Or also:

A methodology is the way to systematically solve a problem. It is a combination of the methods chosen to achieve a desired result and the logic underlying these methods. The methodology is therefore a guide for the user to solve a problem. It restricts creativity as it is based on a predefined set of rules.

A framework, on the other hand, is a logical structure for classifying and organising complex information and therefore a structured approach to solving problems. Frameworks provide the structural components needed to implement a method. It is a basic framework around which something can be built. A framework is also a collection of reusable components. Some frameworks are very rigid and contain clear rules, while others offer more room for creativity (Kuster et al., 2023; Schenk, 2025).

It is important that everyone involved in the collaboration is talking about the same thing. A common definition and perspective are therefore helpful!

## 2.7 Maturity Levels

The maturity level of the participating organisations, particularly in relation to IT and the business processes that are to be supported by IT, plays a decisive role in the context of a tender. Before discussing the reasons for this, the terms maturity level and maturity level models should first be introduced.

Maturity levels or a maturity model assesses the maturity of a unit, e.g. a process, a process group or an organisation, in several stages. Each unit can be assigned a maturity level that it currently fulfils by possessing certain capabilities and characteristics. If this is not already the highest maturity level, the maturity level to which the unit can be gradually improved is also shown. The maturity level therefore represents a performance requirement for the respective unit that needs to be achieved. It is important to maintain the capabilities of the previously achieved performance level. The organisation must therefore not unlearn or forget (Lincke, 2024).

The maturity model therefore comprises specific stages, starting with an initial stage in which the required process does not yet exist in the organisation, through to complete process maturity with a continuous improvement process. As maturity increases, the quality of the unit under consideration improves continuously. Individual maturity is usually determined by comparing it with the requirements of the respective maturity levels.

At a certain point in time, observations are collected on the objects to be assessed in order to record the initial maturity situation. Suggestions for improvement and recommendations for action can then be derived from the determined actual situation. With the help of the maturity model, which, as described, comprises various maturity levels and their characteristics, processes, developments, or even specific objects can be better understood and evaluated. It enables complex issues to be broken down into graduated dimensions and their characteristics to be assigned to maturity levels. A five-level scale, as shown in the following table, has become widely accepted (Table 2.2).

Probably the best-known maturity model is the Capability Maturity Model Integration (CMMI), which was originally developed for software development, but is now available in three variants for development (CMMI-DEV), for services (CMMI-SVC) and for procurement (CMMI-ACQ).

However, maturity models not only include the representation of the individual levels, but also the measures that must be taken to move from one level to the next—a descent is of course also possible. Normally, however, development always takes place in stages, i.e. no stages are skipped, as such a change in the organisation is only possible in exceptional cases. A maturity level is therefore only considered to have been reached when both the requirements assigned to it and the hierarchically lower requirements of the previous levels have been demonstrably and reliably fulfilled (Lincke, 2024).

**The challenge**

When organisations work together, they and their way of working together are strongly influenced by the respective maturity level of the processes. Challenges and problems arise in the following areas:

- *Communication challenges:* Organisations with a higher level of maturity may have clearer communication and a better understanding of processes and expectations. When working with less mature organisations, this can lead to misunder-

**Table 2.2** Maturity levels

| | |
|---|---|
| 5 Optimised | *Stable and flexible.* The organisation is focused on continuous improvement and designed to focus innovation and respond to opportunities and changes. In addition, errors and problems are systematically analysed and rectified. The stability of the organisation provides a platform for agility and innovation. |
| 4 Quantitatively managed | *Measured and controlled.* The organisation is data-driven with quantitative performance improvement targets (intensive use of KPIs) that are predictable and aligned with the needs of internal and external stakeholders. |
| 3 Defined | *Proactive instead of reactive.* Company-wide standards provide orientation for projects, programmes and portfolios and make it easier to share experiences. |
| 2 Managed | *Managed at project level.* Projects are planned, implemented, measured, and controlled. Functioning project management is the basis for all further improvements. |
| 1 Initial | *Unpredictable and reactive.* Work is completed but is often delayed and over budget. There are no requirements for processes, programmes, and portfolios. |

standings if expectations are not clearly communicated or communication channels are not used effectively.

- *Differences in efficiency:* While more mature organisations often have efficient processes and workflows, less mature organisations can be slower and require more resources to achieve similar results. This can lead to frustration if the partner organisations have different speeds or work rhythms.
- *Quality standards:* More mature organisations often have established quality standards and controls in place to ensure the consistency and quality of their products or services. When working with less mature organisations, compliance with these standards can be challenging and require additional monitoring or support.
- *Exchange of knowledge and learning opportunities:* Working with organisations of different maturity levels can be an opportunity for both sides to learn from each other. More mature organisations can share their best practices and support less mature organisations in improving their own processes. At the same time, less mature organisations can bring in new perspectives and innovative ideas that can inspire more mature organisations.

Overall, collaboration between organisations with different levels of maturity requires careful planning, clear communication and coordinated efforts to achieve successful results.

**Service provider**

Service providers, especially the larger ones, are usually at maturity level 4 or 5, although it should be noted that the maturity level does not always have to be the same across all processes and portfolio elements of the service provider (there are usually differences here). If service providers can offer their standard and implement it for customers, the customer can assume that the maturity level of the service is quite high. For the larger service providers, the maturity level in their standard should be 5.

However, it becomes problematic when the customer demands that the service provider adapts and modifies its standard. There is an extremely high risk that this will also reduce the level of maturity!

**Customers**

Service providers have customers at all levels of maturity. Smaller and medium-sized companies often (not necessarily) have a low maturity level of between 1 and 2, while large companies (including larger medium-sized companies) usually have a higher maturity level. Here you also come across companies with a maturity level of 4 or 5. It can generally be assumed that customers with a low maturity level (between 1 and 2 or below) are unable to assess their own maturity level.

**Case study**

A customer with a maturity level between 1 and 2 invites tenders for a service desk with ITIL Service Management services such as Problem Management. The customer's requirement is that the service provider carries out problem management independently and assumes full responsibility for this service, as the customer is not able to do this themselves due to their maturity level.

The service provider agrees and provides the service desk with various ITIL service management services, including problem management.

During operation, problems now arise in the customer's infrastructure that need to be investigated more closely and, above all, in greater depth. To this end, the service provider requests units of the customer and other service providers of the customer to carry out various investigations. The customer's other service providers do not respond to the service provider's request and the service provider has no contact person at the customer who feels responsible for problem management. After all, this service was outsourced. As a result, problems are not solved, and the customer is dissatisfied because they are paying for a service that is not being provided.

In this case (example from practice), the service provider should not have taken responsibility for this process and should have insisted that there is a role at the customer that can also give instructions to the customer's service providers.

Different levels of maturity therefore often lead to things being assumed that are not possible to fulfil or implement in practice. In this case, the (immature) customer will never be satisfied with the services provided by the service provider.

**Example** When presenting a service desk offer, the customer said at the end that they were nice slides that others had also presented to him in the same way. He had already outsourced his service desk three times to different service providers but had never been satisfied with their performance. When asked what was supposed to be different with the fourth contract award, he was unable to give an answer. It was then agreed to work with him to design a service desk that met his requirements so that the subsequent tender and service provision would be to the customer's satisfaction. Whilst working together and investigating the client's requirements, it was realised that the service provider's poor performance was due to the client's immaturity and not due to poor performance by the service provider. This realisation then led to the customer's maturity level being investigated in more detail and an internal initiative being launched by the customer to increase the maturity level before the service desk's next tender.

Many customers use the practices from ITIL to increase their maturity level. However, the practices from ITIL reach their limits at maturity level 5 (in our view), or there are more mature frameworks and methods for introducing and implementing continuous improvement at maturity level 5. We will therefore look at the three most common frameworks: CIP, Lean, and Six Sigma.

### 2.7.1 CIP

In our view, the CIP (Continuous Improvement Process) is the most rudimentary form of introducing and implementing continuous improvement in a company. In our experience, the CIP is also used as a process. It begins with a defined event that must be reported via a defined input channel and ends with a decision to do or not to do something (Bertagnolli, 2022).

In our opinion, only the existence of such a process is continuous and therefore the worst option (but still better than no improvement!).

Companies often offer bonuses for improvements that have been implemented and have (measurably) saved the company money.

Wouldn't it be better if all processes, procedures, products, and activities were subject to continuous improvement by the employees who deal with them on a daily basis? And that these improvements become part of the corporate culture?

This is possible with the following frameworks and methodologies.

**Kaizen**

The term "Kaizen" comes from the Japanese and is made up of "Kai" for change and "Zen" for the better (looser translation: "replacing the good with the better"). Kaizen is used in lean management, where it is backed up by methods. It refers to the continuous improvement of activities, processes, procedures, or products by all employees of a company. The focus is not on major innovations or fundamental changes, but on the involvement of all employees, the large number of daily suggestions for improvement and their rapid implementation. The successes of Kaizen should be visible to everyone.

The main focus here is on avoiding waste (muda) and focussing on value creation. Kaizen also emphasises the reduction of overloads (muri) and irregularities (mura) (see Sect. 2.7.2) (Bertagnolli, 2022).

In Western companies, Kaizen is often equated or translated with the term Continuous Improvement Process (CIP). In this way, supporters of Kaizen and CIP distinguish themselves from the traditional and often cumbersome company suggestion scheme, which has a long but often unsuccessful tradition in Western companies.

**Process orientation**

The Kaizen way of thinking means turning away from a pure results-orientation towards a process-orientation. In this context, process orientation means the documentation and continuous improvement of process standards. The ultimate goal is to optimise the overall result, but this is only possible if customer satisfaction is high, as acquiring new customers is more expensive than retaining customers. To ensure a high level of customer satisfaction, the above-mentioned factors take centre stage. A process-oriented organisational design and the application of continuous improvement methods such as Kaizen can have a positive influence on a company's innovation performance.

**Customer orientation**
Kaizen considers both internal and external customers. External customers are end users, internal customers are, for example, departments within the organisation. If an organisational unit manufactures a product that has to be further processed by another unit, this unit is considered an internal customer. Problems often occur at these interfaces, which is why the implementation of Kaizen objectives is focussed there: quality assurance and improvement, customer satisfaction and cost reduction by employees. Customer surveys are carried out in order to eliminate deficiencies and provide better services.

**Quality orientation**
As part of total quality management, continuous quality control is carried out in which quality is permanently monitored during production and in a complex measurement process. The quality indicators and measurement procedures are described and defined in demanding quality standards.

**Criticism orientation**
In Kaizen, criticism is seen as an opportunity for continuous improvement and is therefore not only permitted but even encouraged. Every employee is encouraged to make suggestions for improvement, which are constructively received by management and implemented wherever possible. In Kaizen, suggestions for improvement are requested, checked, and evaluated in order to integrate them into the company processes if the overall assessment is positive. The result is a continuous cycle of planning, implementation, review, and improvement, known as the PDCA cycle (Plan → Do → Check → Act). The aim is to continuously analyse and improve all processes in the company (Bruhn, 2023; Ćwiklicki, 2023).

### 2.7.2 Lean

In general, lean management should be understood as a corporate culture. If a company decides to introduce lean management, it should be implemented throughout the entire organisation and integrated into the corporate culture.

The key aspects of lean management can be summarised as follows:

1. the alignment of all activities, processes, and objectives with the needs of the customer.
2. the definition of value and added value from the perspective of the end customer.
3. the elimination of waste in all areas of the value chain.
4. the continuous optimisation of all activities, processes, goals, and people.
5. focussing on people as a central component of value-adding services and processes.

Lean and lean techniques are presented in many different ways in the literature. However, the five lean principles should always take centre stage:

- Value: Specification of values from the customer's perspective (customer added value)—customer-centred and customer-oriented focus
- Value Stream: Identification of value streams—process optimisation
- Flow: Creating a continuous flow by avoiding waste
- Pull: Orientation towards customer needs
- Perfection: Kaizen—striving for perfection through continuous improvement

Lean management is generally attributed to the car manufacturer Toyota in the 1950s. However, today's lean management combines many methods that appear to have their origins elsewhere. In the literature, there are repeated references to Taiichi Ohno and Sakichi Toyoda, whereby Sakichi Toyoda studied the problems in practice and got to the bottom of them in order to solve them. As a result, inventions that arose from practical experience could be used more successfully in practice. This principle has significantly characterised Toyota and the Toyota production system and is known today as Genchi Genbutsu.

The original goals of lean management are

- Avoidance of waste (Muda)
- Elimination of imbalance (Mura)
- Reduction of overuse (Muri)

Waste (muda in Japanese) is a key term in lean management. It refers to any activity that consumes resources in any form (labour, space, machinery, etc.) but does not generate value. This can be, for example, overproduction, stock, unnecessary movements, waiting times or errors. By identifying and eliminating waste, a company can utilise its resources more efficiently and increase its productivity.

Mura refers to an imbalance or disequilibrium in a process. This can occur when workload, production rates or material flow are not evenly distributed, which can lead to bottlenecks, overload, or underutilisation. Lean management aims to achieve a smooth and even production flow by eliminating mura in order to improve efficiency and quality.

Reducing the overuse of resources, be it machinery, labour, or other means, is known as Mura. Overuse can lead to wear and tear, fatigue and quality problems. The aim is to optimise the workload in order to avoid overload and create a sustainable working environment in which employees can work effectively without being overloaded.

Lean was introduced at a Japanese IT company in Germany under the name Sense and Respond. As the name suggests, it is about listening very carefully to the wishes and needs of customers, sensing them and responding to them. Digital technology has meant that we have constant two-way communication with every customer contact. This continuous and close communication must be utilised according to lean principles in order to create added value on both sides (Mahadevan & Chejarla, 2023).

**Sense and Respond**

Sense-and-response has been used in control technology for decades, particularly in closed systems such as refineries. Measured values are compared with target values and the system settings are adjusted accordingly in order to minimise the deviation between the two values. Since the early 1980s, the term "Sense and Respond" has also been used to describe the behaviour of certain open systems.

The term "Sense and Respond" as a corporate concept was first used in 1992 in an article in the American Management Association Management Review by Stephan H. Haeckel. The concept was developed by Haeckel at the IBM Advanced Business Institute (Haeckel & Slywotzky, 1999).

The essence of Sense and Respond is to actively listen and recognise what is important to customers. This knowledge is used to find inspiration, to see and think differently, and to drive value creation and the elimination of waste.

It responds to customer needs by implementing innovations and adapting services to successfully support customers in a rapidly changing environment.

**Lean principles**

As already explained, lean should represent the core of the corporate culture, i.e. the "spirit" of the company. In our case, the central aspects and principles of lean listed above can be extended to the following seven principles, which again clearly place the customer and people at the centre, but also include the topics of learning, measuring and managing (Mahadevan & Chejarla, 2023).

- Understanding the customer benefit: The focus is on first understanding what is really important to customers, delivering this and then continuously improving it.
- Eliminate waste: By eliminating wasted time and labour in processes or services, resources can be freed up for improvement. Identifying and reducing waste makes organisations more competitive and increases customer satisfaction.
- Standardisation: Standardisation and the exchange of best practices are promoted in order to improve efficiency and quality.
- Learning by doing: Knowledge is acquired through practical experience and the assumption of responsibility in a real working environment, together with colleagues and customers.
- Involve everyone: Success is created when all employees are involved. It is not about doing things for individuals but about creating a framework that enables each individual to improve their daily work and build success for themselves and their customers.
- Measuring what counts: Care is taken to ensure that only what really contributes to added value, as perceived by employees and customers, is measured.
- Manage visually (manage performance visually): Visual management makes the invisible visible and draws attention to what is important for employees and customers.

Furthermore, there are several high-impact techniques for lean, which are used to avoid waste and increase added value. By focussing on these techniques, it has been possible to repeatedly reduce time and workload, drastically improve quality, reduce costs, save time and create added value (Table 2.3).

For more in-depth insights into lean, we recommend "The Machine That Changed the World" by James P. Womack, Daniel T. Jones and Daniel Roos. It was first published in 1991 and describes the fundamentals of lean manufacturing, based on observations at Toyota (Womack et al., 2007).

### 2.7.3 Six Sigma

Another method that has established itself alongside lean management is Six Sigma. This method was developed at Motorola in the USA in the 1990s. The mathematical process originates from the engineering sciences. The focus here is on quality assurance, which is to be achieved with the help of statistical tools and precise data analysis.

It should be noted that Six Sigma, unlike Lean, always requires a separate organisation within the company and is used in specially defined and selected areas and projects. Lean, on the other hand, can be understood more as a culture within the company.

With Six Sigma, process-relevant data such as process indicators, failure modes and parameters are recorded and statistically analysed.

The Six Sigma organisation consists of the Master Black Belt, the Black Belt and the Green Belt. There is also a Yellow Belt and a White Belt. Six Sigma is implemented as a project. It therefore does not generally exist across an entire company.

The term sigma defines the measure of process capability. Six Sigma therefore means six times the standard deviation, whereby the sigma values are set in relation to the measured variable ppm "parts per million". The target is 6σ, i.e. 3.4 ppm. Six Sigma focuses on improving a process flow that runs in five phases, the so-called DMAIC cycles (Niemann et al., 2024).

The DMAIC cycle comprises the phases:

**Table 2.3** High-impact techniques for Lean

| | |
|---|---|
| Shift-Left (shift to the left) | Reduces repeated handling and multiple handovers. |
| Demand analysis | Eliminates repetitive and unnecessary work requests. |
| Automation | Creates a flow—eliminates excessive quantities and reduces overall waiting time. |
| Voice of the customer | Creates value from the outset by understanding the current situation. |
| Visual Management | Enables the current situation to be presented as quickly as possible so that decisions can be made on the basis of facts. |
| Workplace organisation | Creates an up-to-date, easy-to-find source of truth. |
| Standardisation | Eliminates different, error-prone procedures with a way of working that everyone can understand. |
| Mistake prevention | Increases error prevention from the outset, corrects errors or draws attention to errors. |

- *Define*—In this phase, the project contract is drawn up. The tasks and objectives for the teams are developed and defined.
- *Measure*—This is where the hypotheses are first formulated and then the corresponding measurement methods are determined. This is followed by data collection, whereby the feasibility of data collection is clarified in advance at.
- *Analyse*—The measurement is followed by the analysis phase, in which causes are identified, verified, and quantified. An attempt is made to draw conclusions about the causes of faults from the measurements and to confirm the validity of the results.
- *Improve*—In this phase, a low-cost and effective solution to the problem is sought. Measures are also defined to quantify the financial impact of the improvement. A risk analysis and an implementation plan are also drawn up before the improvement is realised.
- *Control*—This is where the sustainability of the improvement is checked. The actual KPIs are compared with the target KPIs, deviations are recorded and documented. Finally, the changed process is integrated into the process standard and new projects are defined if necessary.

## 2.8 Cynefin

The Cynefin Framework was originally developed by Mary E. Boone and Dave Snowden in the context of knowledge management and corporate strategy. It quickly found favour in the areas of agility and IT service management, as it helps to categorise problems according to their complexity. Cynefin is a Welsh word that can be translated as "habitat".

In complex contexts, the relationship between cause and effect is not known in advance and can only be analysed retrospectively. The greater the uncertainty, the greater the risk of pursuing the wrong strategy. For this reason, it makes economic sense in complex environments to minimise the implementation effort until the added value of the idea has been validated. As expertise alone is often not sufficient for complex problems, short iterations with "safe-to-fail" experiments must be carried out. The hypotheses can then be validated in order to derive the next steps from the knowledge gained.

Cynefin focuses on the unpredictability and quality of decision-making, enabling the customisation of processes. For adaptive services, Cynefin is a valuable tool for exploring alternatives. One of Cynefin's strengths is that it can be used productively after 2 min of training and still offers new aspects after 2 years.

Cynefin is divided into five areas or domains, which we will discuss briefly: (Fig. 2.5)

1. *Clear* (Obvious or Simple)

   There is a clear causal relationship, and the alternative courses of action are largely predetermined: sense → categorise → respond (best practice).

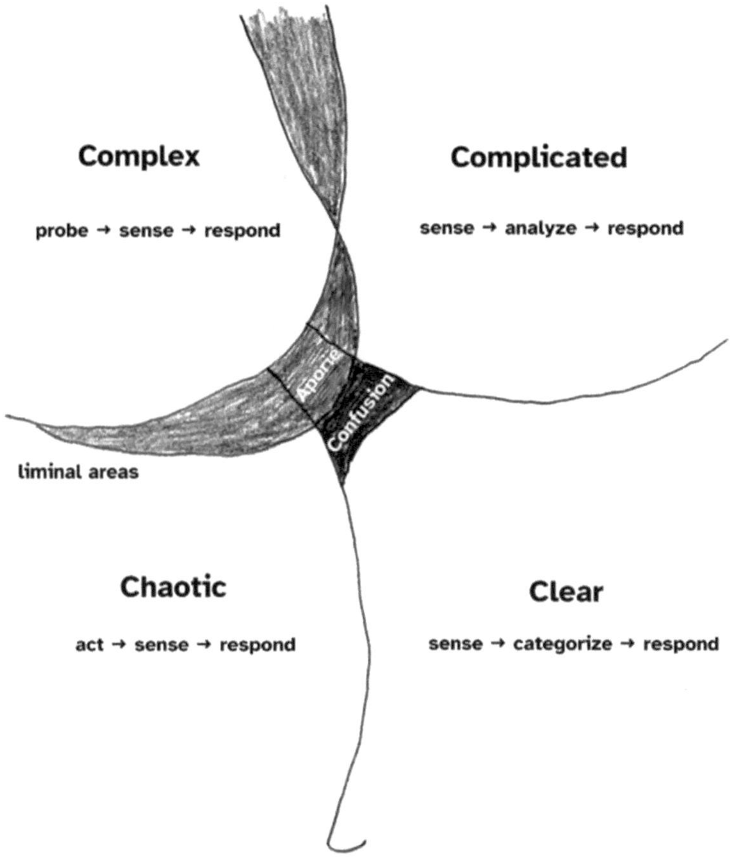


**Fig. 2.5** Overview Cynefin based on Snowden (2020)

2. *Complicated*

   There are many factors to consider, but the framework conditions are clearly defined. Cause–effect relationships can be sufficiently analysed by experts. Options for action and results are known: sense → analyse → respond (good practice).

3. *Complex*

   There is a large variety of networked system elements as well as external and internal dynamics. The cause-and-effect relationships cannot be sufficiently analysed in the situation; later ex-post analyses may be informative. However, the system behaves continuously within a certain framework. The solution direction is known, concrete goals are known, the solution method is possibly unknown. The solution path is found experimentally: probe → sense → respond (emerging practice).

4. *Chaos*

   The system is highly dynamic and turbulent, cause and effect are indifferent. The causality of the system is not recognisable. Measures must be taken to avert damage and zones of stability are sought: act → sense → respond (novel practice).
5. *Disorder*

   This is the state in which the nature of causality is unknown. Disorder is divided into confusion and aporia. The boundaries are desirable transition zones and are open at the top. Aporia refers to a problem in which several conflicting and contradictory results occur.

It is important to understand that the assignment of categories is always context-, time-, and subject-related. For one company, a task may be simple because it has built up the relevant expertise over time, while for another company the same task may be complex. The same applies to the time factor. If there is little time available, a task can be complex which, after lengthy analysis and with the help of specialists, can also be solved in the simple category. For a more in-depth look at Cynefin, we can recommend public videos by Dave Snowden or one of his books such as Snowden (2020).

## 2.9 Objectives and Key Results

Objectives and Key Results (OKR) is a method for agile strategy implementation, a target management method and a management system for target-orientated employee management. It is a framework for setting objectives and measuring key results. OKR was developed at Intel in the 1970s and has also been used at Google since the 2000s

The "Probe–Sense–Respond" approach forms the core of the OKR framework and can therefore serve as a lifeline for complex challenges. Working in short OKR cycles (3–4 months)—with the approach of experimenting (Probe), measuring (Sense), and reflecting (Respond)—promotes a hypothesis-based approach instead of prefabricated solutions. This enables an adaptive implementation of the strategy.

Objectives and key results are the core elements of the OKR framework and are related to each other through a framework process. Based on the vision and mission, which are intended to express the company's medium and long-term goals, objectives and key results are harmonised and formulated at regular intervals both company-wide and at team level.

Both objectives and key results are to be understood as "goals" in the sense of the framework. However, they differ, on the one hand, in terms of their content and, on the other, in terms of their methodological significance. "Objectives" can also be described as "small visions". They are intended to make the strategic impulses of the corporate vision more tangible for a manageable period of time and, if necessary, for individual areas of the company. Objectives generally relate to the entire company for the next 12 months. An example of a goal could be: "Our product A will become the standard solution among CRM systems for estate agents".

"Key results", on the other hand, are targets in the form of measurable results. They form the centrepiece of OKR, as they are defined on a quarterly basis at company and team level and therefore have a decisive influence on operational activities within the company. In the sense of a cascade of content, the key results are intended to take up the strategic impetus of the objectives and enable operational implementation through their results-orientated formulation. An example of a key result could be: "Our product A will go live with 16 customers on 31 March 2026".

The key results therefore form the "how" of an objective.

Cascading, it can therefore be said that the vision and mission are at the top. In order to achieve these, the vision is broken down into smaller goals and specified somewhat. Key results form the lowest level. Depending on the area of application, there can be several levels of objectives and several levels of key results. If, for example, OKR is used in a team and not in the entire company, there will be one vision and mission, 3–5 objectives and 3–5 key results per objective. This number would be reduced if the team is small.

**Good targets are characterised by the following features:**

- Qualitative—not measurable—formulation ("small visions")
- They describe a desirable state in the future.
- There is a maximum of 4–5 destinations.
- Balanced: challenging, demanding, and achievable
- Large projects are subdivided into smaller projects.
- Derived from strategy, long-term goals and team needs
- 60% bottom-up (operational) and 40% top-down (strategic)
- Clear focus on customer benefits and business value

**Good key results are characterised by the following features:**

- There is a maximum of five key results per objective.
- They describe how the objective is to be achieved.
- The driving force for achieving the goal can be easily deduced.
- They are quantitative and measurable.
- They are specifically defined without any room for interpretation.
- They are precisely timed.
- They are accepted by the parties involved.
- They are ambitious and achievable in one cycle.
- They focus on results and not on linked milestones or activities.

**The OKR planning cycle (Fig. 2.6)**

In the planning cycle, it should be noted that the measures contained therein are implemented and agreed jointly and in coordination. This is a key difference to management by objectives (MBO), as explained below. Here, the objectives are not

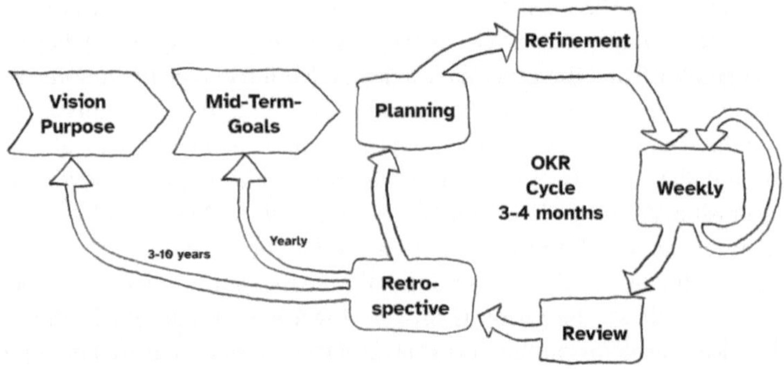


**Fig. 2.6** The OKR cycle

set exclusively by the managers but are also defined by the employees. There is also a commitment to the key results.

For more in-depth insights into OKR, we recommend "Measure what matters: OKRs—the simple idea that drives 10× growth" by John Doerr and "Digital Product Management" by Sascha Hoffmann (Doerr, 2018; Hoffmann, 2024).

## 2.10 MBO

In 1954, Peter Ferdinand Drucker developed the concept of Management by Objectives (MBO), which centres on target agreements between managers and employees. The concept aims to improve employee performance by setting clear objectives and regularly reviewing progress. The targets set in the target agreements are developed with the active involvement of employees (Drucker, 1973).

In the target agreement meeting, managers and employees also jointly define suitable measurement and control systems that can be used to measure target achievement. Once the targets have been defined and recorded in the target agreement, employees are free to decide which measures they want to use to achieve the target within the framework of defined standards.

Focussing on the agreed objectives is crucial. The target agreements should correspond to the SMART approach.

SMART goals are structured and formulated as follows:

- S—specific
- M—measurable
- A—achievable (and accepted)
- R—realistic (or reasonable)
- T—time-bound (planned or scheduled)

Goals should describe where you want to go and not what you want to avoid. No "away from" goals should be formulated. Furthermore, goals should not be expressed as comparisons and should not contain comparatives. They should also not be expressed through negations (Johanning, 2024).

The subconscious does not work with negations. Shouting "Don't fall!" to a running toddler could cause them to trip. Similarly, our subconscious can be misled if our goals are stated in the negative. In order to create clarity, it is often necessary to explain what is not meant by the goal and what is explicitly not part of achieving the goal.

The individual goals of employees are always in line with the company's goals. This serves the growth of the company and the achievement of corporate goals (Doran, 1981).

## 2.11 Vision and Mission

There are no binding guidelines as to what a vision statement or mission statement should look like or what it absolutely must contain. However, our experience can help to describe the purpose and impact of these statements.

Both statements serve as a guiding star for employees in the company and provide orientation in all situations and questions.

**The vision**

A vision is an ambitious description of where the company or division wants to position itself in the medium to long term. In contrast to the mission, the vision is a clear picture of an inspiring future that is to be strived for and achieved together. It always lies in the future and represents a positive challenge without describing the exact path to get there.

**The mission**

The mission defines the concrete steps and courses of action to realise the vision. It defines how the company or sector will achieve its goals and fulfil its purpose. The mission often includes aspects such as the values, principles, and strategies that guide the company, as well as the target groups, products, or services to be offered. It gives employees, customers, and other stakeholders a clear insight into the fundamental direction and purpose of the company and creates a common basis for decisions and actions. Ultimately, the mission serves as a compass that guides the organisation on the path to realising its vision (Becker, 2024).

**Examples of vision and mission**

*Nike Vision Statement:*
To do everything possible to expand human potential.

*Nike Mission:*
To bring inspiration and innovation to every athlete in the world (Pereira, 2025).

*Tesla Vision Statement:*
Accelerating the global transition to sustainable energy.

*Tesla Mission:*
We want to create the most compelling automotive company of the twenty-first century by driving the global transition to electric vehicles (Musk, 2013).

A vision and mission statement are crucial for any organisation as they provide a clear direction and a common goal. A vision defines long-term goals and dreams that motivate and inspire the organisation. It serves as a guiding star that shows all employees where the company is heading and what value it wants to create.

The mission statement, on the other hand, describes how the company intends to fulfil its purpose, and which values guide it in doing so. It defines the fundamental direction of the company and creates a common basis for decisions and actions.

The advantages of a clear vision and mission statement are manifold. As well as helping employees to identify with the company and promoting a common understanding and direction within the company, they also help with external communication by showing customers, suppliers, and other stakeholders what the company stands for and what added value it offers.

A vision and mission statement also make it easier to define outcomes when working with partners. They serve as a point of reference for common objectives and make it possible to clearly communicate and agree on goals and expectations. This promotes successful collaboration and helps everyone involved to work towards a common goal (Reid & Crawford, 2022).

## 2.12 Organisational Change Management

IT service tenders lead to transition projects and bring about changes. Sometimes these changes are minor, because only the service company for a service is replaced, but sometimes they are very big changes for the customer organisation and its employees. The replacement of a service with major changes is called a transformation. In the run-up to transformation projects, strategies must be developed for communicating and implementing these changes.

> **Important** Without additional information and room for manoeuvre, people shy away from change. What is needed is a corporate culture that encourages employees to help shape and implement change. The saying "Culture eats strategy for breakfast" fits in with this. (Culture eats strategy for breakfast.), which is often attributed to the economist Peter Drucker. In fact, Peter Drucker said: "Culture—no matter what it looks like—is singularly persistent". (Culture—no matter how defined—is singularly persistent.) (Drucker, 1991)

The strategy for change must therefore be defined on the basis of the existing corporate culture. A technical or organisational change that aims to radically change an existing culture at the same time is doomed to failure. Cultural change takes time, a lot of effort and perseverance. For this reason, we also advise against a centralised top-down introduction of adaptive services.

There are numerous management methods and literature on the preparation, implementation, and follow-up of change processes. At this point, we would like to highlight some examples of methods that shed light on various aspects of organisational change management. People always surprise us with their reactions during change processes. The spectrum ranges from organised resistance to unexpectedly creative ideas that accelerate implementation or communication in the peer group. Although suitable methods do not allow meticulous planning of the change process, they are good tools for steering and counteracting the process (Huang & Hands, 2022).

### 2.12.1 Emotional Cycle of Change

However well planned a transformation may be, change is always a personal and emotional journey. Each person goes through the cycle of change at their own pace. There are several models that concretise this cycle, one of which is the "Emotional Cycle of Change" model developed by Don Kelley and Daryl Conner from the mid-1970s onwards (Kelley & Conner, 1979). It divides this cycle into five stages, which can be summarised as follows:

1. *Uninformed optimism:* The benefits are dreamed of the effort is not yet recognisable. Usual activities are brainstorming about the next steps and developing a strategy for the future.
2. *Informed pessimism:* The benefits no longer seem so real, but the costs of change become clear. Good reasons are sought for abandoning the endeavours.
3. *Hopeful realism (Valley of despair):* The painful transformation process is palpable, and the benefits seem a long way off. Giving up seems like an obvious option in this phase.
4. *Informed optimism:* The benefits of the approach are beginning to pay off and the costs are beginning to be worthwhile.
5. *Completion (success and fulfilment):* Benefits and costs are understood; the new way of working is more efficient than the old one.

It is not necessary to work exactly according to the five steps of the "Emotional Cycle of Change" by Kelley and Conner, but it is important to deal with this personal aspect of change. For example, people who are enthusiastic about change can go through this cycle very quickly and have little understanding of the fact that colleagues are still stuck in earlier phases months later. People who go through this cycle slowly become important pillars of support, especially in the critical phases, when the leading faster colleagues are already thinking about giving up.

These different speeds therefore require an intensified discourse within the organisation. Levelling the playing field, where managers try to force employees to change at a faster pace with poisonous arguments, only has a superficial effect and does nothing to change the causes. A mutually appreciative exchange can have a positive influence on emotions. The speed of change in the individual, however, cannot.

### 2.12.2 Eight-Step Model According to John P. Kotter

One of the best-known models for managing change in organisations is John Kotter's eight-step model, which was first presented in 1996 in his book "Leading Change" (Kotter, 1996). Based on his own experiences, the book discusses eight steps to change in very concrete terms using case studies. In each step, typical mistakes, their causes and suitable measures are discussed. Although the book dates back to the late 1990s and does not have a strong IT focus, it is still extremely practical today.

1. *Create a sense of urgency*

   In the end, most employees, most managers and practically all top managers must be convinced of the change. To achieve this, it is important to point out weaknesses compared to the competition, make mistakes visible, provide relevant data and enforce honesty in management meetings.
2. *Build a guiding coalition*

   A guiding coalition needs the element of steering by appropriate managers and leadership that drives change. This requires influence, competence, credibility, and leadership that bring about change. The management team must create a climate of trust and develop common goals.
3. *A vision and strategy*

   In several iterations, the management team creates a common transformation vision that is ambitious enough to pull employees out of their comfort zone. A vision that aims for ever better products or services at ever lower costs, that utilises fundamental trends and a moral force that, for example, does not exploit anyone.
4. *Communicate the change vision*

   All employees must have a clear understanding of the vision. Key elements for effective communication are simplicity, speaking in metaphors, analogies, and examples. Many channels such as meetings, memos, and news, but also formal and informal interactions in both directions should be utilised. The ideas of the vision must be communicated again and again. Managers are role models; no one manager should be allowed to step out of line. Existing or apparent contradictions must be actively explained in order to ensure the credibility of all communication.

5. *Empower broad-based action*

   Employees should be shown a path that does not present any major obstacles so that they do not lose sight of the common goal. To achieve this, the company's structures must be harmonised with the vision. Employees must be taught new skills and behavioural patterns so that they can play their part. Information and personnel systems must be aligned with the vision. Managers who undermine the necessary change must be identified and actively influenced.

6. *Generate short-term wins*

   At this point, Kotter uses quick wins to communicate the positive benefits of the change as early as possible in an exemplary manner. Selected successes should be visible to many people, clearly underpin the vision and have a clear link to the change measures. This justifies the initial costs, boosts morale and motivation through positive feedback and turns neutral advocates and hesitant supporters into active participants.

7. *Consolidate gains and produce more change*

   Successes should not be announced too early. Successful measures are used to drive further change. The pace is increased by hiring, promoting, and developing employees. While top management must provide clarity and urgency, the change approach extends to project management and leadership from below.

8. *Anchor new approaches in the corporate culture*

   Anchoring change in the corporate culture comes last, not first. Successfully established changes are the driving force for change in the corporate culture. Only when the new approaches work and are superior to the old methods is the new way accepted, and people are prepared to say goodbye to parts of the corporate culture that are not compatible with the vision. This step requires a lot of communication but is important to ensure that the change is sustainable. All processes must be adapted to the new culture, e.g. recruitment and promotion procedures.

### 2.12.3 GCDA

The GCDA (Goal and Content Dependency Analysis) methodology was developed by Matthias Kreutter and originates from project management. It is a methodology for documenting mutual influences and interfaces and reacting to and controlling them in projects (Kreutter, 2016).

The basis for this methodology is the cause-and-effect matrix (cause-and-effect analysis). This is a tool from Lean Six Sigma that is used to depict and prioritise several factors influencing an error (effect). It is often used to identify and analyse possible causes for a specific problem or effect. It graphically represents the relationship between different causes and their effects by organising the potential causes in rows and the observable effects in columns. With the help of this matrix, teams can prioritise the main causes and develop suitable measures to solve the problem.

In the management of change, it is important to know how the organisational units influence each other and where or who the most influential organisational units are. In this way, the GCDA can create a map of the organisation and support change management as well as the necessary communication with employees and the involvement of organisational units in the change process (Niemann et al., 2024).

## 2.13 Outcome vs. Output

There is often confusion between outcome and output. Not necessarily in the use of the terms, but often in the expectations of the results of an assignment. Especially in the service sector, the outcome is more important than the output. It is very important to distinguish between these two terms. Adaptive services directly target the outcome, while traditional tenders specify an output. In short, output can be described as the scope of services, while outcome serves as proof of impact. We would therefore like to explain the differences in detail here.

Output generally refers to artefacts such as a certain number of documents, a production process, a certain technology or other tangible things. Output is the verifiable result of activities or initiatives. It is the vehicle, so to speak, with which business value is created or increased. The added value for the user or customer is not necessarily directly evident from the output.

Outcome, on the other hand, defines the actual added value for the user or customer. Outcome is based on an output. In traditional business relationships, the IT service provider provides the client with an output. Whether the client can actually achieve the business results planned as an outcome with this output is primarily in the hands of the client.

Concisely summarised:

- *Output* is an easily measurable result that fulfils the requirements
- *Outcome* is the value created in relation to the original plan

**Example** A decline in orders can be explained by internal sales.

An organisation is suffering from a significant drop in orders and the associated loss of sales. When analysing the reasons, it was discovered, among other things, that the internal sales department had lost some employees and that they could not be replaced. This delays some sales processes, especially when end customers have a complaint about the process or even want to prioritise an order. In the past, end customers have approached Sales to inform them that they have ordered from competitors instead.

The company decides to purchase internal "sales as a service" with corresponding capacity planning and service level targets on the market. The plans call for a 20% increase in orders in the first year. After the contracted service provider has taken over the service, the internal sales service is running almost smoothly after 3 months. Test calls, test orders and the required service levels have all been met. This means that the service provider has achieved the required output extremely well.

The outcome, the increase in incoming orders, cannot yet be conclusively calculated 1 month after the go live. Complaints from end customers have at least decreased significantly. At the end of the first year, it is apparent that orders are only slightly up on the previous year. The necessary increase of 20% could not be achieved through the professionalisation of the internal sales team. In terms of outcome-orientation, it might have been better to tackle several alternatives in parallel and gradually promote the most valuable alternatives for increasing orders.

In the area of traditional IT services, it is also particularly important to define the outcome and coordinate it between the customer and service provider. By defining the outcome, the service provider understands what the customer wants to achieve and can better align the output to be created with the customer's goal (Armes et al., 2015).

## References


Al-Saqqa, S., Sawalha, S., & AbdelNabi, H. (2020). Agile software development: Methodologies and trends. *International Journal of Interactive Mobile Technologies, 14*, 246–270.

Armes, D., Engelhart, N., McKenzie, P., & Wiggers, P. (2015). *SIAM: Principles and practices for service integration and management*. Van Haren Publishing.

AXELOS Limited. (2019). *ITIL foundation: ITIL* (4th ed.). TSO.

Beck, K., & Andres, C. (2004). *Extreme programming explained: Embrace change*. Addison-Wesley Professional.

Beck, K., Beedle, M., van Bennekum, A., & Cockburn, A. (2001). *Principles behind the Agile Manifesto*. Retrieved July 7, 2025, from https://agilemanifesto.org/principles.html

Becker, C. (2024). Product strategy—The foundation of product management. In S. Hoffmann (Ed.), *Digital product management*. Springer. https://doi.org/10.1007/978-3-658-44276-7_3

Bertagnolli, F. (2022). Continuous improvement. In *Lean management*. Springer. https://doi.org/10.1007/978-3-658-36087-0_11

Bittner, K., Kong, P., & West, D. (2018). *Mit dem Nexus™ Framework Scrum skalieren*. dpunkt.verlag.

Block, S. (2023). *Large-scale agile frameworks. Agile frameworks, agile infrastructure and pragmatic solutions for digital transformation*. Springer. https://doi.org/10.1007/978-3-662-67782-7

Bovis, C. (2025). Public procurement regulation in EU and UK. In E. Guinchard & C. Panara (Eds.), *The new relationship between the United Kingdom and the European Union*. Springer. https://doi.org/10.1007/978-3-031-70652-3_9

Bruhn, M. (2023). Conceptual basics of quality management for services. In *Quality management for services*. Springer. https://doi.org/10.1007/978-3-662-67032-3_3

Ćwiklicki, M. (2023). Kaizen. In S. O. Idowu, R. Schmidpeter, N. Capaldi, L. Zu, M. Del Baldo, & R. Abreu (Eds.), *Encyclopedia of sustainable management*. Springer. https://doi.org/10.1007/978-3-031-25984-5_377

Doerr, J. (2018). *Measure what matters: OKRs – the simple idea that drives 10x growth*. Portfolio Penguin.

Doran, G. T. (1981). There's a S.M.A.R.T. way to write management's goals and objectives. *Management Review, 70*(11), 35–36.

Drucker, P. F. (1973). *Management: Tasks, responsibilities, practices*. Harper & Row.

Drucker, P. F. (1991, March 28). Don't change corporate culture-use it! *The Wall Street Journal*.

Haeckel, S. H., & Slywotzky, A. J. (1999). *Adaptive enterprise: Creating and leading sense-and-respond organisations*. Harvard Business School Press.

Hoffmann, S. (2024). *Digital product management*. Springer Gabler. https://link.springer.com/book/10.1007/978-3-658-44276-7

Huang, Y., & Hands, D. (2022). Organisational complexity and change by design. In *Design thinking for new business contexts*. Palgrave Macmillan. https://doi.org/10.1007/978-3-030-94206-9_4

ISG-ONE. (2013). *THE RFP WILL NEVER BE THE SAME - Emerging Approaches to Innovative Sourcing ISG WHITE PAPER 2013*. Retrieved July 7, 2025, from https://isg-one.com/docs/default-source/default-document-library/rfs-innovation.pdf

Johanning, V. (2022). Step 4: The sourcing strategy. In *IT strategy*. Springer. https://doi.org/10.1007/978-3-658-38772-3_8

Johanning, V. (2024). The role of IT in the company. In *Organization and management of IT*. Springer. https://doi.org/10.1007/978-3-658-39572-8_5

Keith, B., Vitasek, K., Manrodt, K., & Kling, J. (2016). Embracing codependency: Enhancing success. In *Strategic sourcing in the new economy*. Palgrave Macmillan. https://doi.org/10.1007/978-1-137-55220-4_6

Kelley, D., & Conner, D. R. (1979). Emotional cycle of change. In I. J. W. Pfeiffer & J. E. Jones (Eds.), *The annual handbook for group facilitators* (p. 117f). University Associates Publishers.

Kotter, J. P. (1996). *Leading change*. Harvard Business School Press.

Krause, K., & Schnitzler, T. (2022). Digging deeper. In K. Krause & T. Schnitzler (Eds.), *Business partner management* (p. 87 ff). Springer. https://doi.org/10.1007/978-3-658-37475-4_3

Kreutter, T. (2016). *Projektabhängigkeiten einfach systematisch analysieren: Die GCDA*. Retrieved July 7, 2025, from https://xm-institute.com/xm-blog/projektabhangigkeiten-einfach-systematisch-analysieren-die-gcda/

Krishna Kaiser, A. (2023). ITIL basics. In *Reinventing ITIL® and DevOps with digital transformation*. Apress. https://doi.org/10.1007/978-1-4842-9072-9_2

Kuster, J., Bachmann, C., Hubmann, M., Lippmann, R., & Schneider, P. (2023). *Project management handbook. Management for professionals*. Springer. https://doi.org/10.1007/978-3-662-66211-3

Liedtke, T. (2024). IT service management. In *Information security*. Springer. https://doi.org/10.1007/978-3-658-45711-2_8

Lincke, S. (2024). Governing: Policy, maturity models and planning. In *Information security planning*. Springer. https://doi.org/10.1007/978-3-031-43118-0_6

Mahadevan, G., & Chejarla, K. C. (2023). Lean management principles. In *Lean management for small and medium sized enterprises. Management for professionals*. Springer. https://doi.org/10.1007/978-981-19-4340-9_2

Mandl, C. (2023). Procurement analytics. In *Springer series in supply chain management* (Vol. 22). Springer. https://doi.org/10.1007/978-3-031-43281-1_1

McKenna, D. (2016). *The art of scrum*. Apress.

McKinsey. (2020, October 5). Retrieved July 7, 2025, from https://www.mckinsey.com/business-functions/organization/our-insights/the-journey-to-agile-how-companies-can-become-faster-more-productive-and-more-responsive?cid=podcast-eml-alt-mip-mck&hdpid=b6471911-807d-4c54-bf85-1c6e75267e57&hctky=9960673&hlkid=e2799

Meissner, J. O., Heike, M., & Sigrist, D. (2024). Agile management. In *Organizational design in a complex and unstable world*. Springer Gabler. https://doi.org/10.1007/978-3-658-45022-9_5

Musk, E. (2013, November 18). *The mission of Tesla*. Retrieved July 7, 2025, from https://www.tesla.com/blog/mission-tesla

Myklebust, T., Stålhane, T., & Vatn, D. M. K. (2025). Artificial intelligence (AI). In *The AI act and the agile safety plan*. SpringerBriefs in Computer Science. Springer. https://doi.org/10.1007/978-3-031-80504-2_6

Nicoletti, B. (2018). Procurement processes and finance. In *Procurement finance. Palgrave studies in financial services technology*. Palgrave Macmillan. https://doi.org/10.1007/978-3-030-02140-5_2

Niemann, J., Reich, B., & Stöhr, C. (2024). *Lean six sigma*. Springer. https://doi.org/10.1007/978-3-662-68744-4_3

O'Regan, G. (2025). Outsourcing—Supplier selection and management. In *Guide to software project management. Undergraduate topics in computer science*. Springer. https://doi.org/10.1007/978-3-031-80578-3_10

Oshri, I., Kotlarsky, J., & Willcocks, L. (2023a). Supplier selection, retained management capabilities, and legal issues. In I. Oshri, J. Kotlarsky, & L. Willcocks (Eds.), *The handbook of global outsourcing and offshoring* (pp. 121–151). Palgrave Macmillan. https://doi.org/10.1007/978-3-031-12034-3_6

Oshri, I., Kotlarsky, J., & Willcocks, L. P. (2023b). The IT outsourcing life cycle and the transition phase. In *The handbook of global outsourcing and offshoring*. Palgrave Macmillan. https://doi.org/10.1007/978-3-031-12034-3_8

Palmer, S., & Felsing, J. (2002). *A practical guide to feature-driven development*. Prentice-Hall PTR.

Pereira, D. (2025). *Nike mission and vision statement*. Retrieved July 7, 2025, from https://businessmodelanalyst.com/nike-mission-and-vision-statement/

Reid, S., & Crawford, C. (2022). Crafting the vision statement. In S. Reid & C. Crawford (Eds.), *Entrepreneurial vision. Classroom companion: Business*. Springer. https://doi.org/10.1007/978-3-030-77803-3_13

Roth-Dietrich, G. (2024). Artificial intelligence (AI) for platform business models. In T. Barton & C. Müller (Eds.), *Artificial intelligence in application*. Springer. https://doi.org/10.1007/978-3-658-43843-2_7

Sabharwal, N., Rathore, R., & Agrawal, U. (2022). Introduction to agile frameworks. In *Hands-on guide to AgileOps*. Apress. https://doi.org/10.1007/978-1-4842-7505-4_6

Sarferaz, S. (2024). Sourcing and procurement. In *Embedding artificial intelligence into ERP software*. Springer. https://doi.org/10.1007/978-3-031-54249-7_22

Scaled Agile, Inc. (2024). *SAFe 6.0*. Retrieved July 7, 2025, from https://scaledagileframework.com/

Schenk, B. (2025). *Advanced management information systems. Progress in IS*. Springer. https://doi.org/10.1007/978-3-031-87904-3

Schwaber, K., & Sutherland, J. (2020). *The Scrum guide*. ScrumGuides.org.

Scrum.org. (2024a). *Scaling Scrum with Nexus*. Retrieved July 7, 2025, from https://www.scrum.org/resources/scaling-scrum

Scrum.org. (2024b). *What is Scrum?* Retrieved July 7, 2025, from https://www.scrum.org/learning-series/what-is-scrum/

Snowden, D. (2020). *Cynefin - Weaving sense-making into the fabric of our world*. Cognitive Edge - The Cynefin Company.

Sutherland, J. (2008). *Agile contracts: Money for nothing and your change for free*. Retrieved July 7, 2025, from https://www.Scruminc.com/agile-contracts-money-for-nothing-and/

The Open Group. (2022). *TOGAF® Standard - Introduction - Enterprise Continuum*. Retrieved July 7, 2025, from https://pubs.opengroup.org/togaf-standard/architecture-content/chap06.html

The Open Group. (2024). *TOGAF*. Retrieved July 7, 2025, from https://www.opengroup.org/togaf

Tiemeyer, E. (2020). *Handbuch IT-Management: Konzepte, Methoden, Lösungen und Arbeitshilfen für die Praxis*. Carl Hanser.

Volker, L., & Schotanus, F. (2023). Tendering and supplier selection. In J. Grandia & L. Volker (Eds.), *Public procurement*. Palgrave Macmillan. https://doi.org/10.1007/978-3-031-18490-1_6

Willcocks, L., Oshri, I., & Kotlarsky, J. (2024). The global outsourcing pivot: Advances and challenges. In L. Willcocks, I. Oshri, & J. Kotlarsky (Eds.), *Transformation in global outsourcing. Technology, work and globalization*. Palgrave Macmillan. https://doi.org/10.1007/978-3-031-61022-6_1

Womack, J. P., Jones, D. T., & Roos, D. (2007). *The machine that changed the world: The story of lean production – Toyota's secret weapon in the global car wars that is now revolutionizing world industry*. Simon and Schuster.

# Stakeholder Personas

# 3

We have often seen misunderstandings in tenders because the people involved did not have a clear understanding of the tasks and objectives of the other parties. They prematurely assume that others share their own point of view and goals. By considering the motivations of those involved and understanding their intentions, you can organise your own projects and their implementation more successfully.

In this text, we have attempted to describe the interest groups, their motivations, and their general perspective.

## 3.1 Roles Used in This Book

In this book, generic roles are used to represent the functional areas and responsibilities involved in a tender. However, they are limited to the roles most frequently involved in the process.

For this reason, additional roles may be included in some companies.

Furthermore, it is assumed that all parties involved treat each other fairly and openly and that the motives are known and accepted by all parties involved (Fig. 3.1).

Unfair dealings with one another do occur in reality, but will not be considered here in order to keep the complexity within a mappable framework. Procedures or behaviours that take advantage of a partner without considering the consequences, or the concealment of aspects that a party has not considered or overlooked in order to take advantage of them later or to claim possible penalties, are excluded here.

Benchmarks are also not discussed in detail. This is because invitations to tender are often sent out even though all you want is a comparison of the current partner to check whether the service is being provided at a standard market price. The tender will then take a different course, and as a service provider, you will usually receive a rejection soon after the offer has been delivered.

Our experience has shown that overreaching a partner leads to the partner trying to compensate for the disadvantage. The authors have found that this leads to



G. Köhler et al., *Adaptive IT Service Tendering*, Management for Professionals,
https://doi.org/10.1007/978-3-658-49726-2_3

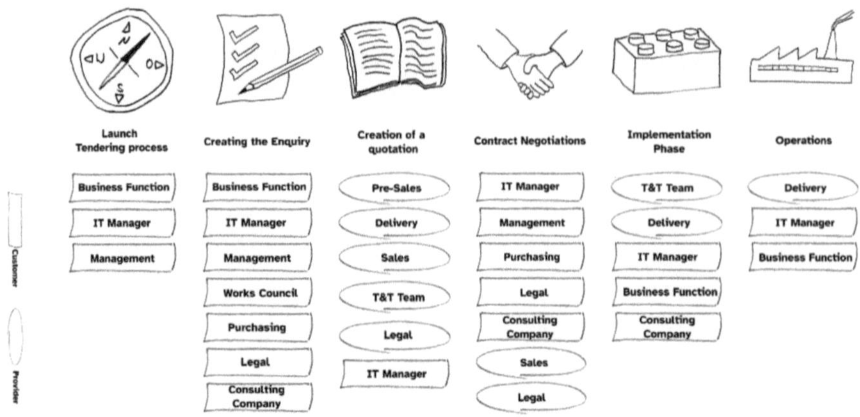


**Fig. 3.1** Participants in a tender at the various stages

claiming and can put a strain on a business relationship. Claiming refers to the search for topics or areas in which one can claim inferior performance or similar from the other party in order to compensate for one's own deficits.

In terms of stakeholders, a distinction is made between the roles on the customer side and those on the provider side. External consultants of the customer are categorised as belonging to the customer side, as they do not represent their own interests in relation to the specific tender, but those of the customer.

In companies where there are other external partners (so-called third parties) in the provision of IT services (e.g. outsourced data centres, technician deployments for repairs, etc.), these are usually involved in some way in the provision of the tendered service. This may be through interfaces in IT service management tools, or as customers of services that are put out to tender, or of services that are required to provide the tendered service.

In reality, it can also happen that the management of external partners is not optimal or, in rare cases, hardly takes place at all, or that they are not taken into account in the tendering process. But this is also not the subject of this book.

As mentioned, we assume that everyone treats each other fairly and openly and works towards the same goal, namely, to provide the best possible services for the customer. Furthermore, we do not take into account the roles and functions of the stakeholders of external partners or do not go into them in detail. As a rule, roles and functions can be held by several people. If we were to take all of the above factors into account, it would be difficult or impossible to depict the complexity here. For this reason, we limit the analysis and only refer to additional functions that can be used.

## 3.2 On the Customer Side

On the customer side, seven roles or functions are usually involved in a tendering process. These roles are (Fig. 3.2):

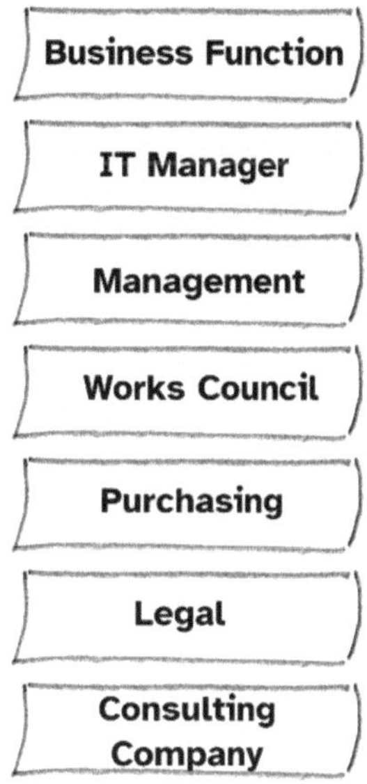


**Fig. 3.2** Participants on the customer side

**The Management**

Management is used as a collective term for the customer's decision-making level with regard to the tender. It focuses on the goal of supporting the company with the tender.

**The Business Function**

The business function may also consist of several departments. It also serves as a collective term for the recipients or consumers of the advertised services. As the recipient of the services, the business function primarily supports its individual business objectives.

**The IT Manager**

The IT manager is the person at the customer who is ultimately responsible for performance and quality within the customer organisation. His or her main focus is to ensure that the service is subsequently operated smoothly and with sufficient quality by the provider.

**The Purchasing Department**

The purchasing department usually acts as a department according to standardised processes and procedures. Several people from the purchasing department may be involved in each tender. The focus is on the cost of the services, particularly the challenge of identifying the best offer in terms of both price and quality.

**The Legal Department (Legal)**

The legal department usually consists of in-house lawyers (the number of whom depends on the size of the company). However, external lawyers can also be commissioned to advise on tenders. The main focus is on safeguarding the company's interests and ensuring compliance with the legal framework.

**The Works Council**

The works council represents the employees and is also made up of employees from the company (in principle from all hierarchical levels up to middle management). It endeavours to protect the interests of the employees. Its activities are based on the Works Constitution Act, collective agreements and agreements concluded within the company between the employees (works council or employee representatives) and the employer. The works council is elected by the employees and generally seeks re-election. In Germany, Austria, and the Netherlands, works councils have a special legal framework and can help determine company policy with regard to employees' interests. In all other countries, there are different legal frameworks, or none at all, and these workers' councils are generally not as powerful as those in these three countries.

**Consultancy Firm**

Consultancy firms often have their own consulting approaches that can help to structure complex tenders and make them contractually describable. Their task is to support the tenders with their experience from other projects to ensure the best possible process and optimum subsequent performance, quality and price.

### 3.2.1 The Management

Management here stands for the decision-makers and initiators of a tender, i.e. the management or the Executive Board (the initiator of a tender can also be an expiring contract or similar). In this context, we are looking at the management's steering and control function with regard to the company's business orientation. (Fig. 3.3) Communication and feedback with the company's IT department, the

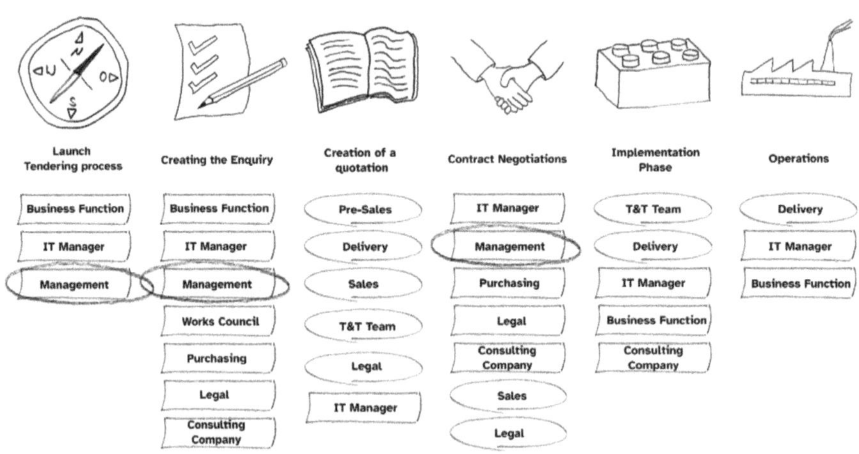


**Fig. 3.3** Phases of management involvement

business functions, etc. can take place via a close personnel network or via a formal system.

This refers to guidelines and written specifications that define a specific purchasing strategy. For example, management makes a "make-or-buy" decision based on requirements and the company's direction. Here, "make" stands for the in-house provision of a service by the IT department, for example, and "buy" for the commissioning of the service by an external service provider. Management decisions are made on the basis of information from the respective specialist and responsibility areas and the general approach on the market.

The company is also often managed by means of a vision and mission (long-term) or a mid-term plan (medium-term). Implementation and control are then carried out by management using a management technique such as management by objectives. The objectives of a tender and the tendering process must comply with these corporate guidelines and are managed in accordance with the management technique.

We do not envisage any direct intervention by management in the tendering process in our analyses. However, this can easily be deduced, as only the role would change in our analyses, but not the decision.

Let's take the example of an owner-managed company in a challenging financial situation. Normally, the management is only involved in tenders to the extent that it specifies the objectives to be achieved. In some situations, the financial situation of a company may mean that the IT service has to be reduced to the essentials. This then also affects the service providers who work with the customer.

We therefore assume that the company is financially secure enough to fulfil its obligations to the provider.

**Overview** Goals and influencing management:
**Objectives**: Services support the company's goals. IT fulfils the role defined in the company. Service providers fit into the partner concept.
**Influencing**: Specification and control via corporate vision, business requirements, organisation and management techniques. Feedback from the requirements of the business functions. Behaviour of comparable companies on the market, e.g. from the Gartner Magic Quadrant. Interests of all company stakeholders. State of the company.

### 3.2.2 The Business Functions as Customers of the Services

The business functions are the consumers of the tendered service. They define what they need (catalogue of requirements or specifications). As a rule, they should not specify how a service is to be provided (specifications) (Fig. 3.4). In practice, however, this does happen, e.g. in the form of direct and personal relationships between business functions and sales or IT managers from an external service provider.

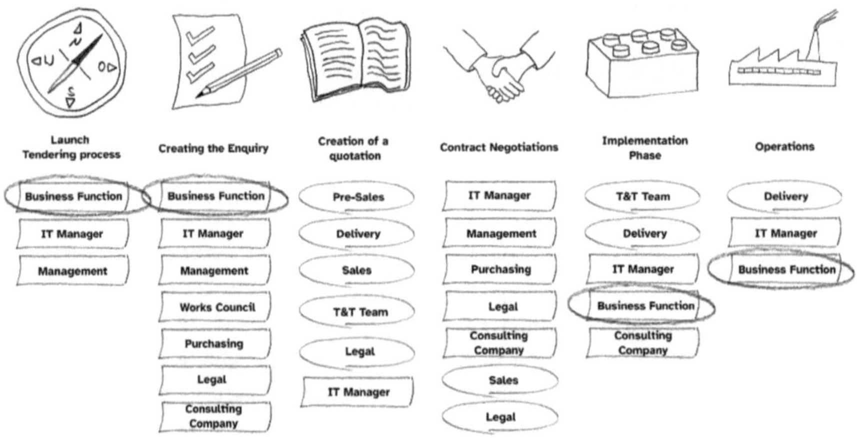


**Fig. 3.4** Phases of business functions involvement

For this reason, many companies emphasise the importance of having vendor management (supplier or partner management) control the business relationships between the business function and third parties. The departments assess their needs based on the requirements of their business objectives and, often, on negative experiences in which, for example, the previous service of a provider did not fulfil the business objectives or even prevented them from being achieved.

Occasionally, experience from the market (trade fairs, consultations, studies by consulting companies) is also incorporated into the assessment of how a service can be provided more effectively and efficiently for the business function. As a rule, the business functions are not involved in offsetting the direct costs of a service, but rather indirectly via cost allocations, as an IT service is usually used by several business functions and this usage is only very rarely charged on a cost-by-cost basis (often for reasons of data protection).

Here we assume that there are no personal preferences of the business functions for a third party and that the requirements of the business function can be formulated to achieve the business objectives of the business function.

**Overview** Goals and influencing the business function:
**Objectives**: The best possible support from the IT service to be purchased in achieving the company's own business objectives.
**Influence**: Own goals, negative experiences in the provision of services, own experiences from the market.

### 3.2.3 The IT Manager

The IT manager is responsible for bundling the services required by the business functions and requesting them from the provider. They are usually also responsible for creating the technical part of a tender (Fig. 3.5). This is (in the best case) developed from the requirements of the business function. However, general company objectives, such as the financial situation, etc., also play a significant role here. The corporate culture also has an influence. This involves topics such as: How do employees relate to each other across departments; how are external providers generally viewed, etc.?

In case of a physical product (keyboard, mouse, PC, etc.), this would be (more or less) simple, as such a product can usually be precisely defined and retains its specifications over a longer period of time. The situation is different for services (services or intangible products).

Companies are constantly changing and the working methods in companies and departments are also subject to an ongoing process of change. This is due to various factors. On the one hand, the company's customers change, and on the other, the customers' requirements of the company's products and services change. The further development of the advertised services, for example through technological progress, or changes in the environment can also lead to an adaptation of the services.

The factors mentioned above make it difficult to fully describe a tender at a specific point in time, as the time of publication of the service to be tendered does not necessarily coincide with the time of service provision. For the provider, the time at which the service begins is usually several months to a year in the future. In this

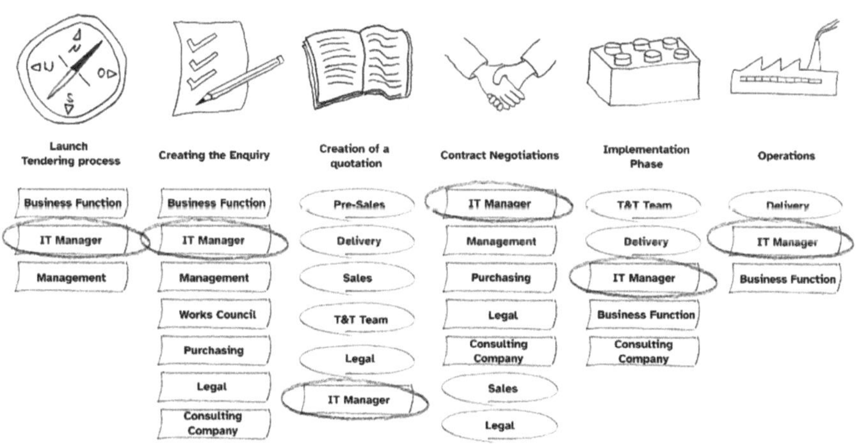


**Fig. 3.5** Phases of IT manager's involvement

context, supplier management is responsible for achieving the qualitative and monetary targets of the purchased service vis-à-vis management and the business functions over the entire period.

**Overview** Goals and influencing the IT manager:
**Objectives**: A technically comprehensive tendering process that manages without escalations in the provision of services.
**Influence**: Goals of the business function, corporate goals, corporate culture, market and environment, technological progress.

### 3.2.4 The Purchasing Department

The purchasing department plays a very central role in the awarding of contracts, regardless of whether these are in the area of products or services (Fig. 3.6)

The task of purchasing in most companies is to compare products and services and make the best choice for the company. The term "the best choice" generally leaves a lot of room for interpretation. This choice is traditionally based on a monetary evaluation.

If the products and services are comparable in terms of quality (the quality characteristics are defined beforehand or agreed with the parties involved), the decision is very often made in favour of the cheaper product or the cheaper service. The comparability, i.e. the requirements that are to be compared, must be defined in advance. There is also room for manoeuvre here.

Before an invitation to tender, the purchasing department will therefore usually agree with the business functions and management how the incoming offers from

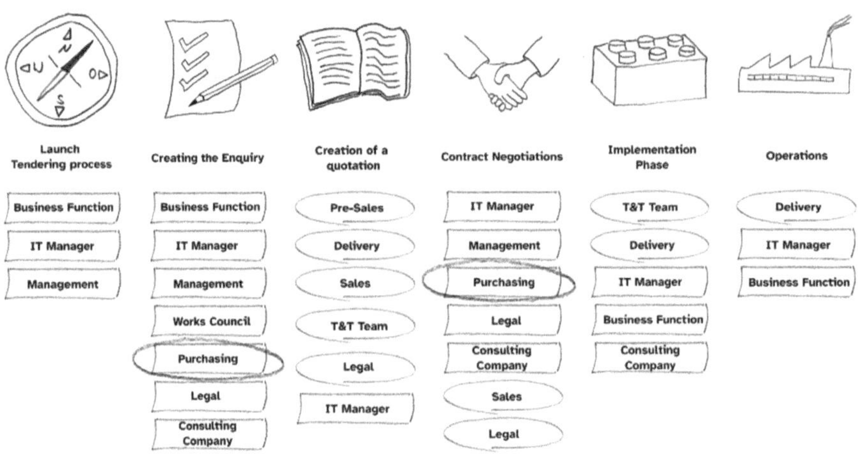


**Fig. 3.6** Phases of purchasing involvement

providers are to be evaluated. A matrix is often used for the evaluation: On the one hand, an attempt is made to evaluate functional and non-functional aspects; on the other hand, the price is evaluated. This is often mapped in a utility value analysis or a scoring model, i.e. a non-monetary analysis method.

The more value is placed on a feature (quality feature or price), the more points can be awarded for it. It is therefore crucial that the customer and supplier have the same understanding of the relevant aspects. This factor will play an important role later on.

In many companies, the targets of employees in the purchasing department are linked to the level of discounts they can negotiate with partner companies. Flexible salary components are often also linked to the achievement of these targets.

However, the purchasing department can only make good decisions when evaluating quality if the business function and the IT manager provide a sufficient and good basis for evaluation. The quality of this evaluation basis depends heavily on the expertise of the business function. Purchasing on the customer side is usually involved until the contract is signed or in the case of monetary service adjustments.

> **Overview** Goals and influencing the purchasing department:
> **Goals**: Negotiate a high discount or rebate, achieve measurable savings.
> **Influencing**: Specification of professional standards or criteria for evaluation by other departments.

### 3.2.5 The Legal Department (Legal)

The legal department has the task of negotiating the contracts to be concluded in a legally secure manner and to prevent future damage to the company (Fig. 3.7).

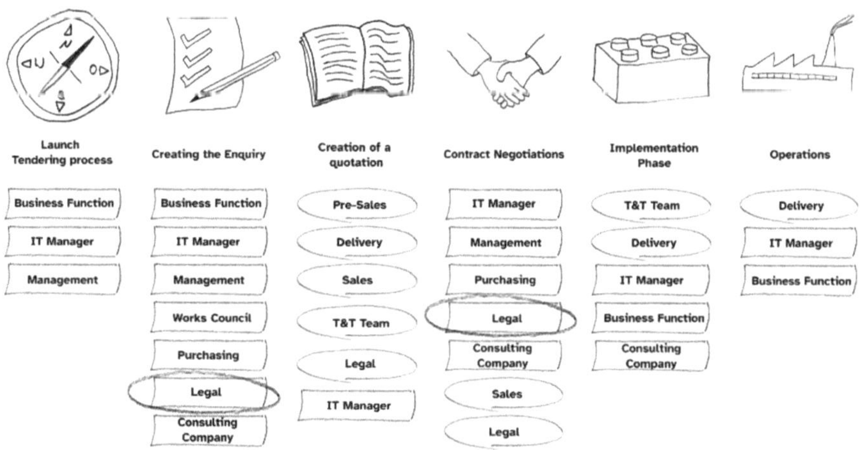


**Fig. 3.7** Phases of legal involvement

Firstly, compliance with regional and international laws must be ensured. Secondly, it must be ensured that no events occur that conflict with the company's objectives. For example, the transfer of employees to a provider that is to provide a service previously provided internally is not necessarily desirable, or it is explicitly desired. In such cases, the legal departments often draw on past experience.

The undesirable events from the past are then excluded with corresponding clauses. The checks to be carried out in a tender can be very extensive and affect several areas of law, such as export law, tax law, commercial law, etc., depending on the scope of the service to be tendered.

In most cases, the responsibility that arises during the provision of a service should also be secured via the provider. The same applies in particular to the company's objectives. The selected provider must support the company's objectives towards its customers.

In the case of tenders, the time required to finalise contracts until it is ready for signature is often underestimated. As a result, employees in the legal departments are often under considerable time pressure. For the sake of simplicity, we will limit ourselves here to the conclusion of contracts for the provision of services without international law, export law, etc. Legal is generally not involved in the implementation of a tendered service. Legal's involvement typically ends with the signing of the contract.

**Overview** Goals and influencing the legal department:
**Objectives**: Avoidance of future risks and legal certainty of the contracts to be concluded.
**Influence**: Laws, personal experience, company orientation and goals, goals of the company's own customers.

### 3.2.6 The Works Council

**Important** The way in which employees' interests are secured varies from country to country. However, in the Netherlands, Austria, and Germany, the government has its own special laws for regulation on how the interests of employees are to be secured. In Germany, Austria, and the Netherlands, some decisions of a company will be legally effective only after the works council has agreed to them. In most other countries, the works council has to be informed or consulted before a decision can be made.

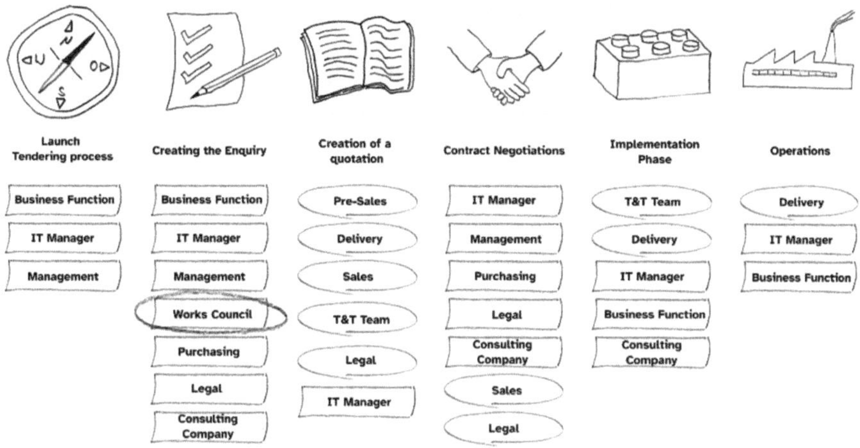


**Fig. 3.8** Phases of works council involvement

The works council is elected by the workforce to represent their interests vis-à-vis the company (Fig. 3.8). In many areas that affect the interests of employees (their working methods, their work performance or its measurement, their salary and their social benefits), the works council must be consulted on changes, or its consent is required. As soon as a tender affects or changes the work of internal staff, the works council must be consulted.

The works council often represents the interests of the employees vis-à-vis the interests of the employer. In order to be prepared for conflicts, the employees in a works council are practically non-terminable during its term of office and for a corresponding period thereafter.

In order to be able to represent interests in a holistic manner, the works council needs an understanding of the company's current situation. For this reason and to represent their interests, the works councils are represented on various company committees.

**Overview** Objectives and influencing the works council:
**Objectives**: To represent the interests of employees vis-à-vis the employer and to be re-elected.
**Influence**: Laws, personal experience, company orientation, goals, status of the company (is the company doing well or badly).

### 3.2.7 The Consulting Company

Consultancy firms are used to compensate for a lack of experience or routine in tendering and to coordinate the internal units and stakeholders (Fig. 3.9).

Consultants and consulting firms often bring their own tried-and-tested procedures, developed and refined through extensive tender experience. However, consultants and consulting firms do cost the tendering party money. Therefore, it is important to try to keep these expenses within reasonable limits.

Using defined and proven procedures helps to take a generalised approach. However, this can result in individual details and special features being overlooked. Also, consultants are contracted for a defined period of time and have a defined budget that cannot be increased at will.

In the general approach of a consultant, the focus is more on procedures and methods than on specialised technical topics or managed services themselves. Considering the many different specialist topics of full IT outsourcing in the workplace alone, such as service desk, service management, IT security, data protection, software distribution, software packaging, on-site technicians, licence management, managed print, office applications and networks (LAN, WAN and WLAN), not to mention telephony, it becomes clear that even the best consultant cannot be an expert in all of these areas.

However, the business functions on the customer side also only have their own perspective and knowledge, which is often gained through years of service. The consultants work together with the customers to develop the tender and sometimes (depending on the company's requirements) also support the implementation during the transition phase.

Another limitation of the consultant is their knowledge of the customer. The more insight a consultant has into the customer's processes and, above all, the

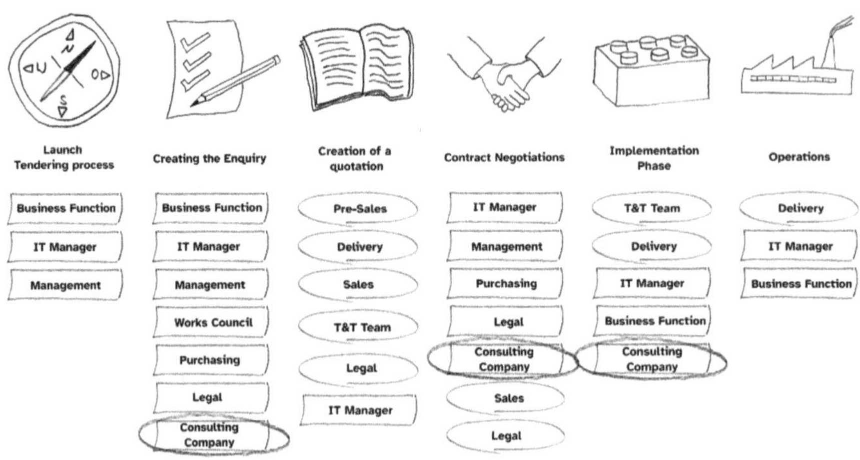


**Fig. 3.9** Phases of consulting company involvement

restrictions to which the customer is subject, the more successful they can be. However, this is limited by the time factor, which in turn is determined by the available budget.

**Overview** Goals and influencing the consultant:
**Objectives**: Realisation of the agreed scope to the satisfaction of the client.
**Influence**: Personal experience, specialised knowledge, knowledge of specific processes or customer requirements.

## 3.3 On the Provider Side

On the provider side, we look at the roles and functions that are directly involved in the tender process. There is also a management team that is usually responsible for approving offers, solutions and concepts for service provision. The requested services must also align with the company's objectives. However, this will not be considered here, as the focus of this book is about tendering and not about the provision of services by providers in particular (Fig. 3.10).

**Sales**
Sales are the provider's salespeople. They are responsible for presenting the provider's services to customers. The main focus is on selling the services offered by the company with the aim of increasing sales volume and margins.

**Pre-sales**
The employees in pre-sales receive the customer's tender and have to adapt the service provider's own services to the requirements. This means configuring the company's own IT services accordingly, or using external subcontractors, so that they

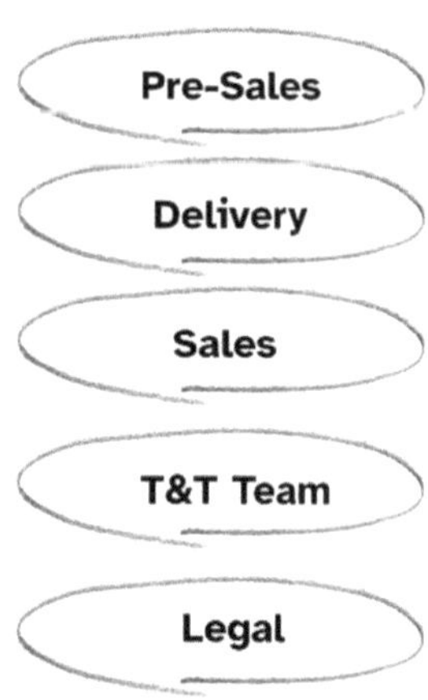


**Fig. 3.10** Participants on the provider side

meet the customer's requirements in terms of quality and price. The aim is to always offer your own services in the same standardised way wherever possible.

**Legal**

Legal is the legal department and usually (depending on the size of the company) consists of lawyers who are employed by the company. However, external lawyers can also be commissioned to advise on tenders. The department's main focus is safeguarding the company's interests and ensuring compliance with the legal framework.

**T&T Team**

The T&T (Transition & Transformation) team consists of project leaders and managers who establish the services sold to the customers by the providers or sub-suppliers within the agreed time and cost framework. This is done in such a way that subsequent operation of the services purchased by the customer is possible. The main aspect is adherence to the time and monetary framework.

**Delivery**

Delivery is the unit (or units) at the provider, including sub-service providers, which must provide the agreed service(s) to the customer in the agreed quality and at the agreed price. The focus is on the delivery of the services and, if possible, on increasing own synergies and ensuring compliance with the agreed services.

### 3.3.1 Sales

Sales is a broad term. There are sales representatives, account managers, account directors, sales representatives and all sorts of other titles. What we mean here is the person responsible for sales volume in a company for a particular customer, in its entirety (Fig. 3.11).

This means not only for a defined service, but for all services that a provider can offer a customer. Sales maintains contact with customers and should endeavour to provide them with services and generate business for the provider.

In most cases, as in this case, this is part of the sales objective, which is also reflected in the salary. Here, too, there are various models. In some cases, a salesperson's salary consists of a variable portion based on the number of contracts concluded with the customer. This often amounts to 30% of the total salary, but it can also be significantly higher or lower.

The measurement of success can also vary depending on the provider's business objectives. In some cases, success is analysed on a monthly basis, in others on a quarterly basis, or even for the fiscal year. However, the fiscal year plays a role in most cases. In this case, the end of the fiscal year is also relevant.

For many regional companies, the financial year ends with the calendar year. For some, it ends after the first quarter (i.e. the end of March), and for others, it ends after the third quarter. Why does this matter? In this case, the motivation of the sales

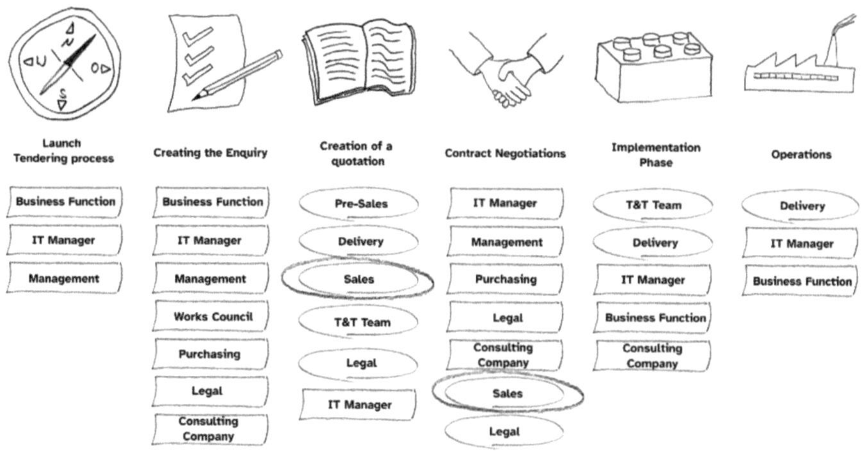


**Fig. 3.11** Phases of sales involvement

staff plays a role. If the targets are aligned with the fiscal year and the sales force has already achieved its targets, i.e. received the maximum salary, this is often reflected in their willingness to take risks and efforts to conclude new contracts with a customer.

In some companies, this effect is exacerbated by the fact that the targets achieved or their over-fulfilment (if any) are carried over into the targets for the following year. This leads to lucrative and promising tenders being rejected or not pursued further for certain reasons so as not to affect the company's own targets for the coming financial year.

Another aspect that often plays a role in the decision for or against a tender is the strategy of a company's services. In IT, these services are often divided into areas such as data centre, workplace services or cloud, etc. If a company decides to shift more towards cloud and data centre services, this is often reflected in sales objectives, as well as in the provider's performance in these areas.

Here we assume that our sales department wants to win the tender and that no negative influencing factors of the provider play a role in the tender.

Sales is also the main point of contact for the customer. Customers will often have unpleasant conversations with them about poor performance or inadequate services. In the event of poor performance, the sales department will have to justify itself to the provider, which may lead to penalties.

**Overview** Targets and influencing sales:
**Objectives**: To increase sales volume while at the same time ensuring the quality of services.
**Influence**: Personal experience, company orientation, personal objectives.

### 3.3.2 Pre-sales

Pre-sales refers to the unit that creates a service design on the basis of the tender and determines the effort (costs) for the subsequent delivery of the service and the transformation (implementation) of the service (Fig. 3.12).

As a rule, these are specialists with technical knowledge of the services to be delivered and the provider's ability to deliver these services. In most cases, there are specialists for individual services, e.g. a specialist for service desk and service management, one for software distribution and packaging, one for network, one for security services, etc.

In full IT outsourcing (although the scope of full IT outsourcing can certainly vary. This is therefore not always clearly defined), it can therefore happen that a large number of pre-sales employees are involved in creating the service design. These individual solutions (designs) must be well harmonised, as they must work together later on.

To put it simply, the task of pre-sales is to bring together the services, workflows and technological features that have developed over many years at the customer into a holistic solution design in just a few weeks. They also have the task of calculating the expenses that will be incurred by the provider in a few years' time and summarising them in an offer that takes into account both the customer's requirements, which have been written down in a document by a person unknown to the pre-sales team, and the provider's requirements.

> **Important** The many unknowns or possible interpretations always became apparent to us when we received different questions and interpretations from different providers in response to one and the same customer requirement, despite very detailed tenders from different providers.

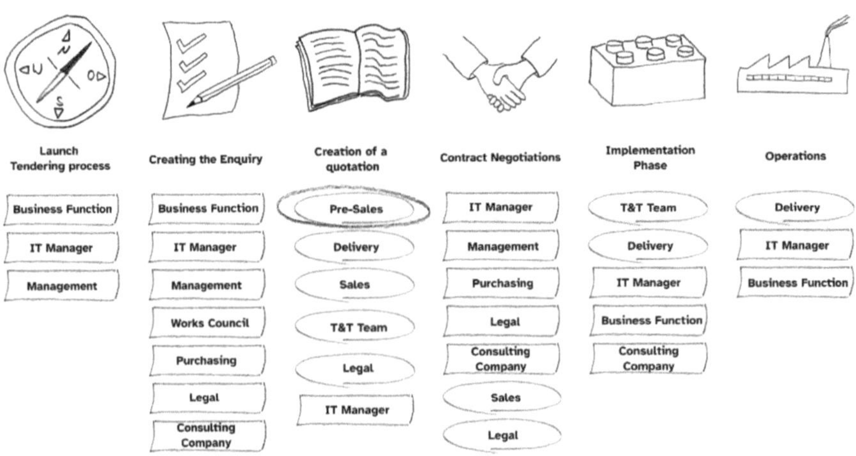


**Fig. 3.12** Phases of participation for pre-sales

On the provider side, it is the task of pre-sales to design a service with its dependencies on other services or functions that fulfils the technical requirements in order to be provided within the framework of the defined parameters and to survive a (hopefully never occurring) dispute.

On the other hand, there are customers who have often established some service management processes (e.g. incident management, etc.), but never really a service with its dependencies. The different levels of maturity and perspective become clear here.

The remuneration of pre-sales representatives varies greatly. At some providers, pre-sales are involved in the successful response to a tender (i.e. dependent on winning tenders), while at others they are involved in the success of the company as a whole. In terms of the roles involved in a tender, the role of pre-seller is one for which there is no dedicated training (as of 2024). Most people in this job have gained a wide range of experience or are trained by the provider through on-the-job training.

The fact is, however, that pre-sales is a cost factor in the preparation of quotations. For larger bids, these costs can quickly amount to a six-figure investment for the provider. Many providers therefore check in advance whether it makes sense for the provider to participate in a tender and prepare an offer.

**Overview** Goals and influencing pre-sales:
**Objectives**: Creation of the design and calculation within the offer deadline. A solution design that works in subsequent operation. Winning the tender.
**Influence**: Personal experience, company orientation, personal objectives.

### 3.3.3 Legal

The legal department has the task of negotiating the contracts to be concluded in a legally secure manner and preventing future damage to the company. On the one hand, compliance with regional and international laws must be ensured. (Fig. 3.13) On the other hand, it must be ensured that no events occur that conflict with the company's objectives. For example, transferring employees to a service provider for a service that was previously provided internally is not necessarily desirable or is explicitly desired.

This may also be the case for hardware that the customer wishes to transfer to the service provider. Here, the legal units usually draw on past experience. The undesirable events from the past are then excluded with corresponding clauses.

The checks to be carried out in a tender can be enormous and affect several areas of law, such as export law, tax law, commercial law, etc., depending on the scope of the service to be tendered. The legal clauses must harmonise with the service to be provided. Conflicts often arise here, as the customer's requirements do not always harmonise with applicable law. Legal employees are confronted with risk

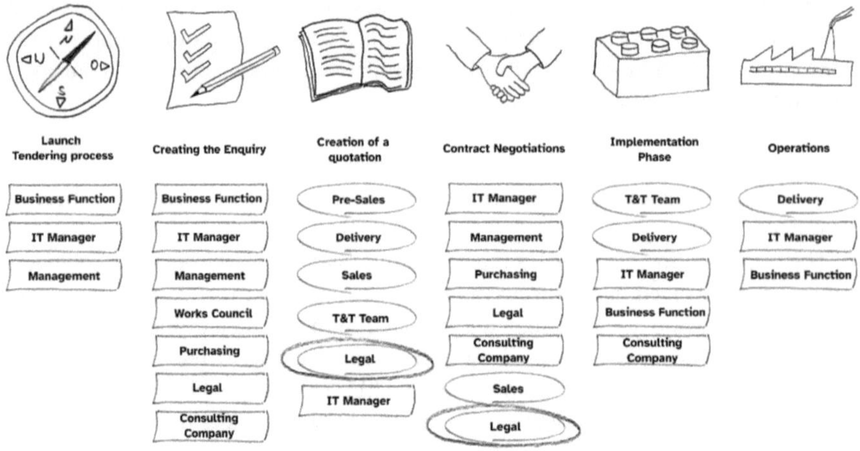


**Fig. 3.13** Phases of the provider's legal department involvement

assessments. They have to weigh up the risk and, if possible, do so without circumventing regulations or changing the requirements of a service.

In tenders, people often underestimate how long it takes until contracts are ready to be signed. This means that employees in the legal departments are often under considerable time pressure to avoid "work at risk" (provision of services without a legal framework).

For the sake of simplicity, we will limit ourselves here to the conclusion of contracts for the provision of services without international law, export law, etc. As a rule, legal is not involved in the implementation of the tendered service. Legal's involvement generally ends when the contract is signed and only begins again if the contract is to be amended during its term or extended after expiry.

**Overview** Goals and influencing the legal department:
**Objectives**: Avoidance of future risks and legal certainty of the contracts to be concluded and services to be provided, avoidance (reduction) of the assumption of responsibility by the provider.
**Influence**: Laws, personal experience, company orientation.

## 3.3.4 T&T Team of the Provider

The provider's T&T team (Transition and Transformation Team) carries out the transition and transformation of one or more services after a tender has been won. In many companies, this team is also simply referred to as the project management team (Fig. 3.14).

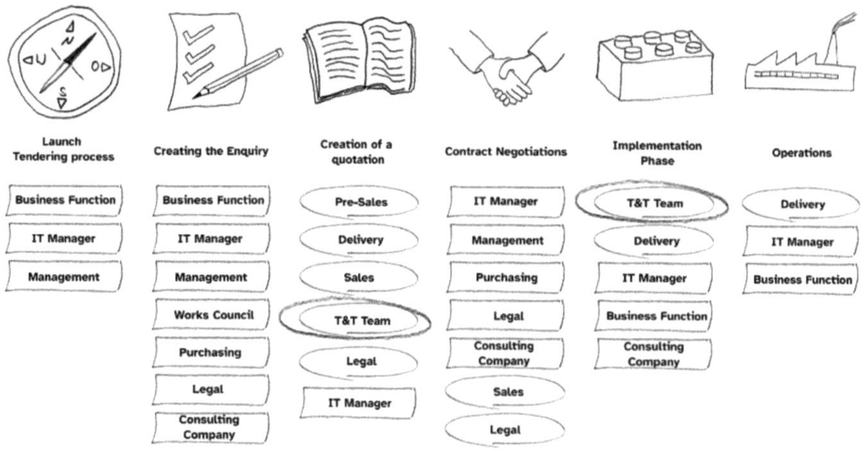


**Fig. 3.14** Phases of T&T team involvement

A transition here means the takeover of the services by the provider without changing the way in which they are provided. A transformation refers to the change of a service. It is currently provided in a certain way. The change makes it provided in a different way. This distinction between transition and transformation has serious implications, particularly with regard to liability.

In a transition, the tenderer has already proven that a service as it is currently provided works and can be delivered with sufficient quality. In a transformation, i.e. a change to the service, this is not the case, and the responsibility often lies with the provider.

Once the contract has been signed, the T&T team has the task of implementing the services agreed between the client and the provider. For many providers, the subsequent T&T team is part of the solution design (i.e. also pre-sales). This has the advantage that much of the solution design and "what was meant" is known to the T&T team. However, such an approach also increases the provider's costs when preparing the offer. The provider must therefore make advance payments without being entitled to compensation for its expenses.

Project management (as of 2024) is often carried out using methodologies based on the waterfall principle. A project is started and at this point the starting point of the project is described and defined, as well as the path that the project will take and the costs that will be incurred.

Furthermore, a basic principle of the methodology, such as PRINCE2, is the separation of project governance (i.e. the management of the project) from the technical implementation. Depending on the size of the upcoming project, this can lead to undesirable costs, but also to a significant difference in project costs if this methodology is also applied to smaller projects.

If you compare full IT outsourcing with the outsourcing of a single service desk, the coordination and management costs of such a separation in accordance with

PRINCE2 remain comparatively high (compared to the costs incurred when transferring a single service desk to full IT outsourcing).

T&T teams rely on this methodology to ensure that the starting point is precisely described and that no additional work is required to reach the starting point. In addition, the path of the project must be defined and must not deviate due to unforeseen changes.

The starting point should also not have changed by the time the project starts. Many of these projects are planned long before they are launched and extend over several months, or even several years in the case of very large projects. If you now consider the rapid development in IT and society, the difficulties in the precise description and calculation of such projects quickly become clear.

Nevertheless, the T&T is contractually fixed, and the calculated costs are set out in the budget of both (or several) partners. Changes to the budget during the year usually result in unpleasant questions and procedures on both sides, which the parties involved on both sides try to avoid. This can quickly lead to the so-called claiming and put considerable strain on the relationship.

**Overview** Goals and influencing the T&T team:
**Objectives**: Realisation of the fixed project plan and (or with) the fixed objectives within the agreed budget.
**Influence**: Personal experience, contractually agreed objectives, technological development, environment.

### 3.3.5 Delivery of the Provider

There is no one delivery that is the same for all providers. Rather, it is a collection of IT units that support or perform certain services for the service to be provided. These services are then provided by defined processes, procedures, and rules, by people with specific experience and by a range of different tools (Fig. 3.15).

The individual units of a provider will have the most diverse compositions of the above-mentioned characteristics. In most cases, they have evolved historically from projects.

**Important** Therefore, there is no provider that is 100% comparable with exactly the same performance. Even if they offer the same services, providers will always differ from one another.

Delivery is responsible for ensuring that the services are provided at the previously calculated costs. At the same time, a delivery must continue to develop in order to remain attractive for future and existing customers. However, the agreed benefits and services cannot simply be changed at a delivery's discretion. This requires the consent of existing customers.

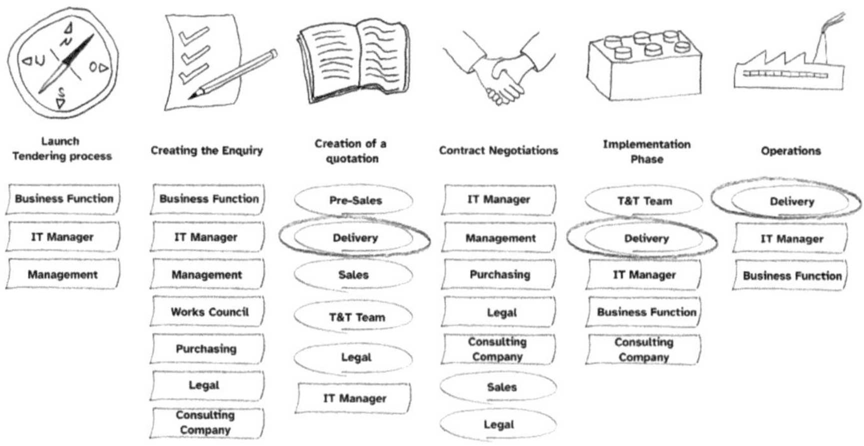


**Fig. 3.15** Phases of delivery involvement

The further development of services often requires a change in the customer's behaviour. This is not always desirable. As a result, a delivery organisation repeatedly finds itself caught between innovation and preserving the status quo of its many different customers.

Another challenge of delivery is the different maturity levels of customers. Some customers have standardised their IT services and their processes are reproducible, predictable and measurable and are subject to continuous improvement (maturity model according to CMMI2 Level 4 or 5).

Some customers only respond to unplanned interruptions that are non-reproducible, unpredictable, non-measurable, and without continuous improvement (CMMI2 Level 1 to 2). In both cases, the contractually agreed service must be provided, whereby one case requires more attention than the other.

**Important** It is a challenge to assign companies to a maturity level, as an assessment of the maturity level by the companies themselves or by professional experts is not the norm. In addition, there is a risk of misjudgements when companies carry out their own assessments.

**Overview** Goals and influencing delivery:
**Objectives**: Realisation of the agreed service at the agreed costs in the agreed quality for different customers.
**Influence**: Personal experience, contractually agreed objectives, different levels of maturity of customers, different technological development of customers.

## 3.4 Summary

There are many factors that influence tenders and their responses: personal experiences and goals of those involved, departmental goals, company goals and a wide range of external influences.

The nature of the objectives also has an influence on a tender or its response. As does the corporate culture of both the tenderer and the provider. Many of these influencing factors are not known or disclosed to everyone involved in a tender. Nevertheless, they have a considerable influence on a tender and also on its response and the subsequent provision of services.

It can happen that even very detailed tenders with several hundred pages are answered or planned differently from provider to provider in the response and also in the subsequent delivery.

The tendering process is further complicated by media disruptions in communication between the customer and provider and different interpretations of terms that are not standardised in an ISO standard. The objectives of the customer and the provider can often be (and in some cases are) contradictory. Compromises must be found and made by both sides.

# 4 Tendering and Awarding Today

In this chapter, we would like to look at the procedures as we generally find them in practice today. We will explain the common procedures and how they are generally handled. Specifically, we will examine these procedures with regard to IT services. We will therefore also focus on these services and procedures in the following section.

Furthermore, we try to give an insight into public procurement law, as some of the regulations and laws there are similar to the procedures in the private sector or are often derived from them. However, this can only be an insight and can only reflect the state of the law at the time of publication of this book. However, it shows how heavily regulated and sometimes complicated public procurement law is (sometimes for good reason).

This book was originally written in German and was based on German law. We have internationalised, so to speak. Therefore, you will find many laws that may not exist in your country or that differ from those described here. However, to describe all the legal bases from all countries would definitely go too far and go beyond the scope of this book. Our focus is on fostering a general understanding of tenders in the public sector, and how they also have an influence on tenders in the private sector.

We describe how a tender is created, the challenges we have faced in our various careers with tendering procedures and how a tender is created in the first place. We have also looked at the history of tenders and the principles that are generally applied today.

It should be noted that a very important decision has to be made before an invitation to tender: will the service be provided by the company itself or will it be outsourced? This pre-tender decision is also known as the "make-or-buy" decision.

This is often not finalised even during the tendering phase, as it is not known exactly how much the service will cost or how much effort will be required to support the service provider. Or you simply need arguments to be able to continue providing the service internally.



G. Köhler et al., *Adaptive IT Service Tendering*, Management for Professionals,
https://doi.org/10.1007/978-3-658-49726-2_4

Suppliers often only find out at the end that the customer has decided in favour of "make", i.e. the independent provision of the subject of the tender. In the public sector, however, this decision must be made before an award (invitation to tender) is published.

Regardless of what the customer decides at the end of this question, it can be assumed that this question was preceded by doubts about the company's ability to provide the service itself, or the realisation that the service cannot be provided in-house.

Service providers should have a lot of experience in providing services, even under different circumstances, because no two customers are the same. Many customers want to use this expertise to get out of their own, often limited view and experience.

This leads to today's common and widespread practice of tendering and its various procedures such as RFI, RFQ, and RFP, which will be discussed in detail later, or the laws and regulations in the public sector.

**Important** At the beginning of this chapter, we would like to point out that outside the public sector, there are no regulations or laws governing the organisation of tenders. The procedures described here will vary from company to company. Similarly, readers with more experience of tendering may have different views.

In our opinion, the following section merely reflects the need for a new methodology, which we will explain from Chap. 5 onwards.

## 4.1 History of Tendering and What AI Says About It

There are probably no reliable records of when people started to compare goods and services with each other in a defined process. At least we have not found any studies or scientific papers in our research that we would like to refer to here.

However, since the urge to get the best option for oneself and for one's area of responsibility is probably older than the first coins, we can assume that the history of tenders is probably old in an indefinite variety and has been perfected by people over the course of time.

In addition, we commission others to make the best choice for us. In our experience, people then often tend to place these decisions (selections) in predefined procedures and make them transparent and comprehensible. It is therefore a question of trust or lack of trust as to whether we work with these tendering procedures.

People's interest in making the "best choice" can also be recognised by the number of reports and features comparing goods, services, or even entire service providers these days. Not to mention the countless sites on the Internet that compare products such as mobile phones.

It should be noted that most websites and reports present the comparison from a certain perspective. If a consumer has a different perspective or other features are more important to them, these comparisons can quickly become worthless or misleading.

During our research for this book, we discovered that, in Roman times, it was probably customary for the price of a service to exceed the original price by a maximum of 20%, so that the provider did not lose their head. Looking at some recent projects, we are sure that some customers today would be delighted if they could fall back on similar measures.

The most prominent examples in Germany are probably projects in the public sector, such as airports or opera houses. But we can assure you that deviations of over 20% are not uncommon in today's implementations, especially in the area of IT outsourcing or outtasking (and whatever other names there may be).

This rarely occurs with physical goods, as production is predictable in most cases. Only in the case of services, such as transport, can significant deviations occur, as we have seen in the recent past due to the pandemic or the outbreak of war in Europe.

As this book will be published in 2025, we would also like to ask an artificial intelligence (AI) about this topic at and share this information with you:

***The question to the AI***:

**Question** Explain the history of tenders. Where and when did the first tenders take place? Which products or services were involved? Who was the client and who was the service provider? How can the concept of tendering be categorised historically?

***Answer:***

The history of tenders goes back a long way and is closely linked to the development of the economic system and procurement practices. The first documented tendering process took place in ancient Rome. The Roman government used tenders to award construction contracts, for example for the construction of temples, roads, and public buildings. In this case, the clients were the Roman authorities, while the services were provided by various craftsmen and construction companies.

Throughout history, tenders have been used for various products and services. In the Middle Ages, for example, tenders were issued for the construction of castles, cathedrals, and fortresses. In the 19th century, tenders took off in the course of industrialisation and were increasingly used in the field of infrastructure construction, such as the construction of railways and canals.

The concept of tendering can historically be seen as a method of selecting the best offer for a particular contract or service. It is a type of competitive process, in which potential providers are invited to submit their proposals and prices. This is intended to ensure transparency and fairness, as all potential providers have an equal chance of winning the contract.

With the advent of modern government and the increasing complexity of projects and procurements, the tendering process has evolved. Today, tendering is used in many areas, including construction, information technology, public sector, healthcare, research and development, and many more.

The concept of tendering has historically established itself as an effective method of finding the best suppliers for specific contracts or services. It encourages competition, allows a choice between different options, and contributes to efficiency and quality in procurement. It also helps to prevent corruption and favouritism by establishing clear and objective criteria for the selection of service providers.

***And further***:

**Question** Did the Sumerians, Phoenicians, or Egyptians also have tenders?

The availability of historical sources from the Sumerian, Phoenician, and Egyptian periods is limited, and it is difficult to find specific information about tendering in these civilisations. However, there is some evidence that tender-like practices may have taken place to some extent.

In the case of the Sumerians, who were one of the earliest advanced civilisations of ancient Mesopotamia, they are known to have undertaken complex building projects such as temples and palaces. It is assumed that they hired craftsmen and labourers for these projects, possibly using informal tendering processes. However, there is no direct written evidence of formal tendering in Sumerian culture.

The Phoenicians, a seafaring nation of the ancient Near East, were known for their trading activities and maritime expertise. It is possible that they may have used certain selection procedures in the procurement of ships and trade goods. However, there is also limited information on formal tendering procedures in the Phoenician civilisation.

In ancient Egypt, tender-like practices were more likely. Egyptian civilisation developed into a highly organised society with complex building projects such as temples, tombs, and palaces. There is evidence that the pharaoh awarded contracts to contractors to carry out these projects. However, it is not known exactly whether formal tenders were used to select the contractors or whether contracts were awarded by other means.

It is important to note that the available information on these ancient civilisations is limited and many aspects of daily life and trading practices have not been fully documented. While there is evidence of certain procurement procedures, we cannot be definitive about whether formal tendering procedures existed in the form we understand them today.

**Question** And with the Chinese?

Chinese history offers several examples of tender-like practices, especially during the Han dynasty (206 BC to 220 AD) and later dynasties.

During the Han dynasty, there was an organised state and a centralised government that carried out public construction projects such as the building of roads, canals, palaces, and defences. It is assumed that contracts were made with selected construction companies or individual craftsmen for such projects. These contracts could be seen as a kind of tendering process in which the best offers were selected.

During the Tang dynasty (618-907 AD), further developments in procurement practices were observed in China. The Chinese government introduced a system known as "Baoding". Under this system, contracts for public works such as temples, pagodas, and canals were awarded to those who could submit the best proposals and bids. This system is very similar to a tendering process where contracts were awarded to the best bidder.

[Our research has shown that the "Baoding" system is very likely a hallucination of the AI. This means that although the result is convincingly formulated, it does not appear to be justified by training data and is objectively incorrect. Although there is a Chinese city with this name, we were unable to find a source for a system for procurement practices].

Throughout Chinese history tendering procedures continued to be used in various fields including the construction of palaces, temples, bridges, fortresses, and canals. The Chinese government and local authorities often played the role of the client while construction companies craftsmen and architects acted as service providers

It is important to note that Chinese history spans a variety of dynasties and periods during which the political and economic systems have evolved. Therefore, the specific practices and procedures may have changed over time. Nevertheless, there is historical evidence that tender-like practices were used in China, especially in public works projects, to select the best service providers and ensure the quality of projects.

**Question** And with the Maya, Aztecs, or Incas?

Among the Maya, Aztec, and Inca, the major pre-Columbian civilisations in Central and South America, the use of competitive bidding is not documented in historical records. Information on the procurement practices of these civilisations is limited and there are no specific records or evidence that formal tendering took place.

The Maya, who lived in what is now Mexico and Central America, are known for their impressive temples and palaces. The construction of such monumental structures was probably carried out by specialised craftsmen and construction companies. However, there is no specific information on whether formal tendering procedures were used to select the contractors.

The Aztecs, who founded the Aztec Empire in what is now Mexico, were also known for their advanced architecture and urban infrastructure. They carried out complex building projects such as the construction of temples, palaces, and canals. However, there are no concrete historical records of how the contracts for such projects were awarded or whether tenders were used.

The Incas, who built the largest pre-Columbian empire in the Andes in South America, were known for their impressive fortresses, temples, and terraced fields. It is believed that the Incas were highly organised and had a centralised system of government. They may have employed specialised labour and contractors for large construction projects. However, there is no specific information on whether formal tendering procedures were used.

At the time of our enquiry, the AI did not have relevant sources for its statement. However, the most we found were statements about the Roman Empire.

Let us now return to our personal experiences from our practice!

## 4.2 Tendering Procedures

Tendering procedures are usually based on legal requirements. In the European Union, European law applies, followed by the law of the member states.

### 4.2.1 Regulations of the European Union

The objectives set out in the EU treaties are to be achieved with the help of various legal acts. Some of these legal acts are binding, others are not. Some apply to all EU countries, others only to certain countries. These legal acts are:

**Regulations**

A regulation is a binding legal act that all EU countries must implement in full. For example, when the EU regulation on the abolition of roaming charges within the EU expired in 2022, the Parliament and Council adopted a new regulation that was intended to be clearer than the previous one—and also to ensure a harmonised approach to roaming charges for another 10 years.

### Directives

A directive is a legal act that sets out an objective to be achieved by EU countries. However, it is up to the individual countries to enact their own legislation to realise this goal. One example is the EU directive on single-use plastics: it reduces the impact of certain plastic products on the environment, for example by restricting or even banning the use of disposable plastics such as plates, drinking straws, and beverage cups.

### Decisions

Decisions are binding and directly applicable to those to whom they are addressed (e.g. an EU country or an individual company). For instance, on 1 January 2023, the Council adopted a decision on the introduction of the euro in Croatia, affecting this country alone.

### Recommendations

Recommendations are not binding. For example, the Commission's recommendation on internal safeguards for editorial independence and transparency of media ownership had no legal consequences. In a recommendation, the institutions can express their views and propose measures without this being legally binding for those to whom the recommendation is addressed.

### Statements

In an opinion, the institutions can comment on a matter in a non-binding form. It therefore does not constitute a legal obligation for the addressees and is not binding. Opinions can be issued by the most important EU institutions (Commission, Council, Parliament) as well as the Committee of the Regions and the European Economic and Social Committee. In the course of the legislative process, the committees submit opinions from their respective regional, economic, or social perspectives. For example, the European Economic and Social Committee has submitted an opinion on the Next Generation SME Strategy.

> **Important** In the case of tenders in the public sector, within the EU member states, we speak of directives.
> At the time this book was written, the public sector was subject to the:
> DIRECTIVE 2014/24/EU OF THE EUROPEAN PARLIAMENT AND OF THE COUNCIL
> of 26 February 2014 on public procurement and repealing Directive 2004/18/EC
> (European Union, 2014)

The agreed directives and their articles should therefore be understood at a higher level. To illustrate this, we will show the definition of contracting authorities in Article 2 of the Public Procurement Directive and then provide an insight into German legislation on public procurement. In comparison, it becomes clear that the legislation of the respective member state should always be taken into account when awarding public contracts/tenders.

## Definition of Article 2 of the Public Procurement Directive

**Legal** Article 2 Definitions

1. For the Purposes of This Directive, the Following Definitions Apply

(1) "contracting authorities" means the State, regional, or local authorities, bodies governed by public law or associations formed by one or more such authorities or one or more such bodies governed by public law;

(2) "central government authorities" means the contracting authorities listed in Annex I and, in so far as corrections or amendments have been made at national level, their successor entities;

(3) "sub-central contracting authorities" means all contracting authorities which are not central government authorities;

(4) "bodies governed by public law" means bodies that have all of the following characteristics:

(a) they are established for the specific purpose of meeting needs in the general interest, not having an industrial or commercial character;

(b) they have legal personality; and

(c) they are financed, for the most part, by the State, regional, or local authorities, or by other bodies governed by public law; or are subject to management supervision by those authorities or bodies; or have an administrative, managerial, or supervisory board, more than half of whose members are appointed by the State, regional, or local authorities, or by other bodies governed by public law;...

Section 2 of this Directive defines the thresholds above which this Directive applies. Below these thresholds, the legislation of the respective Member State applies.

**Legal** Section 2 Thresholds
Article 4 Threshold amounts
This Directive shall apply to procurements with a value net of value-added tax (VAT) estimated to be equal to or greater than the following thresholds:
(a) EUR 5,186,000 for public works contracts;
(b) EUR 134,000 for public supply and service contracts awarded by central government authorities and design contests organised by such authorities, where public supply contracts are awarded by contracting authorities operating in the field of defence, that threshold shall apply only to contracts concerning products covered by Annex III;
(c) EUR 207,000 for public supply and service contracts awarded by sub-central contracting authorities and design contests organised by such authorities; that threshold shall also apply to public supply contracts awarded by central government authorities that operate in the field of defence, where those contracts involve products not covered by Annex III;
a) EUR 750,000 for public service contracts for social and other specific services listed in Annex XIV.

### 4.2.2 International Public Procurement Law

International procurement is even more complex. This is because the different trade agreements between countries or the European Union and the countries or regions must be taken into account.

Trade between the European Union and Canada are governed by the CETA free trade agreement. CETA was signed in October 2016 and has been provisionally applied since 2017. CETA was then ratified on 20 January 2023.

Trade between the USA and the European Union are to be regulated in the TITP free trade agreement. Negotiations are currently (as of 2025) on hold.

Trade between the European Union and Switzerland is governed by the Agreement between the European Community and the Swiss Confederation on certain aspects of government procurement.

Trade between the United Kingdom of Great Britain and Northern Ireland and the European Union is governed by the Trade and Cooperation Agreement (TCA). The TCA was signed on 30 December 2020 and came into force on 1 May 2021.

There are other agreements that we will not go into in detail. In our view, however, the Government Procurement Agreement (GPA) of the World Trade Organisation (WHO) forms the basis for all contracts and trade agreements concluded between individual countries or associations.

**Important** Quote:
The GPA is the only legally binding World Trade Organisation (WTO) agreement on public procurement. Negotiations on updated procurement rules and supplementary market access commitments were successfully concluded on 15 December 2011; the final text of the revised GPA was signed on 30 March 2012. The revised agreement entered into force on 6 April 2014.
The Convention currently has 20 contracting parties (the European Union in relation to its 27 member states, plus Armenia, Australia, the Dutch Caribbean island of Aruba, Hong Kong (China), Iceland, Israel, Japan, Canada, Liechtenstein, Moldova, Montenegro, New Zealand, Norway, Switzerland, Singapore, South Korea, Taiwan, Ukraine, and the United States). In addition, 36 other countries have observer status....

International trade is therefore quite complex.

In order to deepen this a little more, a brief insight into German public procurement law follows, which regulates the regulations of the European Union in even greater detail for the awarding of contracts within Germany.

### 4.2.3 Regulations in Germany

The procedures in Germany and to some extent in other European countries can be divided into two main categories.

On the one hand, we have public procurement (tenders). These are restricted by public procurement law and the procedure is regulated by EU, federal, and state directives. On the other hand, there are tenders in the private sector. We'll start by looking at the regulations in the public sector, using Germany as an example, to help us understand tenders in the private sector (BMWi, 2017).

The following is an insight into public procurement law by BMWi (2017) (Fig. 4.1).

This is now so complex that larger service providers have their own specialists who deal almost exclusively with public procurement law and incoming tenders from the public sector. The public authorities also have employees who are well versed in public procurement law and there are the awarding bodies that then publish an award (invitation to tender).

The awarding of public contracts is essentially regulated by the Act against Restraints of Competition (Gesetz gegen Wettbewerbsbeschränkungen GWB), the Public Procurement Ordinance (Verordnung über die Vergabe öffentlicher Aufträge VgV) and the Sector Regulation (Sektorenverordnung SektVO). In addition, however, the Act to Combat Illegal Employment (SchwarzArbG) (§ 21 Exclusion from Public Contracts), the Posted Workers Act (AEntG) (§ 21 Exclusion from Public Contracts), and the Minimum Wage Act (MiLoG) (§ 19 Exclusion from Public

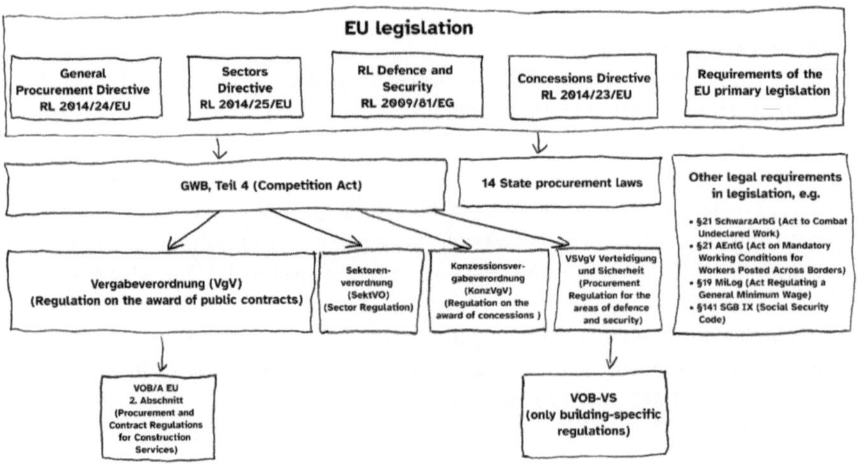


**Fig. 4.1** Tender procedure based on BMWi (2017)

Contracts) must also be observed when awarding and participating in public contracts.

However, public procurement law only regulates how something is to be procured, but not what is to be procured. Here, the contracting authorities are free to make their own decisions. Procurement becomes easier if a public body wishes to co-operate with another public body (regulated in § 108 GWB).

The legal texts cited here are taken from the publications of the Federal Ministry of Justice (BMJV) and of the Federal Ministry for Economic Affairs and Energy (BMWi) on the Internet, for example at:

(Federal Ministry of Justice (BMJV) 2023), (Federal Ministry for Economic Affairs and Energy (BMWi) 2015), (Federal Ministry for Economic Affairs and Energy (BMWi) 2016), and (Federal Ministry for Economic Affairs and Energy (BMWi) 2017)

## What Exactly Is a Contracting Authority?

In principle, this is described in the Act against Restraints of Competition (GWB) and is divided into three different areas.

There is the contracting authority, as described in §99,
the sector contracting authority according to §100, and
the grantor of the licence in accordance with §101.

Public clients (Contracting authorities) are:

**Legal** Act against Restraints of Competition (GWB)
§ 99 Public Contracting authorities
Public contracting authorities are

1. regional and local authorities and their special funds;
2. other legal persons under public or private law that were established for the specific purpose of meeting non-commercial needs in the general interest, if
   a) they are for the most part financed through a participation or in some other way by entities within the meaning of nos 1 or 3 acting individually or jointly;
   b) their management is subject to supervision by entities under nos 1 or 3; or
   c) more than half of the members of their management or supervisory boards have been appointed by entities under nos 1 or 3;

   the same shall apply if such legal person, individually or together with others, provides most of the financing to another legal person under public or private law, exercises supervision over its management, or has appointed the majority of the members of a management or supervisory board;
3. associations whose members fall under nos 1 or 2;
4. natural or legal persons under private law as well as legal persons under public law, so far as they do not fall under no 2, in cases where they receive funds for civil engineering projects, for building hospitals, sports, leisure or recreational facilities, school, university, or administrative buildings or for related services and design contests from entities falling under nos 1 to 3, and where these funds are used to finance more than 50 per cent of these projects.

The sector contracting entities (Sector client) described in § 100.

**Legal** Act against Restraints of Competition (GWB)
§ 100 Sector client
(1) Sector contracting entities are

1. public contracting authorities under § 99 nos 1 to 3 that carry out a sector activity under § 102;
2. natural or legal persons under private law that carry out a sector activity under § 102, where
   a) such activity is carried out based on special or exclusive rights that have been conferred by a competent authority; or
   b) public contracting authorities under § 99 nos 1 to 3 can individually or jointly exercise a controlling influence on these persons.

(2) Special or exclusive rights within the meaning of sub§ (1) no 2 a) are rights which result in reserving the performance of this activity for one or more undertakings while considerably diminishing the eventuality that this activity will be performed by other undertakings. Rights are not special or exclusive rights in this sense if they have been conferred based on a procedure under the provisions of this Part or based on another procedure for which adequate notice was given and which is founded on objective criteria.

(3) The exercise of a controlling influence within the meaning of subsection (1) no 2 b) is presumed where a public contracting authority under § 99 nos 1 to 3

1. directly or indirectly owns the majority of the subscribed capital of the undertaking;
2. holds the majority of the voting rights attached to the shares of the undertaking; or
3. can appoint more than half of the members of the administrative, management, or supervisory board of the undertaking.

And the licensors described in §101.

**Legal** Act against Restraints of Competition (GWB)

§ 101 Concession grantors(1) Concession grantors are

1. public contracting authorities under § 99 nos 1 to 3 that award a concession;
2. sector contracting entities under § 100(1) no 1 that carry out a sector activity under § 102(2) to (6) and award a concession for the purpose of carrying out this activity;
3. sector contracting entities under § 100(1) no 2 that carry out a sector activity under § 102(2) to (6) and award a concession for the purpose of carrying out this activity.

(2) § 100(2) and (3) shall apply mutatis mutandis.

This distinction is important as the sector contracting authorities are generally private companies. For example, if you apply for a service contract with an energy generation company, you must comply with laws and regulations when publishing and awarding contracts.

The threshold values of an award must also be taken into account. These thresholds determine the point at which a contracting authority must put an award out to tender throughout the EU. The thresholds are defined in § 106 GWB. Here, however, the law essentially refers to the thresholds set by the EU so that the law does not have to be amended every two years when new thresholds are set by the EU. The thresholds for an EU-wide award are:

€ 140,000: Supreme and upper federal authorities
€ 215,000: Other supply and service contracts (new in 2024/€ 221,000)
€ 431,000: Sector client
€ 5,382,000: Construction contracts (new in 2024/€ 5,538,000)

If the (estimated) value of the award is higher than these values, the contracting authority must comply with further and additional laws and, above all, longer deadlines for publication. In short, it becomes more complex and takes considerably longer. This is why contracting authorities and also sector contracting authorities often try everything to stay below these values. It should be noted here that the estimate of the contract value to be awarded may well be completely wrong. The way in which the (incorrect) estimate was arrived at must simply be comprehensible!

Contract awards are divided into several parts. For example, there is the service description, which is regulated in:

### §121 of the GWB

**Legal** Act against Restraints of Competition (GWB)
§ 121 Tender Specifications

(1) The subject matter of the contract shall be described as clearly and comprehensively as possible in the tender specifications so that the description is understandable in the same way for all undertakings and so that the tenders can be compared with each other. The tender specifications shall include the functional and performance requirements or a description of the task to be addressed, knowledge of which is required to prepare the tender, as well as the circumstances and conditions for provision of the performance.
(2) For all procurement which is intended for use by natural persons, the accessibility criteria for persons with disabilities or the design for all users shall be taken into account when preparing the tender specifications, except in properly justified cases.
(3) The tender specifications shall be enclosed with the procurement documents.

Then there are the Supplementary Contract Terms for the Procurement of IT Services (Ergänzende Vertragsbedingungen für die Beschaffung von IT-Leistungen EVB-IT, or in englisch Supplementary contractual conditions for the procurement of IT services). These are the general terms and conditions under which a contracting authority purchases a service. These GTC cannot be amended and are included in the tender documents in the form published by the federal government.

It should be noted here that the GTC are specifications that can, however, be overwritten by details, restrictions, or similar in the service description. This means that the service description takes precedence over the GTC. The following EVB-IT exist:

EVB-IT purchase (without installation)
EVB-IT system delivery
EVB-IT Transfer Type A (unlimited use)
EVB-IT Maintenance
EVB-IT services (training, consulting, support)
EVB-IT Transfer Type B (temporary use)
EVB-IT Care S
EVB-IT System
EVB-IT creation
EVB-IT Service
EVB-IT Cloud
The EVB-IT are available to clients as a download.

However, not everyone is allowed to participate in a public procurement procedure. Unlike in the private sector, there are a number of requirements that must be met and there are grounds for exclusion that preclude a competitor from participating.

### These Are Regulated in §§ 123 and 124 of the GWB

**Legal** Act against Restraints of Competition (GWB)
§ 123 Compulsory Grounds for Exclusion

(1) Public contracting authorities shall exclude an undertaking from participation at any point in the procurement procedure when they are aware that a person whose conduct is imputable to the undertaking in accordance with subsection (3) has been convicted by final judgement or a final administrative fine has been issued against the undertaking under § 30 of the German Administrative Offences Act [Gesetz über Ordnungswidrigkeiten] for a criminal offence under:

1. § 129 of the German Criminal Code [Strafgesetzbuch] (forming criminal organisations), § 129a of the German Criminal Code (forming terrorist organisations), or § 129b of the German Criminal Code (foreign criminal and terrorist organisations);
2. § 89c of the German Criminal Code (financing of terrorism) or for participation in such a crime or for the provision or collection of financial resources with the knowledge that such financial resources will be used or are intended to be used, wholly or in part, to commit a crime under § 89a(2) no 2 of the German Criminal Code;
3. § 261 of the German Criminal Code (money laundering; hiding unlawfully obtained financial benefits);
4. § 263 of the German Criminal Code (fraud), provided that the criminal offence is directed against the budget of the European Union or against budgets administered by the European Union or on its behalf;
5. ...

## §124 Optional Grounds for Exclusion

**Legal** Act against Restraints of Competition (GWB)
§ 124 Facultative Grounds for Exclusion

(1) Taking the principle of proportionality into account, public contracting authorities may at any point in the procurement procedure exclude an undertaking from participating in the procurement procedure if

1. the undertaking has demonstrably breached applicable environmental, social, or labour obligations in carrying out public contracts;
2. the undertaking is insolvent, an insolvency proceeding or a comparable proceeding over the assets of the undertaking has been filed or opened, the opening of such a proceeding has been denied for lack of assets, the undertaking is in liquidation proceedings or has ceased to do business;
3. the undertaking has demonstrably committed grave professional misconduct which renders its integrity questionable; § 123(3) shall apply mutatis mutandis;
4. the public contracting authority has sufficient indications that the undertaking has concluded agreements with other undertakings or engaged in concerted practices which have as their object or effect, the prevention, restriction, or distortion of competition;
5. a conflict of interest exists in the execution of the procurement procedure which could compromise the impartiality and independence of a person working for the public contracting authority in the executing of the procurement procedure and which cannot be effectively remedied by other, less intrusive measures;
6. a distortion of competition results from the prior involvement of the undertaking in the preparation of the procurement procedure, and such distortion of competition cannot be remedied by other, less intrusive measures;
7. the undertaking has produced significant or persistent deficiencies in the performance of a substantive requirement under a prior public contract or concession contract which led to an early termination, damages, or other comparable sanctions;
8. the undertaking has committed a serious misrepresentation or withheld information or is not able to submit the required evidence with respect to the grounds for exclusion or the selection criteria; or
9. the undertaking
   a) has attempted to unduly influence the decision-making process of the public contracting authority;
   b) has attempted to obtain confidential information that may confer upon it undue advantages in the procurement procedure; or
   c) has negligently or intentionally provided misleading information that may have a material influence on the decision of the public contracting authority concerning the award decision, or has attempted to provide such information.

(2) § 21 of the Posted Workers Act [Arbeitnehmer-Entsendegesetz], § 98c of the Residence Act [Aufenthaltsgesetz], § 19 of the Minimum Wage Act [Mindestlohngesetz], § 21 of the Act to Combat Undeclared Work and Unlawful Employment [Schwarzarbeitsbekämpfungsgesetz], and § 22 of the Act on Corporate Due Diligence Obligations in Supply Chains [Lieferkettensorgfaltspflichtengesetz] shall remain unaffected.

If a company has been excluded from participation, this can of course be cancelled. § 125 of the GWB regulates how this can be done as follows:

## Act Against Restraints of Competition (GWB)

### § 125 Self-Cleaning

**Legal** (1) Public contracting authorities shall not exclude an undertaking for which a ground for exclusion exists under § 123 or § 124 from participation in the procurement procedure where the undertaking has proven that it

1. has paid or undertaken to pay compensation for any damage caused by the criminal offence or misconduct;
2. has comprehensively clarified the facts and circumstances associated with the criminal offence or misconduct and the damage caused thereby by actively collaborating with the investigating authorities and the public contracting authority; and
3. has taken concrete technical, organisational and personnel measures that are appropriate to prevent further criminal offences or misconduct.

§ 123(4) sentence 2 shall remain unaffected.

(2) The self-cleaning measures taken by the undertakings shall be evaluated by the public contracting authorities, taking into account the gravity and particular circumstances of the criminal offence or misconduct. If the public contracting authorities consider the self-cleaning measures by the undertaking to be insufficient, they shall provide the undertaking with justification for the decision.

§ 126 (Allowable Period for Exclusion) regulates how long a company is excluded from the award:

### Act Against Restraints of Competition (GWB)

**Legal** § 126 Allowable Period for Exclusion

Where an undertaking for which a ground for exclusion exists has taken no or insufficient self-cleaning measures under § 125,

1. if a ground for exclusion exists under § 123, it may be excluded from participation in procurement procedures for up to five years from the day of the final conviction;
2. if a ground for exclusion exists under § 124, it may be excluded from participation in procurement procedures for up to three years following the event at issue.

Anyone thinking "That's a lot of laws and regulations" should realise that this is just an excerpt. The awarding of a contract, i.e. the contract award, is also precisely regulated in § 127 (Contract Award) GWB:

### Act Against Restraints of Competition (GWB)

**Legal** § 127 Contract Award

(1) The most economically advantageous tender shall be accepted. The basis for this is an evaluation by the public contracting authority concerning whether and to what extent the tender meets the specified award criteria. The most economically advantageous tender is determined according to the best price-quality ratio. Apart from the price or costs, to determine this, qualitative, environmental, or social aspects may also be taken into account.

(2) Binding rules on pricing shall be observed in determining the most eco nomically advantageous tender.

(3) The award criteria must be related to the subject matter of the contract. This relationship shall also be assumed when an award criterion refers to processes relating to the production, provision, or disposal of the performance, to trading with the performance or to another stage in the life cycle of the performance, even when such factors do not affect material qualities of the subject matter of the contract.

(4) The award criteria must be specified and defined in a manner that ensures the possibility of effective competition, that the contract cannot be awarded arbitrarily and that it is possible to conduct an effective review on whether and to what extent the tenders meet the award criteria. If public contracting authorities allow variants, they shall define the award criteria in such a way as to apply both to main tenders and variants.

(5) The award criteria and their weighting must be specified in the contract notice or the procurement documents.

§ 127 GWB is then supplemented by § 58 ff. of the VgV (Public Procurement Ordinance).

**Legal** Ordinance on the Award of Public Contracts (Public Procurement Ordinance—VgV)
§ § 58 Contract Awards and Award Criteria

(1) The contract shall be awarded to the most economically advantageous tender in accordance with § 127 of the Act against Restraints of Competition.
(2) The most economically advantageous tender shall be determined on the basis of the best price–performance ratio. In addition to price or cost, qualitative, environmental or social award criteria may also be taken into account, in particular
1. quality, including technical merit, aesthetic and functional characteristics, accessibility of the performance, especially for people with disabilities, compliance with "Design for all" requirements, social, environmental, and innovative characteristics, as well as sales and trading conditions;
2. organisation, qualification, and experience of staff entrusted with performing the contract, where the quality of the staff assigned can have a significant impact on the level of performance of the contract; or
3. availability of customer service and technical assistance as well as delivery conditions such as delivery date, delivery procedure, and delivery or execution deadlines.

The contracting entity may also specify fixed prices or fixed costs, with the result that the most economically advantageous tender shall then only be determined on the basis of qualitative, environmental, or social award criteria, according to sentence 1.
(3) The contracting entity shall indicate, in the contract notice or procurement documents, the relative weighting that it assigns to the individual award criteria in order to determine the most economically advantageous tender. This weighting may also be expressed in the form of a range, with an appropriate maximum spread. Where weighting is not possible for objective reasons, the contracting entity shall indicate the award criteria in decreasing order of importance.
(4) As regards proof of whether and to what extent the tendered performance meets the required award criteria, §§ 33 and 34 shall apply mutatis mutandis.
(5) In general, at least two representatives of the contracting entity shall take part in the decision to award a contract.

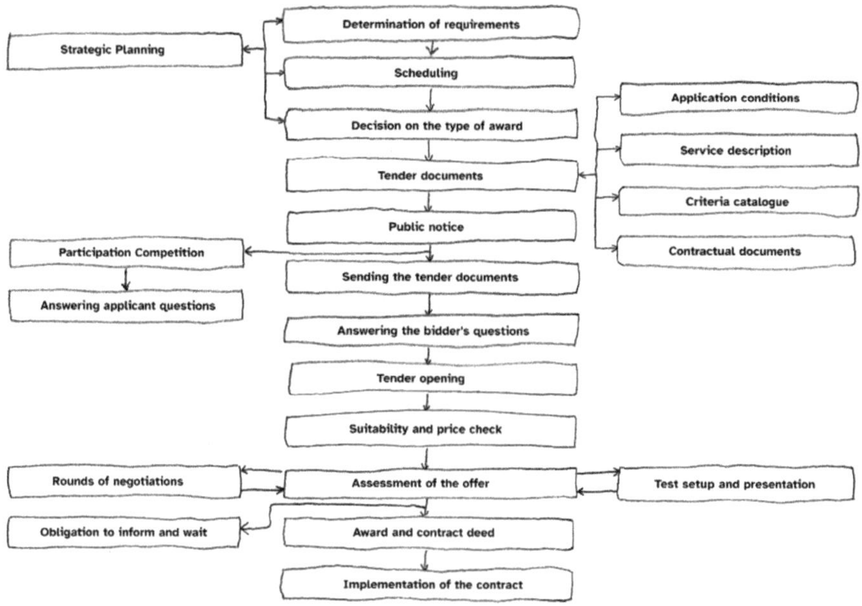


**Fig. 4.2** The possible sequence of an award procedure based on Heuermann (2014)

The course of an award procedure is usually as shown in the diagram above (Heuermann, 2014) (Fig. 4.2):

This shows how complex public sector procurement can be and how long it can take.

Nevertheless, the written word is always open to interpretation, even if it has been cast in law. But on the whole, public procurement law is of course intended to protect the interests of the community and prevent cronyism and camaraderie and, if possible, prevent this. Public procurement law should also enable fair competition.

Public procurement law sets out how services are tendered and the deadlines that must be met at each stage. Some employees of public authorities and service providers take creative approaches to circumvent the regulations or at least extend the boundaries.

We do not want to imply that the community is or should be harmed in every case. In some cases, the limits in public procurement law appear to be quite inappropriate and very often make services more expensive. For example, you can switch to a rental model when purchasing software and then only put it out to tender for 2 or 3 years, even though you know internally that you want to use it for longer.

This leads to a reduction in the volume of tenders, which in turn can mean that the software may not have to be put out to tender across Europe or that a tender can be avoided altogether.

We could list a few more of these creative approaches that we have encountered in practice, but we will leave it at that and turn our attention to the actual topic, tenders in the private sector.

You might think that private companies would be on the other side and that things would work completely differently there than in the public sector. This may be the case for small and medium-sized companies, especially if they are family-run. For all others, it is a question of proving that everything was done in the correct way when the contract was tendered and awarded.

For this reason, guidelines apply in these companies and the purchasing departments, or rather the purchasers, ensure that they are adhered to. A key difference between purchasing in the public sector and in private companies lies in the objectives of purchasing. In the public sector, the primary objective of purchasing and the procurement department is to comply with the applicable laws and regulations.

In the private sector, employees in purchasing often also have the measurable goal of how many savings they have been able to achieve for the company through renegotiations in tenders. This sometimes leads to interesting processes. For example, an IT manager who has to adhere to a very tight schedule can shorten the duration of purchasing negotiations by negotiating with the supplier in advance and asking them to deliberately add a surcharge of 10%, for example, to the first offer, depending on the purchasing department's objectives.

The purchasing department will then negotiate with the supplier and ask for a discount. The supplier quickly agrees to a 10% discount. Assuming that all employees (including the IT manager) act in the interests of their company, everyone wins in this case.

The process has been shortened, the supplier can deliver at an acceptable price and the purchasing department has achieved the targets set by its company. At this point, you can see for yourself whether this makes sense in this process.

## 4.3 Conflicting Interests

Anyone involved in tenders will have already recognised from the above why problems often arise in the provision of services after the tender.

From a bird's eye view, it can be said that public procurement law aims to commission the best offer. The challenge is that the best offer means the most favourable offer in accordance with the tender criteria.

The tender was either prepared by the contracting authority itself or with the help of a consultancy firm. In the first case, there is often a lack of relevant market knowledge about the current possibilities of a service and the corresponding requirements. In the second case, the intermediary can cause suitable solutions and providers to lose sight of their capabilities and, more importantly, their performance limitations.

If the invitation to tender is not precisely tailored to the requirements and is not clear for the providers, discrepancies can quickly arise during implementation. This is particularly the case in public procurement procedures, where acceptance of the tender by the public body already includes the conclusion of the service contract. No further renegotiations or agreements are then possible.

We have never seen a tender for a service that was not open to interpretation in at least some respects, and for which there were no queries. Therefore, the quality required to go directly from the invitation to tender to the provision of services is not always present.

**Important** In a large public administration in Germany, this behaviour once led to an invitation to tender for software in the printing sector and one provider submitted such an outrageously low bid, around 20% below the market price, that it was awarded the contract. All market participants were astonished, as this software could never deliver the required performance. Not even with additional services in the implementation phase.

The competitors' objections were not taken into account in the decision. In the end, the authority was left with cheap but unsuitable software that could not fulfil the actual requirements. The contractual penalties provided for in the tender did not materialise and could not be enforced. As a result, two to three years after the tender, the authority was forced to accept the inadequate performance features that this type of software was intended to deliver.

In the private sector, the objectives of the purchasing department and those of the business functions often get in each other's way. After all, the "cheapest" offer is not always the best for the company.

We have found that the purchasing department is stronger than the IT department when the IT department reports to the Chief Finance Officer (CFO) of a company and there is no Chief Information Officer (CIO) on the management board who is equal to the CFO.

To be fair, it should be noted at this point that the companies that put IT services out to tender are companies whose core business is not IT, but usually the production of goods or non-IT services. Therefore, in many companies, the CFO (who manages the company's financial resources) is considered to be more important than the CIO.

However, we can see that this is changing in many companies in times of high threat from cyber-attacks and that greater importance is being attached to IT. Especially if these companies are subject to legal requirements such as KRITIS (the law for the protection of critical infrastructures in Germany, based on the IT Security Act 1.0 of 2015 and the IT Security Act 2.0 of 2021) or NIS-2 (the law for the protection of critical infrastructures at European level). Of course, current cyber-attacks and media coverage also play a corresponding role in the assessment of a company's IT.

## 4.4 The Various Tendering Procedures

There are actually three common and widespread tendering procedures today. In addition to the actual invitation to tender, the Request for Proposal (RFP), which usually ends with a commissionable service and a legally valid contract, there is also the Request for Information (RFI) and the Request for Quotation (RFQ) (Fig. 4.3 and Table 4.1).

In addition to these common procedures, there is now also a Request for Service (RFS) and other procedures which, in our view, were developed by consulting companies but have not really become established outside the consulting services of these companies.

We have seen the RFP most frequently in our practice. The second most common was the RFI and occasionally there was an RFQ.

However, as there is no standardisation or official standardisation of tenders, such as a DIN or ISO standard, there are often mixed forms of these procedures. One exception to this is the laws in the public sector for the awarding of services

**Fig. 4.3** The various tendering procedures

**Table 4.1** The various tendering procedures

| RFI<br>Request for Information | RFQ<br>Request for Quotation | RFP<br>Request for Proposal |
|---|---|---|
| Query suppliers for concepts of specific services | Query suppliers for concepts of certain services and their possible costs | Query suppliers for one or more dedicated services and their exact costs |
| With an RFI, customers ask providers for expertise on how certain services are currently provided, whether there are new concepts for service provision, and whether these are marketable<br>This also provides customers with inspiration on how to organise their own tender in order to improve the current service with a new service provider, including for their own customers | In an RFQ, the requested services are usually described in general terms, but without going into detail. The standard of the service provider and the expected costs are also frequently asked for.<br>RFQs are used to estimate the budget required for the service and to enter it into the budget.<br>RFQs can also be used without a prior RFI. In this case, the purpose of the RFI is usually included in the RFQ | In an RFP, the expected services are described precisely in the way they are to be provided by the service provider in the future. The exact volumes of the service are defined, and the service provider specifies a price for which the customer can purchase the tendered services |

described above. Especially in the market exploration phase, for which the RFI is a good procedure, it is usually mixed with an RFQ. In the characteristics of the services described, it can also sometimes be mistaken for an RFP.

This often depends on the circumstances a company is faced with. For example, if there is not enough time to first carry out a detailed market survey and tailor it to the company's needs before requesting a quote (i.e. an estimate of the costs), the outcome can be unpredictable.

In practice, there are also different forms of application for the RFP. As a rule, however, an orderable service or an orderable good is at the end of this process.

It can therefore be concluded that there is no "right" form for an RFI, RFQ, or RFP, apart from the requirements of public procurement law. If the client has ultimately achieved what it set out to do, the form chosen was probably the right choice.

### 4.4.1 The RFI

**Overview** Objective: To gather information on "state-of-the-art" solutions and possibilities.

As already mentioned, tendering procedures often start with a market exploration (Fig. 4.4).

Of course, the companies know what their projects are about and what they want to put out to tender. As mentioned earlier in the text, companies that do not come from the IT sector in particular put IT services out to tender. As a result, the best ways to provide a service or the latest methods and tools to support the service are often not known or cannot be used or implemented due to a lack of experience. Another reason is that companies have already failed in the application of these methods or tools.

In an RFI, a company describes the task ahead of it that needs to be mastered and asks the companies contacted for possible solutions to these tasks. It is widely used and, in our view, advantageous to ask what the standard of the company contacted is for solving this task. This can give the customer an initial indication of whether the partner's solution might be suitable or whether the solution described deviates from the customer's expectations and, above all, requirements.

Based on our experience from many projects, it makes sense to select a partner for a service whose standard comes close to the customer's requirements. If a partner has to change its standards for just one customer, this is always associated with

**Fig. 4.4** The RFI

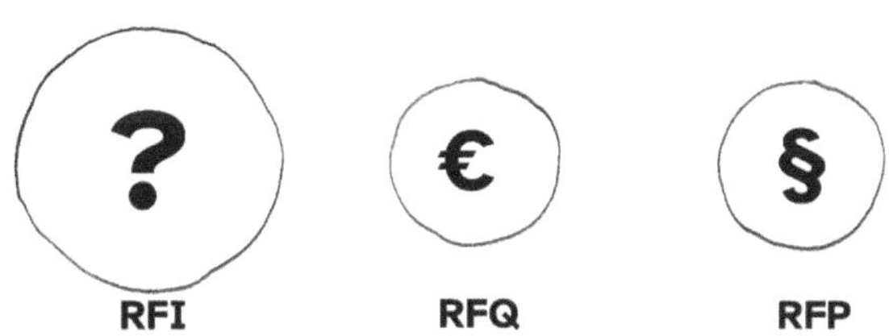

sometimes major internal challenges for the partner. The probability that these partners will not fulfil expectations when implementing the service often increases with the degree of deviation from the provider's standard.

In the years in which we have been involved in responding to enquiries and their subsequent implementation, we have encountered a wide variety of forms and levels of detail. RFIs in particular are very diverse. These range from emails and presentations to elaborate enquiry documents created using word processing or spreadsheet programmes, in which the customers also provide their general requirements for IT security, data protection, or similar.

As a service provider, we have always felt most comfortable with RFIs where we understood the customer's challenge. And where the customer gave us the freedom to respond with "state-of-the-art" solutions that also met our standards or that we had already successfully implemented for other customers.

References are often requested in RFIs (if not here, then at the latest in RFPs or RFQs).

The customers are not comparable in detail. This is because they have different core businesses with different requirements, different levels of maturity to other companies, or the size of the company requires a different IT department.

The labour market for employees from the customer's core business can also have a significant influence on the desired solution. For example, one customer attached great importance to having its service desk located at the customer's site and premises so that its employees always have direct and personal access to the support staff.

The customer said that his employees would expect this and that if he did not implement these and other measures, he would have a hard time finding the right talent on the labour market. This happened despite the fact that the trend in the service desk sector had long been going in the opposite direction and service desks were being relocated abroad or attempts were being made to answer user enquiries automatically with chat bots and AI.

This is also referred to as "shift-left", where in this case the user is on the left, i.e. the most cost-effective resource for solving an IT problem from the point of view of the IT organisation, and on the far right are IT resources such as developers and application specialists, who represent very valuable resources.

As described above, the difference between the companies also makes it difficult to compare requested references (usually the description of customer projects in which the same service was implemented as was requested in the RFI) with the company's own situation. The differences described above and many others that we have not explicitly mentioned make it difficult to compare requested references.

So, if you ask for references, be aware that this can only tell you something about the partner's experience in providing this service. Specify the enquiry, for example, by including experience from other services, such as for the same sector (e.g. banking, retail, etc.). This will increase the ability of the partner you are enquiring about to fulfil your own requirements. Or try to get in touch with the provider's other customers, e.g. to enquire about the provider's flexibility in the event of deviations from contractually agreed services.

Creating an RFI is less time-consuming than creating an RFQ or even an RFP. Nevertheless, companies should think about which service they want to request. In most cases, these are standard services that are constantly requested on the market, such as the services of a service desk or the provision of on-site technicians. Complex services, such as the provision and operation of virtual environments, are rarely part of the expected spectrum of RFIs.

**Important** Redactions in PDF documents
Time and again, we see documents in tenders in which passages are blacked out to protect the names of people, resources or, in one case, even emergency access from unauthorised access. Unsuitable editors are used that merely place black bars over the text and therefore do not effectively protect the actual content. The reader does not have to make any great effort to access the original content.
Make sure that the content is actually no longer accessible. Ask IT specifically how this can be achieved. The most elegant way is to take the original text document, delete or overwrite the content, and then create a PDF document.

### 4.4.2 The RFQ

**Overview** Objective: To obtain information about expected costs.

Now that a company has used an RFI to find out about the market and the solutions available there, it can select the solution that seems most suitable to it, customise it to its situation, and send an RFQ to various partners to get an idea of the expected costs (Fig. 4.5).

In most cases, not all the information that a partner needs to calculate a service is published in these RFQs. Sharing a complete picture with all the necessary information and volumes goes too far for many companies. This information is usually withheld until a valid selection of potential providers for an RFP has been determined.

The RFQ is therefore not very standardised. It is not always labelled as an RFQ when it is sent by a company to potential partners. Sometimes partners only recognise an RFQ because the information is not sufficient to create an orderable offer for

**Fig. 4.5** The RFQ

the customer, but price information is still requested. In this case, it is an RFQ. It is therefore advisable to ask the customer whether the publication of a detailed RFP is planned.

Experienced service providers will not necessarily invest a lot of effort in such enquiries, but will also respond with their standard services, which are already defined in terms of price. Information about the budget to be estimated can also be obtained from this.

In our experience, an RFQ is always useful if the entire tendering process extends over a longer period of time, which is usually the case. An RFQ gives a customer the opportunity to plan their budget for the coming fiscal year with approximate precision.

In our view, this is the only benefit of an RFQ. Using RFQs to categorise or sort out potential partners in terms of price harbours considerable risks because, as already mentioned, experienced service providers generally offer their standard prices. If this then has to be adjusted as part of the RFP, the costs—depending on the adjustment—can deviate considerably from the prices quoted in the RFQ.

### 4.4.3 The RFP

**Overview** Objective: To conclude a legally binding contract with a service provider for the provision of a service.

Nowadays, when a company decides to have a service provided by a partner, an invitation to tender is issued to compare the prices for this service. In some cases, the partner from whom you want to procure a service is already known and you just want to have the feeling that you are not paying too much (Fig. 4.6).

We have encountered situations like this time and again over the years of our practice. If you look at what exactly is put out to tender in the service sector, you can understand why. In contrast to a good, such as a keyboard, the customer's requirements for a service change over time. Sometimes even during the realisation phase of the tendered service. However, the service provider will often want to retain these.

A keyboard is and remains a keyboard. Its characteristics will not change significantly, and you can be sure that they will not change in 5 years' time. In the case of an asset, the company is also free to decide how it is used. For example, whether it is not used for a few weeks, months, or even years.

**Fig. 4.6** The RFP

This is completely different for a service. The surprises of recent years (pandemic or war in Ukraine) make it clear that you need reliable partners who are prepared to go along with changes. Selecting such partners is difficult or even impossible with a tender. Trust is therefore particularly important for many companies when choosing their service providers.

We have also come across all conceivable forms of RFPs in the private sector. In terms of the complexity of an RFP, the differences range from a presentation with five slides (in which the company presents itself on two slides) to RFPs with several hundred or over 1000 pages, in which the requested service must also be integrated into a SIAM (Service Integration and Management) construct.

As an RFP ultimately results in a legally valid contract, experienced service providers endeavour to assess all eventualities that may arise during the term and, if possible, eliminate them. If this is not possible, a risk is identified.

The risk is then assessed in monetary terms and added to the price as a risk surcharge. We have also seen service providers add the risk to the costs. As a result, the customer then also pays value-added tax on the risk.

Here it can be said that the more risk the company itself bears, the lower the price. It is very difficult for a company to assess the risks that a service provider can foresee. This is because this is where the experience of the people involved comes into play. Everything that has gone wrong in their professional lives has great potential to be presented as a risk and valued in monetary terms. This is because trust does not occur in a formal tendering process. However, as mentioned above, this is extremely important for a service if you want to work together successfully over a long period of time.

One of our recommendations to service providers when responding to tenders and, above all, when calculating the price, is that there are also positive risks. In other words, opportunities to expand your own business with the customer and thus increase sales and profits. This can (and should) also be evaluated in monetary terms and included in the price calculation.

No matter how you proceed with an RFP, the result is a legally binding contract. At best, this should set out the services to be provided and the circumstances under which the services are to be provided. As a rule, this is a tight corset into which the customer and partner enter.

In order to change such narrow limits during the contractual term, there is the so-called change process. This is a defined procedure for making changes to existing contracts, for example. As a rule, a change request to an existing contract results in a new offer from the partner. Both parties in such a contract initially try to prioritise their own business, which leads to renewed contract negotiations.

In the end, such a change request to an existing contract with a partner is again an RFP, only usually, but not always, with a single provider. The process is the same as with the original RFP, except that you now have a better understanding of the service and can specify more detailed requirements.

In short, with the traditional approach to an RFP in services, you can suddenly find yourself in a continuous loop of requests and offers. From our past experience, we know of RFPs that resulted in contracts that generated at least five to ten change requests per month during the term of the contract. Both the customer and the partner had to constantly deal with these and provide resources for them.

Especially in banking and insurance sector, there are consulting firms that design RFPs in such detail that it is precisely regulated in every situation what the service provider has to do, when, and how. If the environment then changes or the activities need to be adapted in some way, they have to be re-described by the client and evaluated and offered by the partner. Et voilá, this creates a continuous loop in the RFP process.

**Important** Personally, we can say that this is a potentially nerve-wracking situation, full of administrative work that ultimately does not contribute much to the actual service, i.e. the actual added value of the service provider for the customer. Furthermore, as a customer, you can quickly find yourself in a situation in which the partner exploits its exclusive position to increase its margin.

In the early 90s, a manager once said to me, we generate 20% of our profit with what the customer has advertised. And 80% with what he forgot to put out to tender. This is certainly a very negative example, but it still happens today. This is why trusting cooperation based on a partnership is so important.

## 4.5 How Tenders Often Work

This chapter explains the process of a tender as it is usually found (as of 2024–25) and how the described RFI, RFQ, and RFP procedures are integrated into this process. This procedure ultimately prompted us to develop a better method with which we want to achieve great added value for our customers and have already been able to achieve in initial projects. We describe the classic way of tendering with its six main phases from the initiation of the tender to the performance of the tendered service. In doing so, we will describe the impact of the individual roles involved on each other as well as the obstacles encountered in the individual phases.

In order to emphasise the added value of our method in the following chapter, we will use service consolidation, i.e. the consolidation of several services that are currently still provided by different providers, as an implementation example in this chapter. In our opinion, the positive effects and added value of our method for the customer and the provider are greatest here and in the case of first-generation outsourcing (i.e. the tendering of services that were previously provided by the company's own employees).

We start by describing the company's initial situation and how the decision to outsource was made. We will then go through the individual phases of the tender, the implementation, i.e. the transformation or transition of the services into the desired target state, the operation of the services. We will underpin and illustrate the individual phases with practical examples. The tendering company, in our case the customer, is Customs AG, with its headquarters in Munich and branches in five other major German cities.

As mentioned in the previous chapter, we are presenting an optimal starting situation for the customer here, without personal influences or preferences and without the political currents that usually accompany and influence tenders. If we were to include these influencing factors here, the ramifications that we would have to describe would be too complex. Furthermore, we assume that all contracts of the individual partners of Customs AG expire at approximately the same time. However, the added value of our method becomes clear even in an optimal starting situation.

> **Important** The more chaotic the situation is, the more functions or people are working against each other, the more unclear the goal becomes, and the more people disagree about what should be achieved. As the project progresses, you realise that you should have approached it differently. This speaks even more strongly in favour of an agile approach as opposed to a formalised tender.

During a tender, requirements of various kinds are defined, and expectations are raised. We will show these in the respective phases in order to illustrate the difficulties of the subsequent steps with the defined requirements and expectations.

The individual phases of a classic tender are described below (Fig. 4.7):

The start of the tendering process
How is the decision made?
Creating the enquiry
Who is involved, what methods are there, and how are they frequently used (RFI, RFQ, and RFP)?
Creating an offer

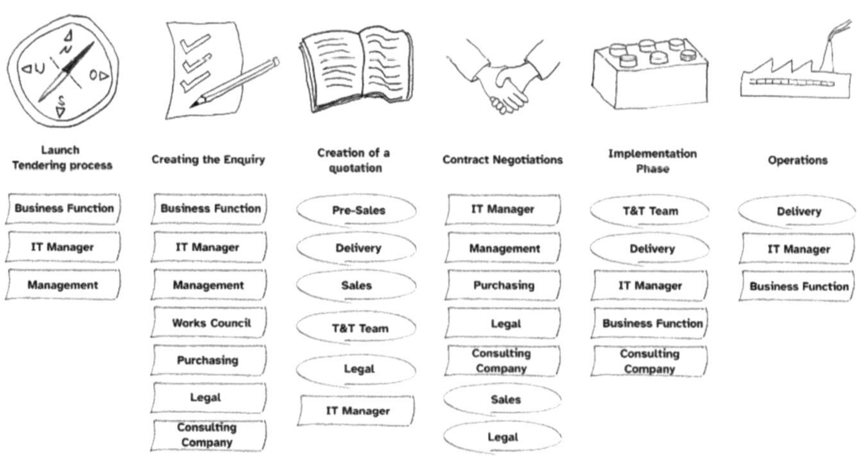


**Fig. 4.7** The phases of a traditional tender

What is the process, what are the roles involved in this step?
The contract negotiations
What happens due to the influence of individual roles and how can this possibly have a negative impact on subsequent operations and why?
The implementation phase (transition and transformation)
Which roles are involved, which methods are used most frequently, and what are their weaknesses?
The operation
What remains of the idea (of the tender)?

## 4.6 The Start of the Tendering Process

The IT services, service desk, on-site service, and the packaging and distribution of software are currently provided by three different providers. These are independent of each other and are managed by Customs AG employees. There is one Customs AG employee per provider who is responsible for this provider and its services vis-à-vis Customs AG in addition to their actual work (Fig. 4.8).

The services provided by the providers repeatedly deviate from the services expected by the business functions. Even switching the individual services to other providers has not yet brought the desired success. Even escalations at management level with the service providers have not eliminated the poor performance in the long term.

The management of Customs AG, together with the IT manager, therefore decided to outsource the services to a single provider. This was expected to result in more consistent processes with considerably faster response times, a significant reduction in costs and greater weight for Customs AG in escalations and change requests to the future provider.

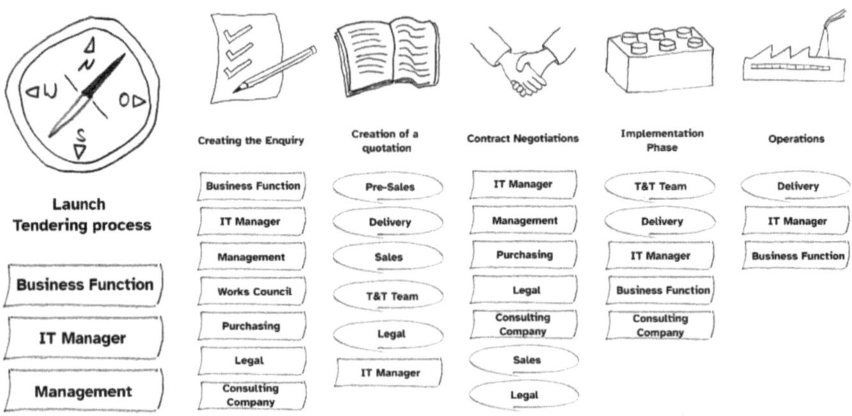


**Fig. 4.8** Start of the tender

In order to ensure that the tender also leads to an improvement in services and relieves the internal employees, who also have to cover day-to-day business in addition to the tender, a consulting company was brought in to support the tender.

### 4.6.1 The Current Services

The service desk is currently provided by a partner whose service desk services are provided from the eastern EU. Customs AG has agreed the following service levels with this partner:

When a Customs AG employee calls the Service Desk, they should speak to a Service Desk employee within 20 s in 80% of calls. Furthermore, the Service Desk should resolve 65% of incoming Incidents directly on the phone.

The on-site service consists of technicians who solve IT Incidents at the Customs AG workstations and the network at the Customs AG sites that cannot be solved via remote maintenance. The on-site technicians also look after the existing hardware at the sites.

The service levels agreed with the on-site service partner are the restoration of Customs AG employees' ability to work within the following working day in the event of an Incident, or within 4 h in the case of VIP employees.

The software packaging partner takes care of creating packages from the so-called standard software, i.e. software that is installed at least 50 times on the workstations of Customs AG employees, which are automatically distributed by the software distribution system and then installed automatically and smoothly.

It was agreed with the partner that the standard software would be categorised into three levels of complexity: Light, medium, and complex. Each of these levels has its own price for the creation of a package and its own lead time until the package has to be created and handed over to software distribution.

Software distribution takes over the distribution of standard software within a certain period of time after the software packages have been released by Customs AG. Software distribution also handles the distribution of normal updates or patches released by Customs AG, as well as the distribution of security patches that have to be distributed directly for certain applications and operating systems.

## 4.7 Creating the Enquiry

In this phase, the parties involved are limited to the tendering company, i.e. Customs AG. The roles involved are the management, which at least lays the foundation for the tender, the IT manager(s) responsible for the services to be tendered, the business functions, the business, which accepts the services, and the consultancy firm (Fig. 4.9).

The management has commissioned the IT manager and the consulting company to issue a tender for the services service desk, on-site service, software packaging and software distribution to a provider. The first step is to compile the desired or

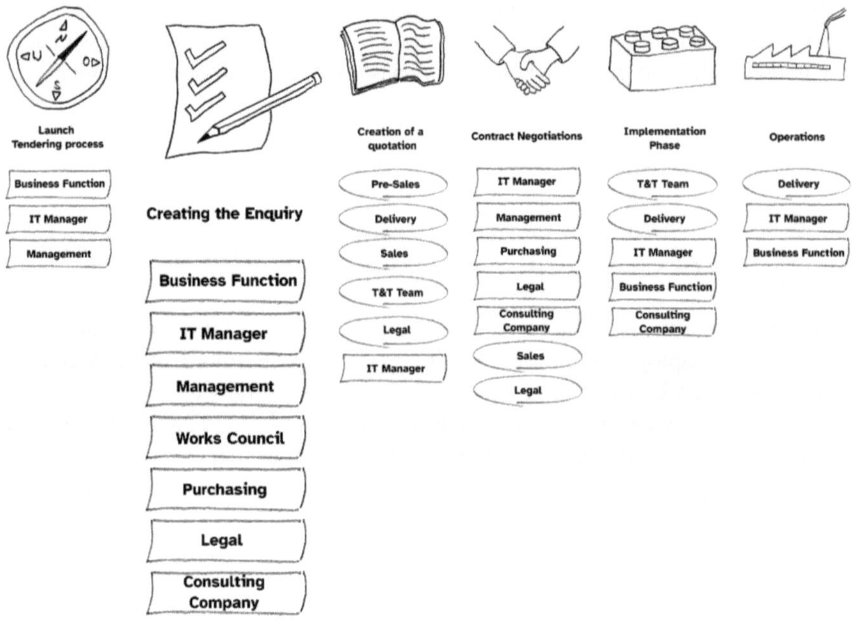


**Fig. 4.9** Creating the enquiry

required services and a list of which departments will accept the services. Furthermore, the existing contracts are scrutinised about terms, service level agreements, and other special features from the agreements with the three partners.

In the next step, the business functions are asked about the services and any requests and urgently needed changes to the services are recorded. This means that the IT manager and the consulting firm have now described the current services and recorded the requirements from the business functions.

> **Overview** Requirements and expectations
> The business functions expect that its communicated wishes regarding the future service will be taken into account and implemented.

## Excursus AI Support Thought Differently

Both customers and providers are currently endeavouring to use generative AI applications in tenders. In most cases, the aim is to use AI to make high levels of complexity more manageable. For example, providers are trying to filter out the quintessence of 5000 requirements in order to be able to create an offer more quickly. On the customer side, hundreds of pages of quotation documents are compressed into just a few pages using AI. The results still need to be improved, but we will see AI applications specialising in tenders in the future.

However, the use of AI to cope with ever-increasing or unpreventable amounts of data could go in the wrong direction. If consistent data consolidation succeeds in reducing the number of irritations and deliberate errors, a tender will better support the business purpose than uncontrolled data collection with AI post-processing. Let's stick with the above examples of many requirements and text summaries. 5000 requirements collected by humans are not self-contradictory. If a customer–provider relationship based on such a contract goes badly, e.g. because the costs for additional services are disputed, some providers will look for precisely these contradictions in order to force the customer's hand.

Providers will work to find the inconsistencies among the 5000 requirements. Whether these results are actively used in the tendering phase or rather kept in the background is a question of the culture in the provider's organisation. This risk can be counteracted by collecting as few requirements as possible, i.e. focussing on the most important requirements, possibly even clustered according to the principle of must and can criteria (see MoSCoW method → Chap. 8). However, this risk only exists with classic tenders; with the adaptive tenders presented here, this risk does not exist due to the prioritisation according to values.

The second example, in which customers want to summarise hundreds of pages of quotation text into a few pages using AI, is very relevant. Anyone who has ever read half a dozen hundred-page offers on the customer side will know the challenge. On the one hand, the danger with AI summarisation is that the number of pages selected is too small for the given complexity. If 100 pages are summarised on 4 pages, important elements are lost. On the other hand, today's AI systems tend to include familiar features in such a summary. This means that particularly interesting, unusual or negative characteristics of suppliers tend to be omitted from such summaries.

Our tip: Formulate precise specifications for the required response documents according to the offer phase. 2 pages of management summary (2000 words), 20 pages of solution description, presentation with max. 20 technical highlights or similar. If the providers then summarise their internal documents with AI support, these will certainly be checked by architects after the automatic summary and supplemented with missing innovations and unique selling points.

### 4.7.1 The Request for Information (RFI)

Customs AG's Purchasing department is then commissioned to conduct a market survey to determine how the services to be put out to tender are currently offered on the market by service providers in their standard form.

The purchasing department and the IT manager then compile a description of the services from the information previously collected by the IT manager about the existing services, the associated service levels, and the requirements from the business functions.

The service providers in question should now describe how they would provide the services in question. From these descriptions, the IT manager should compile the new requirements for the services to be tendered in order to map the requirements of the business function as completely as possible and possibly supplement them with innovations described in the RFI.

**Excursus Shared Service in Tenders**
The proportion of personnel is high in many areas of IT managed services, especially in all service and support roles that have to eliminate faults, investigate causes, or implement non-automatable service requests in several degrees of specialisation. At this point, IT service providers offer various organisational models (Table 4.2).

The various models cannot be provided by all IT service providers in any form and across all service providers. The RFI is therefore a good way of analysing the possibilities of individual providers. In particular, different forms of shared services may or may not be suitable for your tender. Take the time to better understand these models, possibly with a reference visit to a delivery centre.

In this case, it is possible to request a small selection of potential delivery models in the tender. However, if only one specific model is requested, only a few providers will be able to fulfil this directly. This can lead to a smaller variety of offers and higher costs. It is also to be expected that individual providers will reinterpret the exact wording of the tender to suit their model. Ask for a precise architecture including roles and personnel resources.

### 4.7.2 The Request for Quotation (RFQ)

After the RFI was created, it became apparent that although the services available on the market could now be queried, the goal of reducing costs could not really be addressed. The information and requirements for the RFI are therefore supplemented by the volumes of the services to be tendered and the minimum requirements for the services to be provided are added.

This should enable the service providers to determine a cost indication in addition to the description of how they intend to provide the tendered services and what added value they will bring to Customs AG. This will enable Customs AG to address and determine the current IT budget for the services to be tendered in good time during the budget negotiations.

**Important** For understandable reasons, the customer's IT budget is already fixed before the contract negotiations with the future providers. The same applies to the requirements of the business functions. These two key points can contradict each other and often lead to tough contract negotiations and changes to previously agreed services.

In most cases, a consulting firm or the purchasing department will be able to directly assess whether an RFI or RFQ should be used.

**Table 4.2** Shared and dedicated service models in tenders

| Model | Description | Advantages and disadvantages |
|---|---|---|
| Dedicated | Personnel, technical platforms and other resources are provided and used exclusively for one customer. The service provider's employees work exclusively for one customer for the duration of the contract. This makes it possible to integrate customer-specific training, certifications, or security checks into the service<br>With small volumes, this model generally leads to efficiency losses, e.g. underutilised personnel during off-peak times or a sharp increase in hardware costs if a resource is fully utilised and an additional component has to be provided | The advantage of a dedicated model is often based on information security, as all data are stored on physically or logically separate machines and staff do not work for several customers<br>Another reason is the individualised customer support, as the provider's employees know all the customer's special features after a certain period of time<br>The main disadvantage of a dedicated model is the higher costs due to efficiency deficits. A certain size is required to be able to map certain service models. For example, a 24/7 service requires a minimum number of staff, which can only be realised cost-effectively from a size of 10,000 end users |
| Shared | Personnel, technical platforms and other resources are shared by several customers. Data and communication on hardware platforms are separated by customer (multi-tenant system).<br>Hardware resources such as computing power are distributed among several customers (tenants), and allocation during peak loads is usually based on the selected service level, e.g. silver, gold, platinum. There are several models for the IT provider's staff, e.g. an employee can work for four customers at the same time and essentially organise their own time. In highly automated environments, employees are assigned individual tasks. The only thing that matters is the employee's skills. There is no limit to the number of customers in this shared model | The main advantage lies in the price, but also in the service models that can be realised in this way. Simultaneous use by numerous customers means that resources can be optimally utilised, resulting in high efficiency in capacity utilisation<br>This also applies to personnel, for example, a night shift in a control centre where a few employees can monitor the services of many customers. This means that even small customers can realise night-time coverage with active personnel at low cost<br>The disadvantage is a largely impersonal service that needs to be highly structured and documented more comprehensively than a dedicated service in order to function. And not all information security requirements can be realised in the shared model |
| Hybrid | This model is a mixture of dedicated and shared service. One example is a service desk that is only staffed by dedicated personnel during office hours. At night, a shared team takes care of particularly urgent cases | A hybrid approach is a good way to weigh up the pros and cons. Wherever staff are deployed for several customers, not all information security requirements can be realised |

The RFQ is then sent to the service providers from the RFI market exploration so that they can describe in detail how the services to be tendered will be provided, what innovations Customs AG can expect from them, and why Customs AG should definitely select them as a partner. All of this should also be evaluated by the service provider with a price per service or a total price. Customs AG leaves it up to the service providers to decide how they price their services. References to other customers of the service providers are also requested.

**Important** We often experience that customers ask for references. This is perfectly understandable. However, a comparison of a reference also presupposes that the customers and the services requested are comparable. This is rarely possible. A reference allows the conclusion to be drawn that the service provider has been providing these services for a long time and has experience, but it does not allow the conclusion to be drawn that they will provide these services of the same quality for the other customer.

Customs AG sends the RFQs to the service providers and sets a deadline of 4 weeks for the service providers to respond to the RFQs.

### Excursus Decision Matrices in Tenders

When it comes to deciding which IT service provider delivers the best overall package, several criteria usually play a role. A catalogue of criteria with an evaluation scheme is drawn up. At the beginning of the tendering phase, the focus is on factors such as price, performance, and quality. Over the course of the weeks, further criteria are typically added, so that a decision matrix can comprise 50 lines or more (Table 4.3).

This is a classic approach in which the most important criteria take up around 60% and the remaining 40% is divided between subordinate priorities. As these lists mature in the project, many small items are typically added because new employees find additional aspects. The percentage for an additional criterion is then initially siphoned off from the larger 5% of the other criteria and because 1% appears indivisible, at some point even percentage points are diverted from the main criteria.

**Table 4.3** Example of a decision matrix

| Criterion | Maximum score |
|---|---|
| Price | 30% |
| Fulfilment of all requirements | 20% |
| Innovative technology platform | 10% |
| Nearby delivery centre | 10% |
| ISO/IEC 20000 certified | 5% |
| Exclusively own employees | 5% |
| .. | .. |
| Until the sum finally equals 100% | |

This means that the distribution of main criteria to secondary criteria drops from 60:40 to 50:50 or less. Whether percentage points are used, i.e. the total score is standardised to 100, or absolute scores are used, makes no difference.

The next challenge is the mathematical evaluation of the qualitative and quantitative criteria, which are often not sufficiently defined. Let's start with the price and assume that a price range of 6 to 8 million euros is expected for the tendered service. Is it then determined that a provider receives the full 30% at 6 million euros, 0% at 8 million euros and all values in between linearly, i.e. 15% at 7 million euros and 22.5% at 6.5 million euros?

What about the next criterion in the table, the requirements:

From what degree of non-fulfilment should 0% be awarded here?

What is meant by a nearby delivery centre?

A nearshore delivery centre may only be a few hours away by plane. Is this criterion about good accessibility because project teams want to make personal arrangements at the delivery centre?

New information could be interesting for the criteria not met, perhaps a provider does not have ISO/IEC 20000 certification but has an excellently certified team.

In practice, such a decision table is constantly being adapted—to the number of points per criterion or to the calculation formulae. For example, this is because it has been established that the most cost-effective provider offers an alarmingly low scope of services and is still ahead in terms of percentage points. Or the best candidate only comes third in the percentage scale because it does not fulfil many unimportant secondary criteria. This is understandable from a human point of view, but it shows the problematic nature of such decision tables.

One assumption is that the simple, mostly linear calculation formulas and certain dependencies, which in some cases heavily weight secondary criteria, are the main cause. As a way out, complicated evaluation models that work with sophisticated statistical and probability functions are sometimes used. We believe that this is not an appropriate solution, at least not for organisations that have little experience with outsourcing.

Here are some practical tips for designing decision tables:

Main criteria are main criteria. Try to be as open as possible in your organisation about which aspect is decisive. Give the main criteria a high score. Some organisations decide strictly on the basis of price, in which case price should be given a weighting of over 70%.

Limit the secondary criteria to 10% or, even better, list the secondary criteria. These are often nice side effects when deciding in favour of a provider.

Do not decide with a calculated total score but place the main criteria next to each other and give the providers in each line a traffic light colour red-yellow-green for the fulfilment of this criterion. Summarise secondary criteria in a red-yellow-green line.

If you want to calculate overall scores, run through many extreme scenarios in advance. If you need to change the evaluation scheme during the tendering process, have this done by a team that does not know the current providers and their bids. For objectivity, anonymise the contents of the matrix for this team.

Experience has shown that, particularly in an organisation's first outsourcing projects, two or three providers with slightly different offerings remain at the end of the process, but all of them are worth considering. One provider has one highlight (strength), the other two have other highlights (strengths). In other words, the number of green cells in the table is similar for all providers, they are just distributed differently.

With such a well-prepared decision, you can listen to your gut feeling when making the final decision (Gigerenzer, 2007). Especially if several people are involved in the final decision. In this case, try to avoid group effects, e.g. by always voting in secret and openly discussing the preferences of the individual.

### 4.7.3 The Request for Proposal (RFP)

The responses of the service providers to the RFI or RFQ are analysed by the purchasing department and an initial ranking list of the service providers is drawn up. The IT manager and the consulting firm now review the responses and the (hopefully) new concepts for providing the requested services and compare them with the prices quoted for these services (Fig. 4.10).

This allows an initial comparison to be made with the planned IT budget for these services. Depending on how many service providers have been contacted and how many have responded, an initial longlist of service providers to be contacted with the RFP can be drawn up. In addition, the services offered by the service

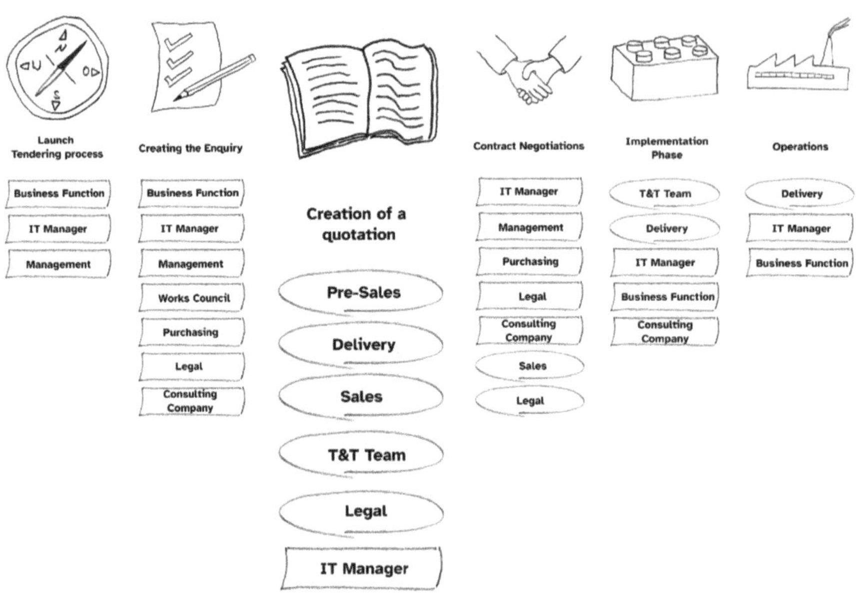


**Fig. 4.10** The enquiry

providers and their costs are discussed with the business functions in order to determine how the services are to be tendered with regard to the requirements of the business functions.

**Requirements and expectations:** The IT budget for the services is often requested here or at least announced to management.

**Important** Most companies that tender for IT services have a different core business and IT is a cost factor that is intended to support the business. The more IT costs, the lower the profit from the actual core business.

Together with the business function and the consulting company, the IT manager now defines the scope of services, the volume of services and important information for the service provider about Customs AG in an RFP. In addition to the service descriptions and the volume of services, further components are added to the RFP.

These are usually requirements of the legal department, e.g. legal requirements that Customs AG must comply with and that are expected of the future service provider. Data protection and data security also have their place in the RFP document. It is not uncommon for the proportion of legally relevant documents to exceed the proportion of the service description many times over.

**Important** The service providers were not aware of these legal requirements when submitting the costs in the RFQ, but they very often have an impact on the price.

After and, of course, during the compilation of the RFPs, an evaluation matrix is created—usually by the consulting company. This enables an assessment to be made on the basis of the facts contained in the offers when the service providers' offers are received.

Depending on how many service providers have been contacted and how much time is left, a shortlist of two to four service providers is formed from the list of all service providers, with whom further negotiations are conducted.

We are assuming the formation of a shortlist with two service providers.

The new RFP is then adapted by the IT manager and the consulting firm from the offers received with regard to the due diligence services.

The request now contains four services: Service Desk, whose requirements do not differ from the current requirements, as well as software packaging and software distribution, whose requirements also do not differ from the current requirements.

With regard to on-site service, Customs AG would like to take up suggestions from one of the RFQs and now offer its employees a front desk at the sites, which is staffed by on-site technicians at certain times and offers employees the opportunity to discuss problems directly with a technician, receive help with operating issues, replace hardware, or collect new hardware. As the front desk is not to be manned at all times, additional cabinets are to be set up at the front desk containing locked compartments that can be accessed using a PIN. Customs AG employees can remove hardware here 24/7.

These performance requirements, together with the remaining documents, such as the data protection requirements and other legal documents, are now sent as an RFP to the companies that have qualified in the RFQ from the point of view of Customs AG.

The requested suppliers are given 6 weeks by Customs AG to respond with an orderable offer. Within these 6 weeks, the suppliers have 4 weeks to ask questions if anything in the RFP is unclear to them. Customs AG has undertaken to answer these questions within 1 week. All questions and answers will be made available to all bidders.

**Important** Most suppliers require an approval process before a bid can be submitted. This process often takes up to a week, or even longer depending on the value of the offer, as higher management levels need to be involved. If a question or answer arises at the end of the question period—i.e. two weeks before the bid is submitted—that requires a new design of the service and therefore a new calculation, this can cause considerable difficulties for the provider and lead to errors in the design and calculation. Errors in the calculation usually lead to considerable challenges in the operating phase, as the provider may achieve a negative result (make a loss). Every provider will try to compensate for this. This is bound to cause considerable tension between the customer and the provider, up to and including the cancellation of the entire service!

From the bids received, Customs AG and the consulting firm will now determine the shortlist participants and inform the bidders whether they will continue to participate in the process or whether they will no longer be considered. The remaining providers (those on the shortlist) are then invited to the due diligence process.

In the due diligence process, these two service providers ask their questions about Customs AG, the services to be provided, and the business functions of Customs AG. This enables the service providers to prepare an offer for Customs AG to order. This is known as a Best and Final Offer (BAFO). Based on this BAFO, Customs AG will decide who will provide the tendered services in future.

**Important** There are companies that enter into contract negotiations with two providers in order to decide at the end of the negotiations with whom the contract will be concluded.

We assume that Customs AG will decide with which of the two providers the contract negotiations will be concluded after the due diligence.

### Excursus: RACI Matrices in Tenders

RACI matrices are often used in tenders and contracts for IT services to describe the roles and responsibilities for operations. They usually describe the division of individual activities between client and contractor. RACI stands for the four key responsibilities: responsible (R), accountable (A), consulted (C), and informed (I).

The following table is a simplified example of a service desk that processes incidents reported by users or systems in Incident Management. In this case, the users and the Incident Management Owner are on the customer side and the Service Desk Agent and the Incident Manager are on the provider side. In practice, the responsibilities of eight to 12 roles can be listed in RACI matrices (Table 4.4).

The RACI principle is a marvellous tool and should definitely be used. In practice, we see two typical pitfalls. Tenders and contracts sometimes contain pages of RACI tables. The idea of the creator is to define every detail as precisely as possible. This often achieves the opposite; the detailed sub-items are no longer clear-cut in some places, so that different responsibilities for an overall activity can be interpreted.

If these page-long wallpapers are copied into the operating manuals during the transition, they are often almost worthless. The original intention of the author is difficult to understand anyway and in an operating situation where you just want to understand where a transition point is located, this would mean hours of study. It is better to keep RACI matrices short. Summarise activities as much as possible and go into detail at the interfaces and transfer points. It may even be useful to highlight these points in colour and comment on them.

The second trap with RACI is to give the service provider an "A" for accountable in too many places in the table or to summarise "A, R" in general. The idea behind this is usually to place as much responsibility as possible on the service provider, but this is often a misinterpretation of the situation. If we stick with the example above, the provider is "accountable" for the incident process and is not only responsible for the result, but also has the freedom to reorganise the process. The provider's complete sovereignty over the incident process is probably unintended and unintentional in the case of service desk outsourcing.

A RACI is about assigning tasks and responsibilities to roles. A description of the delivery item and its scope is certainly already included in detail elsewhere in the contract. In this way, it should already be well established that the IT provider is responsible for the overall service desk performance. Incorrectly placed "A's" in the

**Table 4.4** Example of a RACI

| ID | Activity | Users | Incident Mgmt. owner | Service desk agent | Incident manager |
|---|---|---|---|---|---|
| 1 | Identify incident | R | | R | A |
| 2 | Log incident | C, I | | R | A |
| 3 | Categorise incident | I | | R | A |
| .. | .. | | | | |
| 25 | Review incident process | | A, R | I | C |

RACI matrix are merely confusing. If you are still unsure, why not use "Implementation of the service desk support service" or similar as the first entry in the RACI and give the provider an "A" here?

In some cases, however, the classic RACI matrix has reached its limits. Various extensions have therefore been developed to adequately map more complex tasks and responsibility structures. The reasons for this are manifold:

Multiple decision-makers: In some projects, there are several people who are responsible for the final decision on a task. RACI variants such as RASCI or RACI-VS make it possible to map this shared decision-making responsibility.

External support: When working with external partners or service providers, it can be helpful to include roles such as "Support" or "Driver" in the matrix in order to clearly define their tasks and responsibilities.

Review and approval processes: In regulated environments or for tasks with high quality requirements, it may be necessary to introduce additional roles such as "Verify" or "Signatory" in order to map review and approval processes.

Improved communication: By defining roles and responsibilities in more detail, RACI variants can reduce misunderstandings and unnecessary coordination channels, thereby improving communication in the project.

The most common RACI variants are:

RASCI: Adds the "Supporter" role, which provides support when carrying out tasks.

RACI-VS: Adds the "Verifier" and "Signatory" roles, which check and approve results.

REWA: Distinguishes between "Responsible" for the overall task, "Expert" for the technical advice, "Work" for the actual execution, and "Approver" for the acceptance.

RACIO: Adds the role "Omitted" to explicitly indicate who is not involved in a task.

In addition to the variants already mentioned, there are numerous other adaptations and extensions of the RACI matrix. The choice of the appropriate variant depends on the specific requirements of the project or company. It is crucial that the RACI matrix used is clearly defined and understood by all parties involved (McGrath, 2021).

### 4.7.4 The Contract Negotiations

Due diligence is practically the beginning of the contract negotiations. The two remaining partners can scrutinise all the services they are to provide and also ask other questions about the company. The people currently responsible for the services are usually present to answer questions (Fig. 4.11).

In some cases, there is also an opportunity to speak with the business functions. The providers adapt their offer on the basis of Customs AG's responses. The answers

**Fig. 4.11** The contract negotiations

from Customs AG and the BAFO prepared by the provider form the basis for the contract to be concluded.

**Important** Due diligence (or DD for short) is a phase that should be well prepared by the providers. It can provide insights into the customer and can also provide an opportunity to get to know the specialised departments. Questions can also be asked about other topics related to the contract, such as data security, data protection, etc. As a provider, you should not be cautious here, as both sides have an interest in the future service being provided better and, if possible, more cost-effectively than the current one.

**Overview** Requirements and expectations
After a DD, regardless of whether it is rather short or more detailed, both parties assume that all open questions have been clarified and that the other party knows exactly what their counterpart wants and will provide. Experience shows that today's IT landscapes and the legal and market requirements are so complex that they are usually not conclusively clarified in a DD.

Once the due diligence has been completed, the actual contract is drawn up. Customs AG has decided to conclude a general framework agreement with the remaining provider, in which the actual services to be provided are included as an annex. The annexes describe in detail the services to be provided by the provider, the volumes that the provider can expect for this service in future and the quality characteristics within which the service must be provided.

The systems for the services were finally discussed and agreed by the IT manager and representatives of the business function under the supervision of Customs AG's legal department and consultancy firm and representatives of the provider. The provider's representatives usually consist of the provider's sales manager, pre-sales—who prepared and calculated the services—and the provider's legal department. In some cases, and depending on the provider's culture, representatives from the provider's delivery department also take part in the negotiations.

**Important** In this phase, the different objectives of the individual stakeholders can be clearly recognised and may also lead to tensions. In rare cases, contract negotiations have already been broken off because the parties were unable to agree on key points. This can happen if the previous steps, in particular the due diligence, were not worked out carefully enough. This may be because the time frame was too tight, because the customer did not take the provider into account or because the provider is desperate to win this customer. However, such a situation is unfavourable for both sides and should be avoided at all costs. For the provider, this is because it loses reputation, quite apart from the investment it has made in the tender (often in the six-figure range). And it also applies to the customer, because they may have to admit to the remaining provider that they are the only remaining provider with whom the contract can be concluded in the time remaining, which of course puts the customer in an extremely weak position in the contract negotiations.

These statements make it clear that a partnership-based and open approach is beneficial for both sides.

After the negotiation of the facilities regarding the services to be provided, or in parallel, the remaining contractual documents are finalised. The method of invoicing, place of jurisdiction, special security requirements, geographical scope (locations or countries, etc.), etc. are all agreed.

**Important** The effort involved in this phase of the tender is often underestimated. Especially with inexperienced customers who are looking for first-generation outsourcing, for example. In many cases, the legal departments talk to each other during contract negotiations. Both parties try—in accordance with their remit—to secure and firmly agree on things that are subject to extremely rapid change and will happen many months or years in the future.

Customs AG agrees with the provider on a framework agreement and three service level agreements for the provision of the services. Annex 1 describes the service desk with the requirements from the invitation to tender. These requirements are standard for the market and should also be supplied by the previous provider. Annex 2 describes the deployment of technicians on site to repair workstation and network systems.

Appendix 3 contains the key points for the packaging of software and its distribution to the workstations and server systems of Customs AG. The standard market parameters were also selected for Annex 3. In Appendix 2, Customs AG decided in favour of innovations such as unattended pick-up stations and a front desk physically manned by technicians at times at the five locations of Customs AG.

Furthermore, a fourth system was agreed for the implementation (transition and transformation) of the project. Here, the provider developed a procedure detailing which services would be implemented, the input required from Customs AG, and the milestones to be reached during the implementation process.

The achievement of the milestones and the acceptance of these milestones by Customs AG are also the points in time at which the provider can submit a partial invoice to Customs AG for the implementation expenses incurred up to that point. When the last milestone in the implementation phase is reached, the services are officially handed over to regular operations.

A total implementation period of 6 months was agreed in the annex. The six-month implementation phase ends 1 month before the contracts with the old service providers expire. It is therefore necessary that the implementation phase is not significantly exceeded, as the provision of the services would otherwise be jeopardised.

**Important** The provider usually prepares the planning for the implementation. In doing so, it is absolutely dependent on the cooperation of the customer. The provider now draws up the planning, taking into account the projects mentioned to him that could have an influence on the transition. It often happens that the provider is (unintentionally) not informed of all the projects that have an influence on a transition because the customer is not aware of their influence or because they are being carried out in neighbouring departments that are essentially uninvolved in the tender. These "flight-in" projects can significantly disrupt a transition. In addition, the customer, particularly in the case of first-generation outsourcing, underestimates that its own employees will have a considerable additional workload during the transition compared to normal day-to-day business.

### 4.7.5 The Implementation Phase

The transition of the agreed services from the partners and organisations that previously provided the service (old provider) to the new provider is referred to as a transition or transformation. In general, the term transition is used when the new

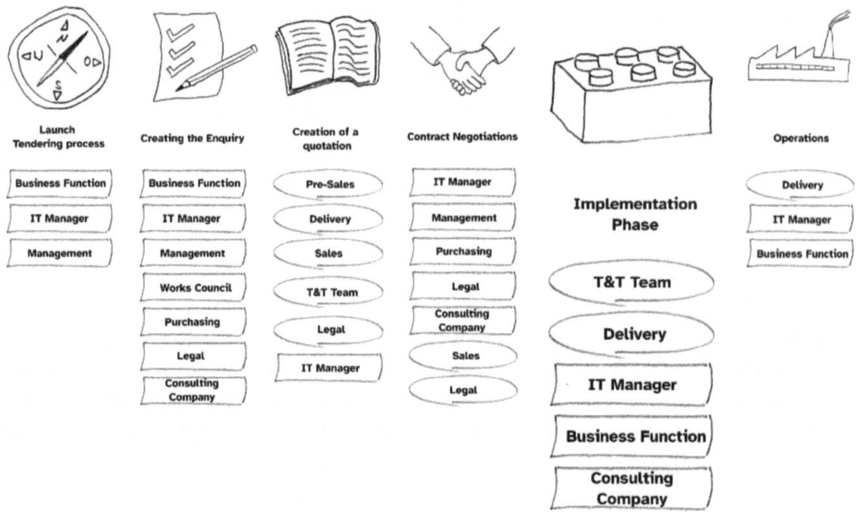


**Fig. 4.12** The implementation phase

service does not differ significantly from the old service. In contrast, the term transformation is used when the service changes significantly (Fig. 4.12).

Depending on the complexity of the service to be provided by the partner, the transition can be very demanding and the planning very complicated. We will refrain from going into this level of detail here and present the process somewhat generically.

Customs AG has decided not to make any significant changes to the service desk, software packaging, and software distribution services, but simply to have them provided by another provider. For the on-site service of the technicians, however, Customs AG has decided to transform the service into a fundamentally different operating model.

The implementation phase usually begins immediately after the contract is signed. If the contract negotiations are delayed and the timeframe for the implementation phase is jeopardised, the provider could start the implementation phase despite the customer not having signed the contract. This is often referred to as "work at risk", as the provider is making advance payments without having received an official order, as the contract enabling the order has not yet been signed.

**Important** Providers are very reluctant to carry out "work at risk" and usually require authorisation from the management, as if the contract negotiations fail, the provider is left with the costs and possibly also the staff hired specifically for the customer. Contract negotiations are therefore under great time pressure.

The implementation phase begins with initial coordination between the two project teams (customer and provider) in order to get to know each other, define responsibilities, and familiarise each other. The operating team at the provider is also established at the beginning. At least, the employment contracts for the new employees providing the services should have been concluded by now (they should already have been negotiated). Depending on the size of the customer or the volume of new services to be provided, this cannot usually be covered by the existing operating team.

The IT manager and Customs AG's consultancy firm have agreed with the provider that the service will not be provided exclusively by newly hired employees, but by a mixture of experienced and new staff.

After coordinating the formalities and getting to know the two implementation teams, Customs AG's new provider begins by looking at the services in their current state and compares the operating manuals with the current state in order to compare the path from the current state to the target state with its own planning.

**Important** Most of the operating manuals that we have come across in the past are outdated and often do not correspond to the processes and procedures currently in place. Only in companies with a high degree of maturity can it be assumed that documentation is up to date. These operating manuals are often provided to the new provider in advance of a DD or are even part of the RFP. In this case, the provider can assume that the documents are up to date, but this does not necessarily allow conclusions to be drawn about the maturity level of the entire company.

The new provider of Customs AG has set up a governance level for the transition and transformation (T&T for short) and specialised areas for the three services.

**Important** According to PRINCE2, the management of a project should be separated from the technical implementation. This enables better coordination. However, it also increases the costs of the implementation phase.

Customs AG, on the other hand, does not have the resources to deploy a 1:1 mirrored implementation team for the project and relies on the new provider's implementation team. This will, as a rule, lead to considerable problems during implementation, and in some projects, this has already led to the failure of the entire project.

The new provider is now required to request and obtain the information it needs for implementation from the employees of Customs AG.

He has now reached the first milestone, built up his operations team, and is in the process of setting up the new services for Customs AG and creating the required reports.

In parallel and so far unnoticed by the implementation project, a division of Customs AG is preparing and implementing a migration of the Lotus Notes software solution to the Microsoft Exchange software solution. The project management on the Customs AG side informs the new provider in one of the management meetings that the preparations have now been completed and the rollout is planned for the scheduled start of operations of the new services.

**Important** In the implementation phases, you often come across the "in-flight projects" mentioned above. In other words, these are projects that suddenly appear, often unnoticed by the provider, and which can have a significant impact on the implementation and sometimes even on subsequent operation. It should always be borne in mind that the core business of the customers discussed here, such as Customs AG, is generally not IT.

The new provider of Customs AG now has the task of planning and supporting the requirements of the new migration project (Lotus Notes migration to Exchange) of Customs AG in addition to the tight schedule for the implementation of its own new services up to the handover to operations (the so-called "go-live"). To this end, it is necessary to work out in which areas of its own new services the migration to Exchange will have an impact.

After examining the impact of the migration from Lotus Notes to Microsoft Exchange, Customs AG's new provider realises that it will affect all new services. For the Service Desk, the number of expected calls will increase considerably, as Customs AG employees are not familiar with the new tool and will ask questions about its operation. The number of errors (incidents) will also increase. The new software has to be packaged and distributed. And the planned front desk will also have to deal with an increased number of enquiries from on-site technicians.

**Important** Examining the effects of such "in-flight projects" is not included in the provider's project costs. Neither is any necessary adaptation of the contracts with the customer. Such new projects often require a change request procedure in order to adapt the contracts. This often leads to tensions, as the project managers at the new provider are often no longer able to realise their project in the planned time and therefore no longer within the planned budget. Tensions arise for the customer, as the provider now tries to get the increased costs reimbursed by the customer, whose project budget now also has to be increased.

Customs AG and the new provider agree to support the migration project and the resulting additional costs incurred by Customs AG's new provider will be compensated by Customs AG. This was agreed by the provider's sales manager and legal department with the Customs AG IT manager and legal department in a corresponding change request procedure.

The remaining milestones up to "Go Live" were completed by the new provider of Customs AG and the services were handed over from the old providers of Customs AG to the new provider. The old providers are now available to Customs AG for another month as a backup and for any questions that may arise.

**Important** The tender is completed at the latest when the new services are handed over to the new provider. Up to this point, the project has lasted one and a half years from the decision to award the services again because they are not satisfied until they have now been handed over. Technological changes or innovations are very difficult or even impossible to integrate into this project. However, they are often part of the customer's expectations of the new provider.

### 4.7.6 Operations

Operation is now the final phase. It continues until the services are outsourced to a new provider. The new provider delivers the services in the same way as they were created and developed during the implementation phase. The new provider's operating team has been trained accordingly and the procedures for collaboration have been established (Fig. 4.13).

Customs AG's current contract with the new provider describes the services to be provided and also contains the date on which the contract with the new provider ends.

Customs AG expects new technologies to be presented and introduced by the new provider.

**Important** The introduction of new technologies usually requires new planning and often also a new version of the contracts. In short: a new invitation to tender with the difference that the initiation then comes from the provider. This means that a large part of the process described above would take place again (albeit no longer over such a long period of time).

In our experience, it is difficult for both suppliers and customers to introduce innovations during the contract period.

This is difficult for the provider as they have to involve employees who offer innovations to customers but are not directly involved in customer projects. The introduction of innovations is therefore not included in their budget. It is also difficult for customers, as they usually rely on the provider to offer innovations independently.

Here, the expectation of such services in later operation, such as the introduction and implementation of innovations, is contrary to the decision within the RFP in favour of a provider with a more favourable price (or one from the mid-price range), as price often plays a significant role in the tender.

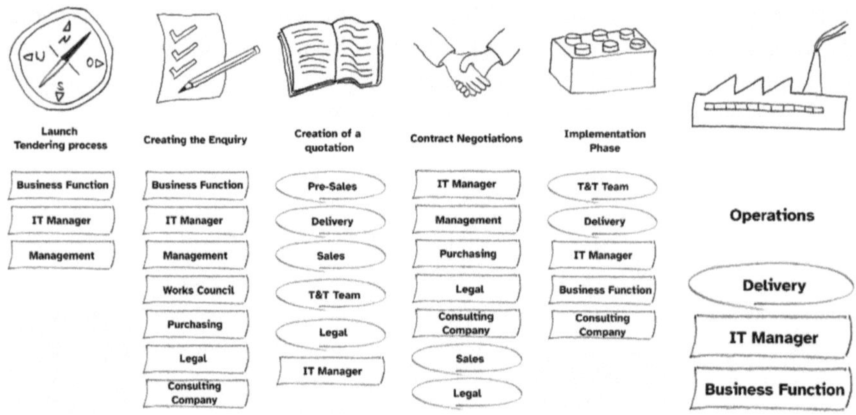


**Fig. 4.13** The operations

But simply working out how innovations can be implemented for the customer and what added value they bring to the customer (i.e. actually an unsolicited offer) costs money. Most providers avoid including these additional costs in the tender, as they increase the price and thus reduce the probability of winning the tender.

Furthermore, many providers prefer to focus on acquiring new customers (i.e. participating in tenders) and only react when existing customers escalate. It should be noted that the resources for introducing innovations and demonstrating added value to different customers are limited. As a result, providers have to manage these resources carefully (apart from the additional costs).

### Excursus Lack of Certification or an Industry Standard

In some business organisations, it only becomes apparent over time that certain standards, certifications, or corresponding data are required. These are not so much international standards such as ISO/IEC 27001, whose necessity for the company should be generally known. These are usually requirements that arise from the client's contracts with its industrial customers. It is not uncommon for deviating requirements or even individual measures of an industry standard to be defined differently in individual contracts. Especially if the IT organisation is not integrated, but is seen as a support unit, such requirements are easily overlooked.

The associated costs are often surprising when, from a management perspective, a small 6-figure sum is charged for a few reports or 30 years of data archiving for a single client. Or when very high personnel costs are charged for accompanying an annual audit. The main reason for such high additional costs is usually that the original design does not fit the new requirements at all and the specifications have to be covered with additional tools and dedicated personnel.

If a cost-effective shared service with integrated central multi-client tools was originally purchased, individual requirements such as specialised reports, log files, or longer data retention times can rarely be configured individually. The limits of what is technically feasible with centralised multi-client tools are exceeded if certain parameters, time stamps, or additional fields are added. A shared team cannot allocate a dedicated person to an audit.

New requirements are often given to the provider as an addition, although alternative solutions could be a much better fit. We therefore recommend collecting these and other new requirements and jointly developing alternatives to the original solution. If necessary, the tasks can be distributed among different teams in order to find a cost-effective interim solution.

## 4.8 AI in the Tendering Process

As this book is being written, AI applications are experiencing a real boom. Numerous projects are being launched by customers and IT service providers to make both managed services and tendering processes more efficient with the help of artificial intelligence. Experiments with generative AI applications from the public cloud quickly reach their limits. Many companies are therefore creating current architectures for their AI environments that consist of public cloud clients and private cloud applications (hybrid cloud) in order to adequately map data protection requirements.

It is to be expected that IT service providers, consulting firms and large internal IT organisations will develop specialised AI applications over the next few years that will support tendering procedures at all stages over time. It is difficult to predict what impact such AI applications will have. As the outcome of IT services is much more complex than the outcome of products, for example, such AI applications will continue to support rather than dominate tenders in the future. The sheer number of publicly accessible tenders and responses from providers is also too small to achieve reliable results, at least for machine learning algorithms.

We see the following areas of application for artificial intelligence in tenders:

### Linguistic Data Processing

Applications to support the creation of tender and offer texts are already common practice today. The support services range from spelling, grammar, and translation tools to the creation of texts based on templates and anonymised examples. AI can also be used for market research and to identify potential providers. On the service provider side, the service descriptions of several individual services can be combined into a complete package. Completely generated texts and presentations are currently only used selectively. These are usually used more for preparation than as a kind of rough draft that still needs to be technically finalised.

In the future, consulting firms and full-service providers, i.e. organisations with a broad range of services, will be able to use many of their text and architecture modules automatically in tenders with the help of AI applications. It can be assumed that this will be more about optimising current methods and practices for responding to tenders.

**Example** There are providers with a high degree of standardisation who bid for tenders with a scope of services that is only more or less suitable from the customer's point of view. The result is a favourable offer that is not optimal for the customer in practice. If such a provider develops an AI application, it will probably compare the tender and the offer, but is more likely to report deviations to an internal risk management system. This way, the customer is not better served, but the service provider can protect itself better.

In the area of contracts, it is conceivable that AI applications will be used in the future to analyse contracts for negotiation and thus support contract negotiations. These applications could recognise catch-all clauses, concatenations, or contradictions and point these out to the individual contracting party. It is also conceivable that AI systems could be used to manage the requirements and quality of the service in accordance with the contract. As a result, providers will be able to focus more on the required service and customers will be able to monitor this minimum service in detail.

### Analysing IT Services

The existing data volumes generated by the technical services offer a broad field of application for AI analyses. Such data is generated by the services for support capability. Examples of such data are log files, i.e. event logs that are used to trace processes. But also trace files, i.e. data for tracing and analysing errors.

There is also data from IT service management. This is data from a ticket system, e.g. about faults, service requests, or changes. Data from service management databases, such as asset information, data records from a configuration management system, contract data, and service level reports. There is also real-time information, such as inventory data from network scanning and monitoring events. In addition, the IT and IT service management processes can be analysed and evaluated by the AI.

All this data can be used to optimise services, whereby the amount of data is already so large in medium-sized environments that optimisation by human personnel is reaching its limits. AI-supported network applications can already analyse misconfigurations or performance bottlenecks in complicated environments and offer suggestions for improvement. Such findings can be incorporated into the requirements of a tender.

If customers were to grant providers full access to this data in future as part of due diligence, providers could have a final assessment of the technical optimisation potential calculated by AI. In today's tendering processes, customers and their consultants tend to be reluctant to provide data. In many cases, this is probably due to the fact that the maturity level of IT service management tends to be low and is reluctant to be disclosed. In addition, there is little structured data available in such environments. Here again, AI can provide support by using techniques such as natural language processing (NLP) and machine learning (ML) to extract relevant information from texts, images, videos, and other unstructured data, recognise patterns, and gain meaningful insights.

### Optimisation of IT Services

The larger service environments are, the more efficiency potential they offer in terms of information and technology. This is already happening today through automation and in future, AI analyses will uncover even more potential for optimisation. AI bots and robotic process automation can already be used to carry out standardised processes and value streams. Specialised AI will continue to advance in operations and support in the future and will also be able to implement complex requests or solve known errors.

In the area of organisation, partners, and people, we see little potential for future applications for current specialised AI applications (weak AI). A general AI (strong AI) that can recognise, evaluate, and solve problems independently under changing environmental conditions is currently not foreseeable.

**Important Weak artificial intelligence** is characterised by the fact that it has neither creativity nor the ability to learn independently in a universal sense. Instead, its learning ability is limited to training recognition patterns (machine learning) or comparing and searching through large amounts of data.

It can be used for clearly defined tasks with a defined methodology to solve more complex but recurring and precisely specified problems. The particular advantages of weak AI lie in the automation and control of processes, but also in speech recognition and processing. Examples include text and image recognition, speech recognition, text translation, and navigation systems.

**Strong artificial intelligence** is a theoretical form of artificial intelligence. It is used to describe a particular approach to the development of AI. A machine that has human-like intelligence and self-awareness can solve problems, learn and plan for the future is called strong artificial intelligence.

The goal of strong AI is to create intelligent machines that are indistinguishable from the intelligence of a human being. However, like a child, the AI machine must learn from information and experience and expand and improve its capabilities over time.

It can therefore be assumed that increasingly high-quality IT services will be offered in the form of an efficient service platform. These are technically fully automated and also offer largely AI-supported processing of service management in the support functions. It is conceivable that the manufacturers of technical products in this area will ensure a certain degree of standardisation across providers. How quickly such services are then accepted by the market depends on the flexibility of customers. Today, higher-value services can be negotiated with all the extras and special customer requirements. Services that are standardised in terms of processes and technology can only be ordered with special requests to a limited extent.

**Example** If you order a transport service for a multi-generational home today, you can instruct the taxi service to accompany children and elderly people to and from the vehicle. Such an additional service is nothing unusual for taxi service providers and can be offered at no significant extra cost. With a fully autonomous robot taxi, this individualisation of the service is inconceivable.

### The Fully Automated Tendering Process

When will the day come when you no longer need this book because everything will be done fully automatically by AI? The possibilities for specialised AI applications are limited if we look at the cases above. These AI applications will be a help, they will radically shorten tasks and time for clients and contractors. Extending specialised AI to the diverse technical and procedural aspects of different client organisations and a variety of providers requires standards above a certain size to fully support a tendering cycle.

In contrast to AI applications in the private consumer sector, which can form clusters and patterns with the help of new training data that arrives daily, there are significantly fewer events and training data for managed services tenders. Standardisation by an AI application that receives unstructured alerts and responses as training data is unlikely or very time-consuming due to the small size of the database. It also requires a certain number of early adopters among customers and providers who are willing to support the development of such an AI-driven tendering process with their data.

This does not even take into account aspects that organisations and people bring to a tendering process. Would a decision-making body decide in favour of the most suitable service provider according to the AI process, even though this service provider is completely unknown to the company? How reliably would such an unknown service provider react to a future problem situation? Perhaps the second-best service provider, which has been known for years for its flexibility and reliability, is the better choice? Human emotions and human strengths play a decisive role here and these cannot yet be replaced by AI.

Speculation remains about the feasibility of a strong AI. Since the 1960s, individual AI researchers have been predicting this for the next two to three decades. To date, none of these announcements have materialised. General artificial intelligences remain speculation. Preliminary forms will probably emerge in certain areas, e.g. in the form of extremely comprehensive weak AIs that provide an adequate solution for 99% of their environmental conditions.

What about an alternative to strong AI for tenders? Perhaps in the next 10 years it will be possible to standardise and reduce the cost of IT services with the help of AI to such an extent that a product-like decision for technology and IT processes will suffice. Perhaps many customers will decide in favour of a transformation to these standards. This will leave individual services, processes, partners, and organisations as a field of application for customised services. It is a wonderful field of application for value creation with adaptive services.

## References

European Union. (26 February, 2014). Directive 2014/24/EU OF The European Parliament and of the Council of 26 February 2014 on public procurement and repealing Directive 2004/18/EC. Retrieved on 7 Jul 2025 from https://eur-lex.europa.eu/legal-content/EN/TXT/HTML/?uri=CELEX:32014L0024.

Federal Ministry for Economic Affairs and Energy (BMWi). (17 February, 2015). Act against Restraints on Competition (GWB)—Part 4 in the version of the Act on the Modernisation of Public Procurement Law [Vergaberechtsmodernisierungsgesetz—VergRModG] of 17 February 2015, Federal Law Gazette I of 23 February 2016, p. 203. Retrieved on 23 Jul 2025 from https://www.bundeswirtschaftsministerium.de/Redaktion/DE/Downloads/V/vergaberechtmodernisierungsgesetz-en.pdf?__blob=publicationFile&v=6.

Federal Ministry for Economic Affairs and Energy (BMWi). (12 Apr 2016). Ordinance on the Award of Public Contracts (Procurement Ordinance (Vergabeverordnung—VgV)) in the version of the Ordinance on the Modernisation of Public Procurement Law (Vergaberechtsmodernisierungsverordnung—VergRModVO) of 12 April 2016, Federal Law Gazette I of 14 April 2016, p. 624. Retrieved on 23 Jul 2025 from https://www.bundeskartellamt.de/SharedDocs/Publikation/EN/Others/VergabeVerordnung.pdf?__blob=publicationFile&v=3.

Federal Ministry for Economic Affairs and Energy (BMWi). (27 July, 2017). Monitoring-Bericht der Bundesregierung zur Anwendung des Vergaberechts (Monitoring report of the Federal Government on the application of public procurement law) 2017. Retrieved on 7 Jul 2025 from https://www.bmwk.de/Redaktion/DE/Downloads/M-O/monitoring-bericht-der-bundesregierung-zur-anwendung-des-vergaberechts-2017.html.

Federal Ministry of Justice (BMJV). (22 December, 2023). Competition Act (Gesetz gegen Wettbewerbsbeschränkungen—GWB). Retrieved on 7 Jul 2025 from https://www.gesetze-im-internet.de/englisch_gwb/index.html.

Gigerenzer, G. (2007). *Gut feelings: The intelligence of the unconscious*. Penguin Books.

Heuermann, R. (2014). *Strategisches IT-Management: in Privatwirtschaft und Verwaltung*. Walter de Gruyter GmbH.

McGrath, S. (2021). Accountability and responsibility. In S. McGrath (Ed.), *Speaking management*. Springer. https://doi.org/10.1007/978-981-16-2213-7_16

# Where We Want to Go: Adaptive and Integrative 5

Perhaps some of you have already experienced the following situation. Requirements are collected for a software product, a suitable team is found, the software is implemented over a period of months, and everyone involved is disappointed at the first demonstration 6 months later. The software does not fulfil the expectations by far. The catalogue of requirements was designed in such a way that people talked past each other or even created contradictory requirements.

Either way, the finished product is disappointing and needs improving. This discrepancy between output and outcome is one of the reasons why agile software development emerged and is now the leading method used by well over 90% of software development companies. In this context, advocates of agile software development methods often refer to an iterative approach, which contrasts with the waterfall model. Although such a waterfall model has probably rarely existed in its purest form, the concept lends itself to comparison.

This agile revolution, which has become an integral part of software development, was seen as a successful model that should also be transferred to other areas. Agile organisations, as described by Frédéric Laloux in his book "Reinventing Organizations" (Laloux, 2014), have been a real hype over the last 10 years. Some of our customers have indeed transformed themselves into agile organisations and have been valuable advisors in the development of the method presented here.

We would like to emphasise that it is not necessary to be an agile organisation to benefit from our method. Our method is suitable not only for agile organisations, but also for traditional companies that may be hidden champions in their core business and wish to understand the benefits and costs involved. Adaptive methods are



G. Köhler et al., *Adaptive IT Service Tendering*, Management for Professionals,
https://doi.org/10.1007/978-3-658-49726-2_5

a valuable tool for gaining insight into values that cannot easily be expressed in monetary terms.

**Important** In addition to financial performance indicators, there are other important values that influence the success and sustainability of a company. These non-monetary values can be intangible in nature and often help to shape corporate culture, customer loyalty and reputation, employee engagement, innovation and creativity over the long term. It is important to understand, measure, and promote these values to ensure a holistic view of the organisation's performance and value.

Organisations that have adopted agile methods for software development and other areas are committed to continuously using and improving these approaches. Therefore, it is reasonable to expect that, as they become more widely adopted, agile methods will also be viewed more realistically. Currently, some companies are not very open to agile methods, considering them disorganised and chaotic. The current debate is highly polarised and lacks real-world examples. The future will show the places where agility adds value.

We began developing our methodology around 2018 and have successively tested it in customer situations. During this time, the outsourcing market has changed significantly. Most customers are turning away from large outsourcing projects in favour of smaller-scale tenders. The resulting diversity of providers is accepted and, in cases of doubt, individual services are transferred back to in-house IT.

Clients from highly innovative industries, whose business is usually closely linked to IT, go one step further and work with providers to develop adaptive services that serve as the basis for innovative business processes. In doing so, they combine new innovative services and standard components that are linked together via integration layers. In such an approach, customers and providers pursue many agile strategies, such as early experimentation, value-adding development, etc.

The combination of standard components and customised components is interesting, especially in terms of development over time. It is easy to imagine starting a completely independent IT operation with a new technology selection for a new, disruptive business area. This allows the greatest possible freedom and design to maximise business value. As soon as this manifests itself after a few iterations, it is worth integrating one or other standard service, as the customised version of this service does not provide any significant added value.

A mix of standard services, innovative variants, and integrations can be created and further developed from the client's existing experience, but above all from a broad-based provider, which provides the necessary freedom but also brings in value from existing services. In addition to cost efficiency, these can be properties

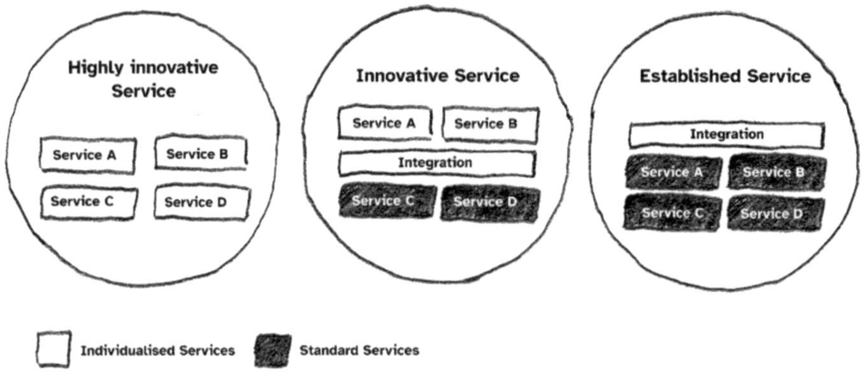


**Fig. 5.1** Development of a highly innovative service over time

such as scalability, security, maintainability, or quality aspects. Adaptive services can be a valuable link here (Fig. 5.1).

**Important** In the past, people often used a combination of various technologies to create highly innovative services to support new businesses. Different programming languages were also used, as were various cloud applications. All of these were used in a similar environment. The aim was to bring a new business idea to market as quickly as possible. Further development then took place within the framework of the ad hoc opportunities created, which quickly led to a high level of technical debt. If the business idea was successful in the long term, the technical platform would eventually be completely converted to a new technology, incurring huge expenses.

Non-functional requirements usually play a major role in such a platform. These requirements address important quality issues for technical systems and the IT services based on them. They deal with issues such as scalability, supportability, performance, portability, security, reliability, and much more. In particular, this means that the above-mentioned ad hoc solutions are not suitable for professional IT operation by a provider. To put it another way, the risks associated with an ad hoc approach are significant, even when the outcome is positive and the business idea is successfully brought to market quickly.

The challenge of bringing business innovations to market quickly through IT services and then developing the components sustainably in the next logical step is an excellent fit with adaptive service portfolio management. In other words, it is a systematic approach to the further development of all individual IT services, applications, development projects, and skills. As shown in the diagram above, individual standards develop over time from services created in the short term.

The further development of individually launched services that have supported a customer's innovative business idea must be actively managed in an adaptive approach. In contrast to a business process-oriented increase in efficiency for an individual customer, an IT service provider can industrialise such innovative services. This means that individual services are made usable for several customers through decomposition and standardisation. In addition to the reuse of pure functionality, the focus is on service capability properties.

This methodology enables you to set up and control an adaptive IT service portfolio management system, treating individual services as alternatives. We hope this excursion into highly innovative industries was inspiring. You will see that getting started with adaptive services is much easier.

Our methods and approaches have two areas of application. Firstly, they are ideal for creating value from existing industrial services. Secondly, they are ideal for focusing value on new business developments, striking the right balance between standards and innovations. This is why we call our methods 'adaptive': they adapt to the needs of the client. This applies whether a client wants to know exactly what value they will receive from IT services or whether they need a platform of services for their innovations.

## 5.1 Values and Benefits of Agile Methods

The methods we have developed build on the central characteristics of agile software development and transfer these advantages to the area of managed services. In contrast to the traditional approach, the agile method requires integrated teams. The following section looks at the benefits of these cross-functional teams in more detail. This is the first hurdle in the transition from the traditional approach, which is characterised by teams working separately at the customer and provider ends. Our experience shows that the added value developed by integrated teams at high speed is worth all the effort.

An iterative and incremental approach is required when designing and developing agile services, i.e. even extensive services are developed in partial steps, and their usability is checked at an early stage. This enables us to swiftly ascertain whether a well-intentioned function is practically ineffective and should be replaced. Early adopters can gradually begin to integrate the delivered service into their work from a certain range of functions. This allows important information to be derived at very short notice, enabling the service to be used productively.

Using this approach, ideas can be tested in practice quickly, for example after a brainstorming session. If significant added value is achieved with the new, unfinished service after a few iterations, word will get around and more people will try to utilise its benefits. People who are curious are often active and productive in driving the main features of the development forward. In contrast to a traditional approach, where almost finished prototypes are handed over to the customer for testing, the adaptive approach can avoid disappointment on the part of the customer if the service works as planned but still has potential for optimisation.

Agile software development uses a vision to make sure that the stakeholders involved in an iterative development do not deviate from their original path. However, as managed services have fundamentally different characteristics, decisions about time investments, resources, training, and licences must be made at specific times. Many basic technologies and licence models have a monolithic character. For this reason, we also need to use a vision. But we need to be much more specific.

A major challenge when switching from a classic, waterfall-based approach is the change in dealing with a centralised architecture. This can be created in the course of the project. Based on the knowledge gained from the values created, a central architecture can also be changed again and again without losing the vision. Enterprise architects are required to develop a sustainable solution without restricting the freedom of the teams. This requires special skills. Architectural specifications must always aim to create value.

Here, we present a value model that can be used pragmatically to create roadmaps for the implementation of the agile services designed and developed. The necessary preliminary work and possible alternatives should also be used for strategic planning or partially for a cultural analysis in the company. Value-steering through services can be established by working with a board of stakeholders from a wide range of backgrounds and experiences.

We see a similar challenge to the creation of value in the design of contracts, particularly on the side of safeguarding value. A framework must be provided to support agile methods in comparison with the conventional approach. This can be done within existing contract models, but these should be based on specific use cases and a schematic architecture. Measurement parameters and possible penalties should be able to accommodate the adaptive value development. This requires adjustments to be made during the contract period, as explained in more detail below.

### Excursus Values Versus Budget

Whenever we teach our methodology, we have noticed that some users tend to focus on familiar content and procedures. This bias leads them to spot familiar parts and pay little attention to content they are unknown with. They wrongly ascertain that: "We used to do it the same way". In doing so, they overlook the crucial differences in the adaptive approach. That's why we try to incorporate key differences between traditional and adaptive methodology as short digressions. Don't rush. It's important to take your time and develop scenarios from your working environment so that you can spot the difference.

A classic industrialised service is a perfect example here. A service like this can be purchased cost-effectively by a typical hierarchical organisation with highly standardised performance features. Let us have a look at SD-WAN-based network services, which are intended to replace an existing, outdated campus network with MPLS lines. The IT organisation is aware of the expiring maintenance contracts of its campus network and wants to replace it with modern technology.

Don't worry if you're unfamiliar with these technologies! You can simply follow the example. You don't need to know much about networking. MPLS (Multiprotocol Label Switching) is a traditional networking technology, which uses labels to forward data and ensure the reliable performance of critical applications. SD-WAN (Software-Defined Wide Area Network) adds a logical control plane that can orchestrate expensive dedicated lines, such as MPLS, as well as cheaper broadband and wireless communication. Mixing communication technologies to suit the individual needs of production sites and offices usually offers significant cost advantages over a traditional MPLS-only WAN. In our example, the organisation connects multiple sites, including remote plants, at a lower cost while providing secure, reliable access to cloud services and real-time data. Centralised management and dynamic traffic routing further reduce operational overheads, making SD-WAN a more scalable and cost-efficient solution for modern industrial networks.

In a budget-oriented organisation, the decision is very simple if the modernisation is more cost-effective than the current solution. Especially if, after a certain investment in the conversion, the running costs of the modernisation enable a quick amortisation. Many companies have a target period in which an investment must pay for itself, so that calculating the return on investment is simple if the running costs are more favourable. Additional sponsors or replanning are only necessary if the conversion costs of the new provider do not correspond to the desired amortisation period.

The entire issue remains stuck in the financial dimension. Only in a few exceptions is there any mention of modernisation or innovation opportunities in connection with the new technological platform. Let's add to our example the consideration that an IT organisation must gradually take care of production-oriented IT (OT). In the past, this was mainly the task of the local production IT teams. Together with the technological renewal, the current network tender should be used to expand the possibilities of OT and anchor it centrally in the IT organisation.

The budget is derived from the annually planned running costs, an innovation cost centre and, as this is still not enough, the IT management is looking for further sponsors within the company. Production IT is currently financed via the cost centres of the plants and product lines. IT management is therefore holding discussions with these cost centres to present the functions of the new OT technologies. They can even provide reference stories from competitors who have also adopted these modern technologies.

The budget question is always whether the new technology and service can be financed. The business areas in question typically must develop and scrutinise the resulting business opportunities themselves, as well as assess the viability of these opportunities and determine the most appropriate way to proceed. Some ideas are discussed early in the process; however, it is a top-down approach. The sponsor is approached based on a technology. Then its department can examine the feasibility. It can also look at possible projects. These are based on the defined service.

**Example** Subsequent production optimisation with OT

Our example company might be a manufacturing company, bringing an end to a period of stagnation by introducing a popular product to the market. With the resources now available, an IT manager convinces various business units to jointly invest in modernising the network. The IT department's slide set wonderfully illustrates the current possibilities and the new technical options that are now available to the individual divisions.

Individual modernisation projects based on the new network infrastructure that are immediately necessary have been specified, but the investment decision is primarily based on future technical possibilities. A detailed examination of hundreds of modernisation projects would not be economically feasible or too costly at the present time.

Now let's look at a single area just a few months after the introduction of this new network service. This production area now wants to equip its production line with a You-Only-Look-Once (YOLO) AI. Such an AI application enables real-time object recognition so that faulty product elements can be sorted out even during very fast production cycles.

It turns out that the YOLO application is suitable for the new network and the object recognition data can be written quickly enough. However, the existing OT elements in this production must be adapted and certified for the selected LAN service. For this particular area, it would have been more favourable to retrofit and invest in other network components for in-house operation. The decision to participate in the central modernisation would have been different due to these subsequently arising requirements.

Of course, our example could also have been optimally positive. The new technology fits perfectly, can be enriched with existing elements such as monitoring, or can even be provided as standard by the chosen provider at low cost. The challenge of a top-down approach remains: Further projects and planning must adapt. A return on investment across all bottom-up projects over the next few months usually fails to materialise or would be too complex once the company reaches a certain size.

The potential new business value resulting from the top-down design of the IT organisation is difficult to determine. The financial stakeholders are responsible for their own part of the investment, so it is assumed that the project is already paying off. Innovations are only actually developed in a decentralised manner. This is if they are developed at all. As already mentioned, our example involves a platform service that can be used as a basis for technologies and innovations. The situation is different with centralised business management systems, such as ERP systems. However, it is not necessarily easier when it comes to the needs of business units.

But let's stick to the platform service and the discussion about the difference between values and budget. A value-based approach works the other way round. Instead of looking for funding for a technology decision, a value-based approach gathers ideas and alternatives for potential value. This means that we talk about changes in products, technologies, processes, or companies that promise higher-value creation in the future.

Ideally, potential value should be expressible in financial terms, but this is not always possible. For example, value can be created from the customer perspective, from the internal process perspective or from the learning and development perspective without being immediately and directly measurable in financial terms. To illustrate the difference between traditional and adaptive services in planning, we return to our example of platform services.

When budgeting for platform services, fixed amounts are planned for the transition and operating phase, which are usually provided with risk buffers of less than 10%. If new lucrative business opportunities arise during the transition and could be developed, the necessary changes cannot usually be realised within the project's small financial buffer or the concluded contract.

Adaptive services are planned based on potential values as a kind of projection into the future and should be planned with business value potentials of 150% to 200%. This means that the alternatives compiled for a roadmap should be planned in such a way that, theoretically, 150% to 200% outcome is achieved if all the added values envisaged are realised. All architecture alternatives contain new business values that can be realised. They compete based on added value, as set out in a metric. For example, as soon as a component of the backlog becomes more valuable, it is favoured.

In a traditional project, such as the transformation of a platform, framework conditions such as resources, time, and requirements are defined in accordance with the project management method. These dimensions are typically given a small risk allowance, such as the 10% mentioned above. This allows the team to compensate for uncertainties. However, adaptive value creation requires at least one free dimension, as otherwise it is not possible to develop new values iteratively. Let's take a look at the three most important dimensions: resources, time, and business value to be created.

In practice, we often work with certain team sizes that should only be slightly expanded by experts. Therefore, scaling via the number of resources in adaptive projects is not a suitable approach. The resources dimension should therefore be regarded as fixed in planning.

In the time dimension, we work with roadmaps that contain the most important ideas in the form of architecture alternatives based on values. These differ from roadmaps that are common in traditional project or portfolio management. Adaptive roadmaps contain ideas and values. The outcome should be clearly recognisable. Outputs, such as activities or minimum viable products, can be developed during the roadmap, for example in a backlog. Even if our roadmaps have a basic cycle of 6 months, values can be moved into the next roadmap. The time dimension is therefore free.

However, the most important dimension is the potential value created. A potential of 150% to 200% serves to maintain freedom in the development of ideas and to guarantee a minimum value of 100%. The outcome is therefore also very flexible, but the organisation's expectation is clearly defined. A value to be achieved of 150% to 200% is an ambitious target that should not be achieved or completed below 100% in terms of innovative strength (Fig. 5.2).

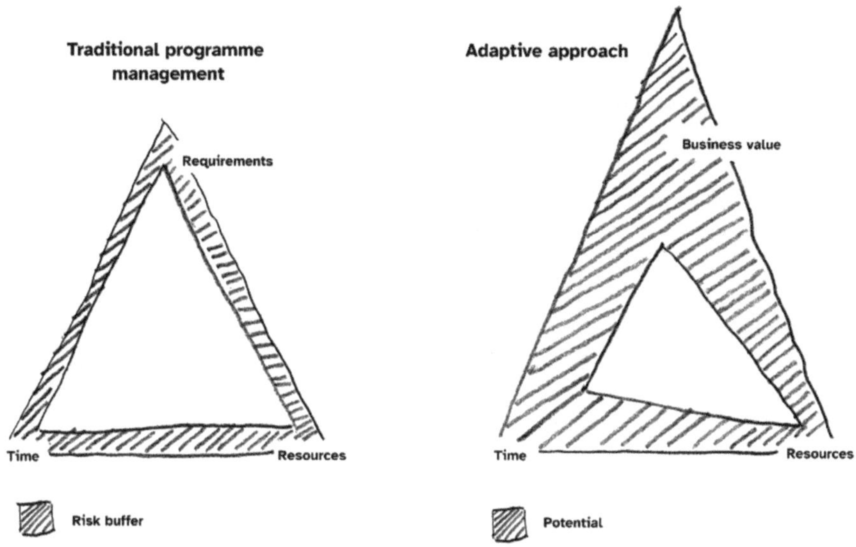


**Fig. 5.2** Comparison of Risk potential vs. Value potential

**Example** One example of such potential value would be service request management. Due to limitations in data, information, and tools, this currently has an error rate of 0.6%. This means that for every 1000 service requests, 6 need to be reworked. The next roadmap envisages a reduction in this error rate as a potential value.

Initial solution ideas and alternatives that have been identified for request fulfilment include improving service quality through process improvements and flexible measurement methods in the value stream. The implementation of all alternatives has the potential to reduce the error rate from the current 0.6% to 0.2% in 1 year. An improvement to 0.2% is therefore a very ambitious target, but one that can be achieved if all the solution ideas work. It is also possible that new, better solutions will be found during the roadmap. Our goal is to achieve an improvement of 200%, whereby an improvement to 0.4% should be aimed for as a 100% target. The assured value contribution can be defined on the basis of this 100% target.

It could be a simple case where the values can be expressed 1:1 in financial metrics and an investment in the renewal of platform services pays off immediately. It is not uncommon. This is especially the case when companies commit to an adaptive model. The savings potential in the initial roadmaps is often large. But let's stick with the example of an IT organisation that wants to take care of modern operational technology centrally in the future. With the focus on values, it is now important to uncover further potential within the company.

To create a roadmap with sufficient value, potential additional value must be identified within the organisation. When looking for internal allies, the question should not be whether they can finance more for a service from their budgets, but whether joint value creation is possible to justify an investment in the roadmap. This can be done very specifically in one of the next roadmaps, but also as a collection of potentials. There is a fundamental problem here in the application of adaptive services when dealing with monolithic technologies, which are historically characterised by budgets and expansion of the intended use (adoption).

In practice, a value-based approach differs significantly from the prevailing budget-based concept. The new perspective contributes in particular to greater participation and control. A combination of value-based and budget-based approaches can be easily reconciled at the beginning if certain core concepts are taken into account. Initially, it can be difficult to determine which compromises preserve core values and which are more damaging. In the following sections, we will explain these core concepts and the methods that will help you to get started with adaptive services.

## 5.2 Overview of Adaptive Services

Adaptive services differ significantly from managed services in some characteristics, but some concepts can still be retained. In our quest for adaptive models, we have found that certain approaches and methods are obvious and simple. Others have taken us over 2 years of accumulated experience and collaboration. Below we present some plain concepts that will be explained in detail in the following chapters.

We hope that the first examples from the previous chapter still leave many open questions that we would like to answer in the course of this chapter. Simple variants of adaptive tenders and services can work well in practice, but are based almost exclusively on mutual trust. Trust is a wonderful and important ingredient for collaboration. Truly successful managed services always start with building trust. However, other factors are relevant for a lasting business relationship; trust alone is not enough. This experience was one of the central guiding principles in the development of our methodology.

Let's first look at a traditional organisation. Then let's consider an IT organisation. This organisation wants to put a central service out to tender. This could be something like Managed Workplace. This service has already been put out to tender three times, with various service providers winning the contract and achieving varying levels of success. Preparations for the new tender are made around 1.5 to 2 years before the end of the contract. The company is aiming for a contract term of 5 years, which may be extended by a benchmarking clause after 3 years.

One of the main criticisms levelled at the current service provider is its lack of willingness to innovate. Within the IT organisation, at least, there is a perception that the service provider is obstructive. Expenditure on the introduction of more modern technologies or leaner processes was always seen as too complicated and cost-intensive by the current service provider. In recent years, this has led to change requests from the business functions being initially scrutinised but rejected in advance for cost reasons.

The situation is similar with the modernisation of IT service management. The existing contract did not provide for any fundamental changes, meaning that neither processes and organisation were changed nor new IT service management tools purchased. A reorganisation or more powerful tools were always associated with high additional demands from the previous service provider. The new tender aims to satisfy both this long-standing demand and the requirements of current and future change projects.

Another area for improvement is a service that is currently fixed in place. This service is far too expensive compared to the rest of the industry. The organisation demands too much of the service, and it demands too much of too many different things, when compared to the market. In addition to the already extensive requirements of the internal departments, a large number of new industry standards have been added over the years, which must also be supported. For the new tender, the IT organisation aims to streamline the service components and reduce costs. The impact on the numerous requirements of the business functions is to be resolved through intelligent compromises.

Two years before the end of the contract, a group of IT experts defines a minimum workplace that meets all legal requirements, standards, and guidelines of the organisation. All additions are reviewed and removed if they are not absolutely necessary. This minimum design is then presented to a committee made up of the most significant departments and key users. The committee was also asked in advance to only add the most urgent requirements. A massive request was made to add as few extras as possible. It turned out that even with the best communication of the need for savings, the plan to tender for the leanest possible workplace is almost impossible to realise. On the contrary, all business functions constantly try to include as many requirements as possible in the tender, with the aim of ensuring that the needs of all stakeholders are met. They have learned from past experience that future requirements are usually rejected due to budget constraints.

Finally, the CTO's advisory body defines what additional requirements must be included due to developments over the next 5 years. These requirements are categorised as future investments. They are not necessary at present. Nevertheless, they serve to provide future services. This is how the future provider is to be brought under control. Unlike existing providers, this provider should not be able to hinder innovation by making excessive financial demands.

The tender is now sent to nine service providers as a Request for Information and then as a Request for Proposal. After a shortlist, only three service providers are considered. To ensure fairness, the client and the providers communicate via a catalogue of questions. The providers' questions are anonymised and sent to all interested parties together with the answers. At the beginning of the tendering process, a presentation of the tender content is held and there is an opportunity to ask questions in a plenary session with all providers.

Once the written offers have been submitted, the three suppliers are invited to present their offers. Unless close relationships have already been established with certain suppliers, this is usually the first moment when trust can be built. This usually happens about 1 to 2 months before the contract is signed, depending on the size of the tender. From this point onwards, two to three service providers work more closely with the company. Mutual insights are provided as part of due diligence.

After due diligence, the three remaining providers work their findings into a final offer with an amended price. The best package is selected from these final offers, and the contract is finalised with this provider. The other providers are either removed or placed in a kind of waiting position. This allows the customer to switch to the second-best provider if the contract negotiations fail. The most favourable price is agreed with the final provider and, in our example, a six-month transition phase begins.

Using the typically 4000 to 6500 requirements, a waterfall-like detailed plan is now created that implements the modernised workplace from the tender. The individual requirements are translated into actions and the transition to the new provider is implemented step by step. The existing service provider and the company provide resources to support this transition process.

Joint tests take place a few weeks before the transition phase is completed. Depending on the schedule for the go-live, the cutover to the new service provider takes place on a specific day. In the following weeks, there is typically a phase of intensive early life support until the services are set up to the satisfaction of all parties and only minor improvements are required.

The chosen example is a typical scenario that we have encountered frequently in our professional experience. At this point, we do not want to go into more problematic customer–supplier situations. Compared to the previous process, we will identify the initial differences using an adaptive approach. Let us therefore go back 2 years and start again in the situation of a workplace service that is already outdated.

Adaptive services differ primarily in their focus on value creation. An adaptive approach begins with the search for waste and previously unutilised business potential. As an existing provider will continue to provide the service for another 2 years and the customer's ability to exert influence has proved problematic, IT concentrates on business potential.

Existing needs of individual user groups, ideas from innovation workshops and information from competitors can be used for an initial collection of potentials. It is important to consider a wide range of ideas. The spectrum encompasses minor proposals and thoroughly advanced business concepts. Also, the degree of elaboration can vary between them. There may be a new business idea that has been developed in a business function for months. This may exist alongside smaller, more technical ideas.

However, unlike a traditional tender, it is important that no detailed technical requirements are added here. The added value for users must always be derived from the descriptions. Use cases or epics, which are common in agile software development, are suitable for generating initial ideas. These are natural language description models that describe with whom and through which interactions a system is used to achieve certain results or tasks. In addition to use cases or epics, it is possible to roughly outline entire systems as building blocks and describe their benefits and value in detail.

The focus should be on formulating the description of the service. It should be clear and comprehensible. A precise definition of the scope of delivery usually comes with good characteristics for the valuation. In the case of adaptive tenders, however, it is problematic to describe the delivery method in too much detail. This refers to requirements that define the individual delivery methods in the traditional sense. Only when you are familiar with adaptive methods can you decompose such classic requirement modules into agile values.

**Important** As you will see later, an alternatives horizon develops from the collection of small suggestions and use cases through to elaborated business ideas. This is a constantly growing collection of architectures that represent value potential. Our method envisages that these alternatives can exist in different stages of development.

Even an idea scribbled down on a napkin can be included in the alternative horizon. However, before including such an idea, the scope of services must be clearly defined, and a description of the desired outcome must be provided. Over time, immature components must be further developed in order to become candidates for a roadmap. However, they can also be realised as valuable details of an architectural alternative. It is important that the alternative horizon is a collection of living elements that will be further developed. These components may therefore be of varying quality and maturity.

One example of an immature idea is: "Before visiting a customer, our sales team should be able to access their current issues and open orders via smartphone at the touch of a button, in order to demonstrate our expertise and engage with the customer". This idea could prove to be a potential added value. However, it means a great deal of effort for everyone involved if all workplace requirements are only recorded at this level.

A maximum-sized solution module could be, for example, a description of how a competitor equips its sales organisation with mobile devices, possibly by naming the components of the solution, which consists of industrial software components. For the adaptive approach, however, it is important to precisely describe the desire, the benefits, and the resulting values. This description should always be in the first position. As the description based on epics can be very detailed, it may be helpful to use this comparative approach in order to focus on the central values.

For an initial roadmap, elements that are too distant or complex should be temporarily excluded. If this has not already been done by individual departments, building blocks and ideas should be summarised in clusters. Some clusters may appear incomplete or sparse. These areas could be put on hold for the time being, or workshop sessions could be used to generate ideas to fill them. This can easily be done later.

With a focus on a specific cluster, discussions can now be held with a limited number of service providers whose willingness to co-operate, experience, and ability to implement are required. Depending on the timing and available resources, the client can start with two service providers in parallel or test the adaptive approach with the preferred service provider. In the event of failure, the first collaboration may be cancelled and the project continued with the second-place candidate.

Negotiations should be held with the service provider to develop a minimum value service. Ideally, this should be realised in two iterations of 30 days each and be designed as a kind of prototype in a limited environment. Even if a minimally functional service should not generally have the character of a prototype, it is permitted here as an exception. The relationship and cooperation with the future service provider should be tested at an early stage. Any difficulties that can be overcome in this initial phase should be minimised as far as possible.

In the first step, a service contract that is billed according to time-and-material expenditure is a suitable form of contract. For the isolated development of ideas, cloud environments can be used as a kind of testing ground (sandbox) for many adaptive services. Cross-functional teams should work together from the outset, including idea generators, responsible IT employees, and key stakeholders who are actively involved in the service process.

After two iterations, a functional service was developed in this example, which provides the idea providers with feedback-ready results. The professional and technical collaboration can be evaluated by the stakeholders in two reviews. The basis of trust and performance of the cross-functional teams can be assessed in at least two retrospectives based on the service. For the basic principle of sprints (iterations), see also → Sect. 2.4.8.

If there is a general consensus that the full scope of services should be developed in collaboration with the service provider, a roadmap will be drafted together. Our suggestion is to plan a six-month roadmap with specific values and to outline the content of further development based on this. In addition, the contracts can be defined in stages at the beginning. The different types of contract and their advantages and disadvantages will be explained in more detail later.

The same company still has 1.5 years until the end of the contract with the current service provider. At this point, a company with a traditional approach would likely release the RFI. Implementing adaptive enhancements with a new service provider can help to build trust much earlier, even if the scope is initially small. In our example, there is still a possibility that there will be a standstill after 6 months, with only some of the services being available.

Typically, after a few iterations, a stakeholder will begin to use the service. The service is still incomplete. The stakeholder will provide intensive feedback. This will be in the form of both criticism and new ideas. This stakeholder is usually an innovator who is socially involved in the company, enjoys a high reputation, and takes risks. Innovators have many resources at their disposal to deal with mistakes and dead ends in innovation development.

> **Important** The user categories used here are straightforward to understand. They are based on a popular model that is used to analyse how and why new ideas and technologies spread. This theory, known as the "diffusion of innovations", was developed by Everett Rogers in the 1960s (Rogers, 2003).

This guides further development, as the applicability becomes more tangible, but also the realisation of the values becomes more tangible. You know, this is often abstract and far removed from a technological perspective. Base services such as Managed Workplace enable the development of a fully usable workplace after just a few iterations. This includes compliance with legal framework conditions and guidelines. However, these challenges for adaptive development will be discussed separately.

After a few months, the first group of users begins to use the new workplace. Our experience shows that they are willing to tolerate missing functions or inconveniences because they trust that their feedback will be acted upon when they communicate directly with cross-functional teams. Compared to the timeline of a conventional tender, the company still has around 1 year until the end of the current contract with the adaptive variant.

Gradually, more and more user groups are switching to the new workplace. Our experience shows that this includes at least all groups that previously received no support for important requirements. It can be assumed that over 50% of the user groups welcome these developments. Furthermore, in this example it is very likely that a certain number of users of the old contract can be cancelled during the term, so that two completely parallel services do not have to be operated.

At the end of the contract with the old service provider, all users must be migrated to the new model. This procedure is not fundamentally different from a conventional transformation. However, any kind of resistance is to be expected with far-reaching innovations, even if the first 50% of users accept the innovations quickly and enthusiastically. A fundamentally new service will always encounter obstacles and is not guaranteed to be a success.

Up to this point, we have shown you two methods of tendering for a new workplace service in an organisation. These two initial examples illustrate important differences between the two approaches. A solid, first adaptive tender should be designed somewhat differently. We have deliberately chosen this example to draw attention to two important differences. When adaptive services are used to establish a new business unit or market segment, the risk lies within the new business model. In this example, however, we are deliberately focussing on core services that the company needs on a daily basis.

Let's look at the issue of trust and risk in relation to a traditional tender. The company representatives do not receive enough information to build trust until late in the process. They hand over a comprehensive package of 4000 to 6500 requirements to the service provider, which they are expected to fulfil within a few months. If this fails in any way, contractual penalties and specific cancellation rights can be applied, but the company is in a massively problematic situation. Trust in the service provider should therefore be examined very carefully.

With the adaptive approach, the period for building trust is much longer. However, an important difference is that the initial trust is not yet very high or stable. It is created gradually on the basis of value streams. At least for the first users, there is an opportunity to actively decide in favour of the new system and switch with little risk. The likelihood of the service provider failing when integrating the last user groups or in the first few months of operation is low. Nevertheless, there are some pitfalls with the adaptive approach, which are discussed below.

In our experience, in addition to the different levels of trust, the acceptance of the solution is also fundamentally different. Whereas in the traditional model, the architecture is agreed with all requirements well in advance and implemented with little feedback, the adaptive approach is an incremental approach to solutions that need to be revised and adapted.

Although a service with a great deal of experience and expertise was suitably and conceptually well thought out and implemented on time and on budget by an excellent service provider, a certain disillusionment sets in when it is used for the first time. This may be due to the fact that the properties appeared better in the imagination or that the business conditions have changed after a year. In our experience, the main cause is usually the wide range of requirements, which ultimately results in a detrimental mix of compromises.

An adaptive approach enables dedicated users to actively participate in development. If good control is ensured, adaptive services implement the highest values first or eliminate the biggest waste. Due to the constant influx of criticism and changes, it is not possible for resource reasons to consider every little thing that is requested. In comparison, an adaptive solution would probably have implemented a smaller number of requirement definitions at the end of the 2 years, but would have made a much greater contribution to value creation.

**Excursus Requirements Versus Increment**

In a large proportion of traditional tenders, an increasing number of requirements can be observed for a tender subject that hardly changes. One reason for the massive increase in the level of detail due to the increase in requirements is dissatisfaction with the previous suppliers. Particularly in the case of cost-driven tenders, discussions were held in previous practice about the performance characteristics contained in the contract. The most economically efficient supplier provides only the services that have been specified in writing in advance. Subsequent features always mean an additional claim for such providers.

Although the number of requirements has increased massively, the desired success rarely materialises. There has been no significant change in either the service descriptions or the scope of supplementary discussions. An analysis shows that clients often do not explicitly know what they need. This gives resourceful service providers the opportunity to discover and exploit existing gaps. The actual situation is likely to be more complex in many cases.

On the one hand, it is challenging for companies of a certain size to clearly define which services a base service should include in order to ensure that both internal and external customers can build their business on it. On the other hand, industrialised services are not usually standardised to be interchangeable. Even with platform services, providers try to differentiate themselves from one another.

There is no such thing as a modular system of services, as it is often depicted on presentation slides with building blocks, in the sense of these interchangeable building blocks. It is certainly possible to gradually purchase various services from individual full-service providers, right up to complete IT outsourcing (ITO). A combination of services from different service providers with or without partial in-house operation does not work according to the simple modular principle. In practice, there are gaps or overlaps between the modules that need to be resolved through customisation and integration.

The task discussed here is therefore clearly complex. Complex problems are characterised by a variety of networked system elements and internal and external dynamics. A clear cause-and-effect analysis at a specific point in time in the present is not sufficiently possible. Small interventions in a complex system can typically be analysed retrospectively (ex-post), as a non-chaotic system behaves continuously and steadily within a certain framework (the classification used here is based on Cynefin → Sect. 2.8).

The aim is to describe a system that will meet the following criteria at a given point in time:

for a continuous period of 3 to 5 years;

for more than 10,000 employees;

from different areas of the company;

Managed Workplace Service defined by more than 4000 requirements

We do not consider this to be a sensible solution strategy for defining this service. In our professional experience, we have met many IT managers who play down the complexity of the situation and the potential difficulties at this point. We would therefore like to explain the problem more clearly. IT managers often say things like: "What's so complicated about it?". This view does not adequately grasp the problem. Defining a cost-effective workplace for around 300 to 500 user groups in different countries with corresponding requirements for manageability, security, and flexibility is clearly categorised as complex in the Cynefin framework.

Many organisations respond to such challenges by simplifying the problem category. This is done, for example, according to the following motto: "I put five of my best people to work on defining the requirements quickly and clearly". The problem is then declared solved. In case of doubt, methods from the "obvious" category are used and an inappropriate solution is defined. Since an organisation has declared the problem solved, there are initially few honest reactions to shortcomings and gaps. Those responsible in the organisation try to play down the defects. This can lead to necessary additional changes being commissioned more or less secretly via a service provider. This approach helps ensure that the hierarchy's solution strategy is not called into question.

Such a project is complex because it is focussed on an unknown future. It involves people, i.e. social systems and a multitude of business requirements that cannot be fully penetrated by a small tender team in a time frame of a few months. Above a certain size, however, this applies to all companies we know. Theoretically, there may be companies that master all of the above parameters so well that a jointly managed workplace falls into the "complicated" category.

The statement "What's so complicated about it?" leads to a simplified domain that does not correspond to reality. Ashby's Law of Requisite Variety states that the variety of the control system must be at least as great as the variety of the disturbances that occur in order for it to perform the control (Ashby, 1956). In other words, categorisation errors are a high risk and deliberate categorisation errors deliberately play with this risk.

As an emerging practice, an adaptive approach is an effective solution for complex issues. Although the solution directions are known, many specific goals still need to be worked out. Such an approach means that solutions are found incrementally and in an error-tolerant manner. Initial solutions are incorporated into the overall solution direction as required, provided they prove to be good and practicable. Developments are tested, evaluated, optimised, or rejected in various directions. Negative results also contribute to improvement as knowledge gained.

In contrast, the collection of requirements is a description of outputs whose added value is usually still transparent for the idea provider. If only the requirements are passed on, it is not clear to those involved in the implementation which deviations from the requirement are acceptable in order to still achieve the benefit. In an adaptive approach, there may also be an alternative component that can achieve the same customer benefit even better and more cost-effectively. In a collection of requirements, such an exchange is hardly feasible for those involved in the implementation.

So far, the procedure is rational, the service provider is supposed to deliver an output, the company's business knows best what is suitable for the company as a technology platform. Unfortunately, the compilation of countless requirements often results in an unfortunate mix. Requirements from different silos within the company are rarely harmonised with one another. Performance requirements with different, sometimes contradictory demands and ideas about the supported business value often result in an unclear picture. The information that a provider can obtain about the values supported by the requirements is blurred.

A well-crafted traditional tender reviews the company's core values and emphasises them. However, these objectives are often lost in a myriad of details. In many tenders, there are even contradictory requirements at a technical or service level. With up to 6500 requirements in the service sector, this is not surprising, as it is no longer possible for a single person to keep track of them all.

If no central values are generated in traditional tenders, the organisations usually ensure compensation. In our experience, this approach tends to work well, particularly during the transition period and in the first few months. During this time, the tendering team and key stakeholders work together to address any disruptions or misunderstandings. Conflicts or major improvements by one of the parties involved rarely occur at this stage. Unstructured, extensive lists of requirements represent a high risk here.

A value-oriented approach differs significantly from a method focussed on output. Here, increments are created step by step from the collected and grouped values, which grow into a minimum viable service after a few iterations. At this point at the latest, the requesters can try out the function and assess whether it actually delivers the desired outcome. Compared to the waterfall-like implementation of requirements, this process offers closer feedback in terms of time. In addition, usable partial results are available at an early stage instead of monolithically building up a service.

In practice, this results in two key challenges. Integration must be found, particularly in the case of parallel cross-functional teams. This can be achieved organisationally using proven standards such as SAFe or Nexus (→ Sect. 2.4). In connection with the provision of services on industrial platforms, some approaches are presented below that can take better account of the special features of managed services.

Another challenge that is also known in the field of agile software development is the creation of a service vision. This vision must be created at the beginning of a development phase that is expected to last several months. It should include an outline of the potential business values of the new service. Increments are created in iterations, whereby each iteration must deliver a functional increment. Parts of the service features must already be usable, and the increment must be potentially releasable. The partition of a service vision into manageable elements, all of which must have a value, represents a major challenge.

In the traditional approach, a complex service design can be developed over months; tests and verifications of the concept only have to cover partial areas. Prototypes that are created to identify new approaches are often independent of the later service and can be discarded at the end like a demonstration object. In an adaptive approach, all elements should be potentially usable and the maximum development time until the next review should not exceed 1 month.

We meet this challenge with the adaptive approach. The architectural alternatives are not assembled into individual monoliths, but are a set of differently abstract components that are interrelated. The services to be developed are generally scalable in one of their dimensions. Decomposition can begin at different levels, starting with the creation of a roadmap of interrelated alternatives with the greatest possible benefit. In addition, creating adaptive services often means additional improvement or innovation of existing services, so increments and minimum viable services can be created early in the roadmap. Due to the interdependencies, it is easier to maintain an overview than is the case with large, self-contained software projects → Sect. 5.3.2.

Nevertheless, this design problem persists regardless of whether adaptive services are used. The methods presented here will help to master it well. But it's important to understand that this challenge is frequently identified as a barrier in real-world situations. Compared to monolithic services that are planned according to requirements, breaking them down into increments seems almost impossible. From the perspective of a traditional tender, this argument may even be correct, but it is based on a false assumption. In adaptive services, development is value-based, and not all properties of an output are fixed at one point in time.

Adaptive services pursue a clear development direction and utilise suitable methods to fill the potential business value space. This guarantees a minimum level of realised value, which is generally higher than in the traditional approach. The paths to value development can be analysed afterwards. This demonstrates the mastery of complex projects.

## 5.3 Dynamising Alternatives: From Vision to Roadmap

If you read traditional tender documents, you will also find a large number of values in the company presentation and the tender criteria. These are often lists with up to a dozen values that cover a broad spectrum. In addition to the subject of the tender, such as meeting demand or the most favourable price, there are statements on quality, flexibility, sustainability, and partnership, according to which the providers and their range of services are to be weighted.

We know from practical experience that these catalogues of criteria for selecting providers are difficult to use. Values that can be easily analysed and calculated in metrics, such as prices, short transition times, or percentage coverage of requirements, are often used. Soft criteria are usually also assessed very softly and favourably or deliberately ignored in the selection process, although they should serve as a basis for decision-making.

An adaptive approach promises that an organisation or a sub-division can align itself more closely with value targets. In this approach, this applies regardless of whether these values are soft or hard in the traditional sense. First, let us consider the ideal case. In this scenario, values can be expressed in monetary terms, such as dollars or euros. For example, the company may wish to increase its turnover by 10% next year. It intends to achieve this with the new service. In practice, however, many important values are very difficult to measure in euros. Let's take the example of increasing the attractiveness of the company for employees.

"We want to become the most attractive company in our sector in our country" can serve as a vision here. A ranking by two market research companies can be used to check whether the target has been achieved. An internal target for this financial year could be to double the number of applications from trainees and career starters. All of these are meaningful metrics that are geared towards a valuable goal, but cannot currently be expressed in financial results in hard monetary terms.

It is acceptable if the vision and mission contain certain values or tasks that cannot be easily defined in financial metrics at first. However, it is advisable to better understand the associated business values over time. Ultimately, any investment should pay off, so effectiveness should be demonstrated at some point in time. In this example, better and more motivated employees should ultimately lead to increased sales and profits. The criteria for such an indirect value-adding improvement to ultimately be the best measure of proof of impact for the organisation may even take several years in a step-by-step approach.

Some companies try to express everything in financial figures, for example to be able to calculate a return on investment for the value "attractive company for employees". The financial levers of these values are usually estimated for this purpose. Due to a lack of experience or data, such estimates are usually not a solid basis. Adaptive methods cope well with values from all perspectives. The beauty of this is that adaptive methods can be used to convert the effects of soft values into financial values. If this is desired.

Adaptive methods are very good at integrating hard and soft values into further development, such as the reorganisation of a managed service. Essentially, the aim is to prioritise the best measure in terms of value over other measures when creating the next evolutionary step. This means that we can cope with relative values in the decision-making process even without absolute values. Of course, even in adaptive environments, directly measurable values that can be represented in financial results are more favourable for decision-making.

In our adaptive approach, we can utilise almost all systems that define values. No matter what they are called in companies: purpose, vision, corporate strategy, North Star, etc. Existing tools can also be utilised at the strategic-tactical level, and we will even be able to fall back on many practical everyday things. The most valuable and obvious basis for decision-making is a vision (Fig. 5.3).

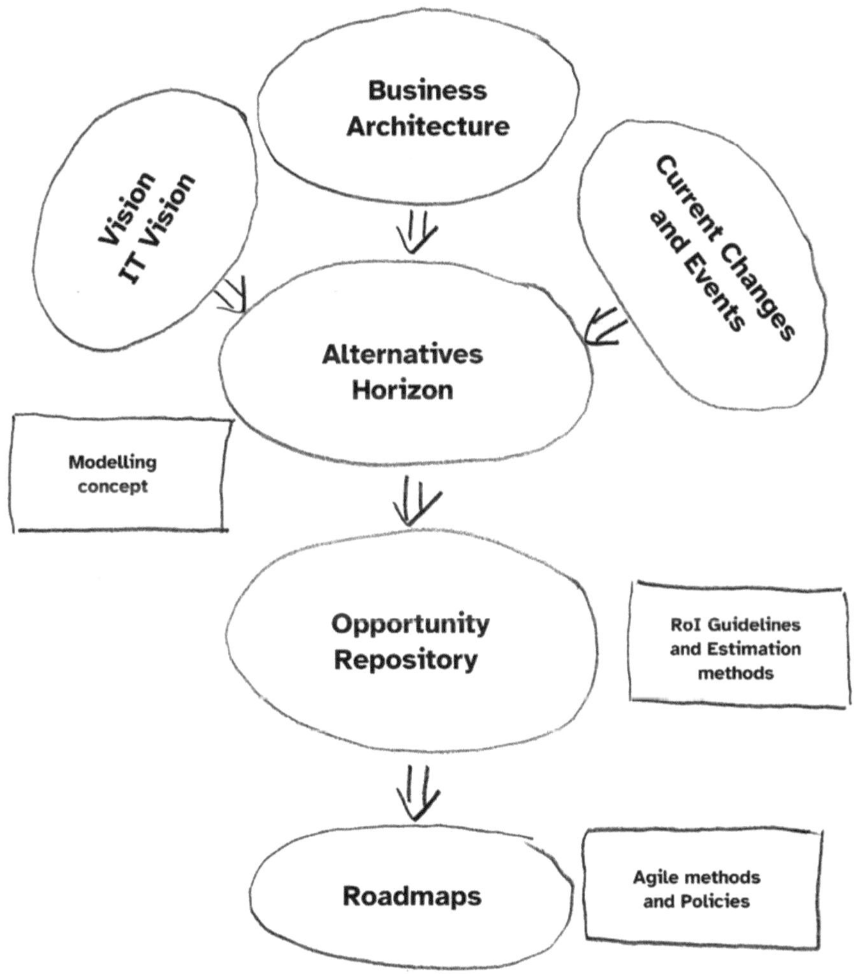


**Fig. 5.3** Overview of the alternatives dynamiser

### 5.3.1 Vision, Business Architecture, and Current Developments

Instead of requirements, we use gathered ideas as input, especially at the beginning, any kind of idea that offers added value. This can be a coarse sketch from a brainstorming session, a prototype from a design thinking meeting, an epic or use cases. You are also welcome to use existing designs, architectures, or parts thereof as a collection for development potential. We call all these valuable elements "alternatives". But first, let's look at the management of alternatives. In an ideal world, a vision would be enough for us (Fig. 5.4).

#### Vision

Corporate visions (→ Sect. 2.11) occur in a wide variety of contexts. We need a vision as a shared dream of the future state of a company or part of a company. The vision should reflect the needs of the market and aim for ever better products or services at lower costs for the company. It must be desirable, achievable, targeted, and flexible. It must be easy to understand and easy to communicate.

A vision can cover anything from the entire company to a specific project. At least one vision is required that covers the core of the value domain. Visions for the core business are ideal, from which targeted visions for sub-domains or projects can be derived if necessary.

We need the vision to develop ideas for values and to structure existing ideas, use cases, requirements, sub-concepts, etc. If you work in agile software development, you may be familiar with project or product visions, but these are not sufficient here. If possible, we need a direct link to the business and its development direction.

If there is no vision or the existing vision is not usable, it is worth developing a vision for the adaptive process. It may be a good idea to give the required vision a name such as "North Star". This is appropriate if the original company vision is too

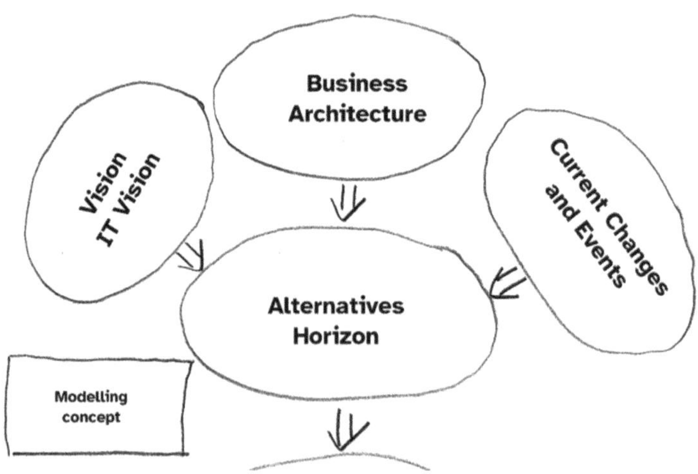


**Fig. 5.4** Input channels for architecture alternatives

flowery, complex, directionless, or difficult to interpret. In a cross-functional team, you will need about 2 days to develop such a North Star.

As many readers will have already encountered the term corporate vision in one form or another, we will not go into more detail here on the development of vision, mission, and strategy. You are welcome to fall back on your established method. If you do not yet have a method for developing a vision or want to replace the existing one, we recommend taking a look at the OKR method → Sect. 2.9.

Objectives and Key Results (OKR) is an independent subject area that is ideally suited to adaptive methods. The OKR methods can be used to develop evidence of outcome value over time. As all OKR books and training courses start with a vision, it is sufficient to read Mission, Vision, and Mid-Term Goals at this point. We recommend the practical book "Objectives and Key Results: Driving Focus, Alignment, and Engagement with OKRs" by Paul R. Niven and Ben Lamorte (2016).

### Business Architecture

Business architecture is a connecting and controlling discipline between management and IT. As part of the enterprise architecture, business architecture creates models for the optimal integration of corporate IT into the corporate organisation. The most widely used framework for enterprise architectures is the Open Group Architecture Framework (TOGAF) (→ Sect. 2.3). TOGAF is covered in this chapter because it provides valuable insights into enterprise architecture, enabling existing architectures to be mapped to models.

TOGAF's process model for the development of technical architectures is called the Architecture Development Method (ADM). ADM models information architectures in the four domains of business, application, data, and technology. It develops modularisation, standardisation and relies on existing, proven technologies and products. Adaptive roadmaps are intended to incorporate part of this governance.

The alternatives introduced by the business architecture can be structured according to vision-compliant values. A defined business value should be consistently visible through the ADM for each artefact, as the vision often covers a smaller scope in practice, deviations from the big picture can occur here. In this context, the most important phases of the TOGAF Architecture Development Method, a) to d), are as follows:

(a) An "**Architecture Vision**" is a briefly summarised target architecture. This architecture vision must support the business objectives, correspond to the strategic objectives, comply with the guidelines and take into account the requirements and objectives of the stakeholders.
(b) "**Business Architecture**" is the first of the four TOGAF architecture domains. It describes the product or service strategy based on the corporate objectives, the strategy, the organisation, and the central business processes.
(c) "**Information Systems Architecture**" develops target architectures for the areas of data and application systems. The data architecture describes the structure of the logical and physical databases, including the resources. The applica-

tion architecture comprises the application systems and their relationships to the company's core business processes.

(d) The "**Technology Architecture**" describes the hardware, software and network infrastructure required for the provision of business-critical applications.

All interim results from all phases provide useful input for our alternatives. TOGAF ADM is a method for summarising and structuring architectures in phase e) "Opportunities and Solutions". If this governance is already established in the organisation, many positive aspects of the enterprise architecture are also useful for our adaptive approach.

### Current Changes and Events

The third type of input channel is current changes and events, which can be upcoming or recently implemented IT changes and small projects. These are so-called "in-flight" projects, i.e. projects that have been planned for some time or are already being implemented. There may also be business units that implement changes largely independently of the IT organisation, e.g. on the basis of the standard IT portfolio or even in the form of shadow IT. Multiple players, including uncontrolled changes, is something else that needs to be considered.

A similar structure to the business architecture with a sub-division into levels can be used here. It is to be expected that the alternatives here are less structured and that the outcome to be achieved is not well documented. It is therefore necessary to initially focus on a few services, products, or projects and analyse these more intensively. New stakeholders can also be included if necessary. In our experience, very few companies have a complete mapping of IT and its utilisation.

Existing change processes and data structures are also an important source of information for us. They are not a collection of new ideas and suggestions, but it is interesting that the collection of alternatives for solved problems creates a different perspective on these solutions. Changes made in the past, for instance, might not have been aligned with the company's vision at all. For example, we may find the further expansion and renewal of the company's own data centre, even though there is a company policy to prefer cloud services.

Analysing these developments provides a deeper insight into where your company stands, what the requirements of day-to-day business are and whether you are on the right track with your current management. In this way, a pool of knowledge can be created that sets the direction for the next architectures. This is an important decision-making basis for future design proposals. Some discrepancies will inevitably be difficult to resolve. These should be given great attention.

It would be wonderful if discrepancies between vision and culture could be quickly eliminated. In fact, such discrepancies can often be managed effectively. Compromises have to be made in the architecture anyway if industrialised solutions are a central component of a solution. An adaptive approach can show a way forward here that represents an interim solution. Provided the vision continues to serve as the central control element, the core values will remain safeguarded.

## Enterprise Architecture Versus Adaptive Model

In a well-established enterprise architecture environment with a robust structure, an agile or adaptive approach to defining roadmaps may be considered incompatible. In particular, the leading process and design sovereignty could be disputed. It is to be expected that it will take some effort to introduce an adaptive method on a level playing field. Let's start with a positive case.

In cross-functional teams, we have had good experiences in developing a compatibility between agile and existing frameworks. The established system can certainly be fully supported. The only important thing is that the adaptive methods are given the necessary freedom. Synchronisation points can be, for example, reviews in which enterprise architects, as stakeholders of the business architecture, coordinate their requirements and provide information on incomplete increments.

The idea is that the adaptive approach will provide the primary development service, supporting all existing interfaces in reporting and governance. Decision structures or specifications can be represented in the reviews by stakeholder guidelines. A minimum viable service can be rejected here because it does not fulfil certain requirements, for example. Insights into value enhancement in previously unconsidered dimensions can also begin in the review and be developed, for example, in the business architecture parallel to the sprint.

An adaptive approach is constantly focused on value, with architectures and their assumptions being amended as necessary. This is not an ordinary way of operating in enterprise architecture. If certain assumptions are called into question early on because certain values cannot otherwise be achieved, a response to these new revelations must be provided by the enterprise architecture. Depending on the type of realisation, this can be a challenge that extends over several phases. If representatives of both methods are interested in integration and the best possible utilisation of their respective methods, far-reaching decisions are also made.

A completely different situation arises if a company does not adapt its existing design practices. In this case, agile methods cannot be integrated, and value creation is unlikely to materialise. There are examples of certain subtasks, which involve many work steps, being handled late in the architecture process using Scrum methods. This happens in a playing field with very strict framework conditions in which a traditional governance model is transferred to agile methodologies. Normally, the development of future values is hindered here by the strict control of simple outputs and a restriction of the necessary freedoms (Fig. 5.5).

It can be difficult to find suitable compromises at the outset that do not restrict valuable freedoms. This is particularly challenging for beginners, who often have to juggle several factors. Later in this book, we will discuss hybrid models and provide examples from this field. These combine adaptive approaches with existing guidelines. These can give a first impression of which freedoms are necessary. If you want to start with a hybrid approach, it's worth gaining some experience and investing in an agile coach.

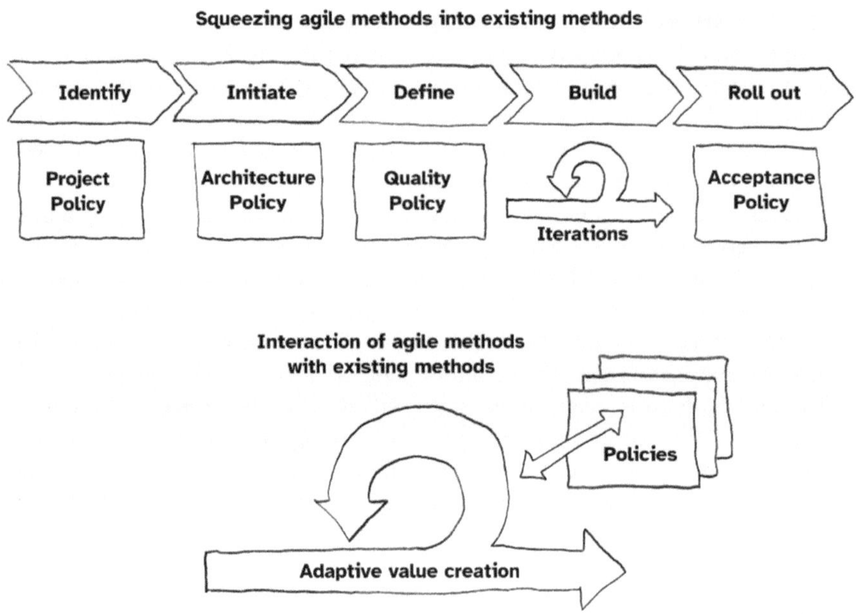


**Fig. 5.5** Governance vs. Leeway

### 5.3.2 Alternatives Horizon

The alternatives horizon is essentially a compilation of alternatives. In practice, these alternatives can come from any input channel that has already been defined. The three channels presented here are typical examples. Regardless of whether three or five input channels are active in your company, it is necessary to differentiate between prospective alternatives, alternatives for the immediate future, and past developments (Fig. 5.6).

As already mentioned, the alternatives can include different architectures, generic ideas, or fragments of architectures—e.g., ideas that cover PoCs. The content can be visionary, business-orientated, current, or future-orientated. The decisive factor for inclusion in the collection is that the value to be achieved is obvious. External experts must also be able to immediately understand the result of a concept.

In the early phases of adaptive projects, the alternatives horizon can serve as a simple repository of alternatives that are closely related to the service to be provided. In an advanced form, it is an organised pool of unevaluated ideas. The broader it is, the more it reflects the perspective of the entire organisation and unfolds its effect not only as a value provider for opportunities.

Up to a maximum number of 100 alternatives, these can generally still be handled in an unstructured manner. From this point onwards, an alternatives horizon is required that provides a structure and can represent relationships between the

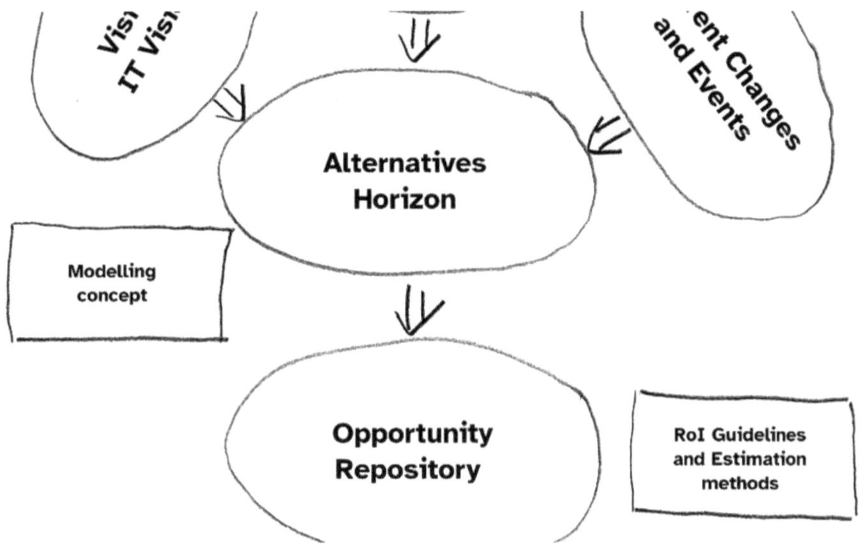


**Fig. 5.6** Alternatives horizon

values. In practice, this can be a smooth transition in the work of a project team. The first alternatives horizon may be created on a pinboard and only takes into account a section of around half of the alternatives.

We suggest structuring the alternatives in a coordinate system. To do this, the alternatives can be divided into four areas on the Y-axis: visionary, strategic, tactical, and operational. It is advisable to group similar or related alternatives in one level. The potential value can be visualised by the size of the grouping. In the next step, the X-axis sorts the alternatives according to their topicality and divides them into past developments, immediate future, and prospective alternatives. If an alternative covers several time spans, it is categorised in the option that extends furthest into the future (on the right of the X-axis).

In the third step, relationships should be established between alternatives on these four levels. On an electronic canvas these are arrows, on a pinboard these can be threads. A tactical alternative should be found for each operational alternative, a strategic alternative for each tactical alternative, and finally a visionary alternative for each strategic alternative. If this is not the case, it is worth analysing and completing the alternatives horizon.

Especially at the start of work on such a project, one element may simply be missing due to the size of the project. If both a strategic and a visionary alternative for an operational alternative are available, a tactical alternative can easily be added in a brainstorming session. If there are no operational alternatives, the gap will most likely be filled by generating suitable ideas at short notice. Operational alternatives may well be missing in the perspective view. It is to be expected that value potentials will continue to develop, and it therefore makes no sense to analyse a distant future too intensively.

If there are no options for assigning visionary alternatives, there are usually more serious reasons for this. In the case of past developments that are not anchored, there is probably a problem within the organisation or in the interaction with partners. For example, an analysis may reveal that existing changes are taking place in silos and do not incorporate a central vision or strategic guideline. This must be taken into account in the further process. It may be necessary to investigate the identified causes as part of a change management project.

If missing allocations in the alternative horizon are primarily due to interaction with partners, this can be of particular interest in the tendering context. In practice, we are familiar with service provider relationships in which the purchased service is not aligned with the client's values. This can go so far that there is a mutual acceptance not to deliver or call off certain service elements. There can be many reasons for such a decoupling of business values in a relationship that has grown over time.

Even if such a problem occurs, it requires comprehensive corrective action as part of a new tender. Our experience shows that it is not primarily a question of finding out who is responsible for the misinterpretation of the service. In this respect, it is much more important to raise awareness and change the social system. In one example of first-generation outsourcing, a contractor convinced the existing team to accept unsuitable, cheaper service elements. The management has now become aware of this issue and has made the decision that this partner will no longer be considered. Simply excluding this partner is not enough in such a case, as a lack of experience, orientation, or even loyalty of the existing team has emerged, which needs to be investigated in more detail and corrected.

Working with dependencies and complexities on the alternatives horizon can generate ideas and lead to levels of abstraction on which these ideas can be generalised or concretised. The alternatives horizon should be understood as a living working tool rather than a fixed structure. Colour coding can be used to represent different states of immature alternatives on the structure, with similar colours marking clusters that are not yet fully aligned. Green dots represent future ideas that can be completed at any time. Yellow dots mark important construction sites for the next steps. Red dots indicate errors that need to be rectified (Fig. 5.7).

As part of tendering projects, the alternatives horizon should always be further developed so that analyses can be carried out at any time. This can be done about once a month afterwards or as part of a retrospective. These analyses can be reflective, to check for any overlooked issues; current, to confirm that we are on the right track; or forward-looking, to explore alternative scenarios. While teams at all levels can perform these analyses independently, they are even more effective when the entire organisation collaborates.

The alternatives horizon should be used for reflection and control when reviewing developments from previous iterations, when changes to requirements arise, or when working on parallel projects. For example, to answer questions such as:

At what level should decisions be made?
What alternative solutions are there in this cluster?

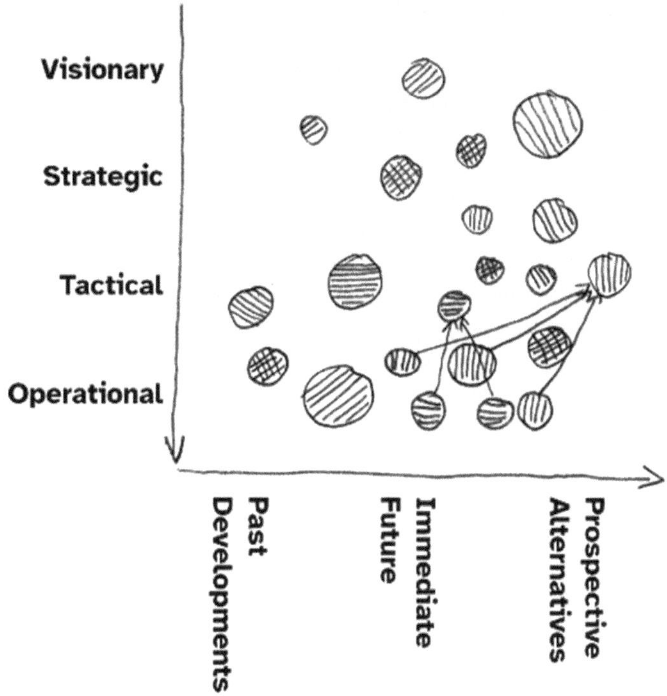


**Fig. 5.7** Example of an alternatives horizon

Do we implement service components according to proven methods or do we use the current change situation to evaluate new technologies?
Can we attract more sponsors who share our mindset and values?
How willing is the organisation to embrace cultural change?
Are we bound by previous practices or are we consistently moving in the direction of our vision?

If an update is combined with an analysis of the alternatives horizon in a retrospective, this can be done within 30 min. Allow 15 min for the update and a further 15 min to analyse the movements on the board. The direction of view from the vision to the operation provides a tendency that can be derived from the culture. However, when alternatives from the operation to the vision are considered, a general trend emerges from the feedback.

At this point, a comparison of two alternatives or a trend is sufficient for many questions. If a trend tends to be more positive than that of the previous month, we are on the right track. The next step is to calculate alternatives based on hard facts. The alternatives horizon should be used regularly to monitor the target direction, this creates permanence, especially if many stakeholders are involved.

**Example** Alternatives Horizon and Enterprise Continuum

The structuring of an alternatives horizon presented here is deliberately kept simple. This enables to plan and implement initial projects. The methodology can be expanded into a complete architecture approach for IT products and IT services. The approach is suitable for customer organisations through to IT service providers—with considerable differences in complexity. This book can only convey the basics. In this example, an idea for an expansion option for the dynamisation of alternatives is presented.

In the following outline, elements of the TOGAF Enterprise Continuum (The Open Group, 2022) are used to provide additional structure to the alternatives horizon. The classification of the TOGAF Architecture Continuum is used to subdivide the alternatives from concrete organisation-specific to abstract architecture principles. In our example, no distinction is made between alternatives and architectures, so that sketches and ideas can also be included in the continuum. For highly regulated industries, external architectures could also be considered as a separate input channel alongside vision, business architecture, and current developments (Fig. 5.8).

## Excursus Alternatives Versus Use Cases

You may be wondering about the introduction of the new term alternative, where in agile environments you work with use cases, user stories and epics and in classic environments with requirement definitions. An alternative usually encompasses more than the terms mentioned; in simplified terms, it could be seen as a generic term for a value description. In addition, an alternative is an architectural element that supports a choice.

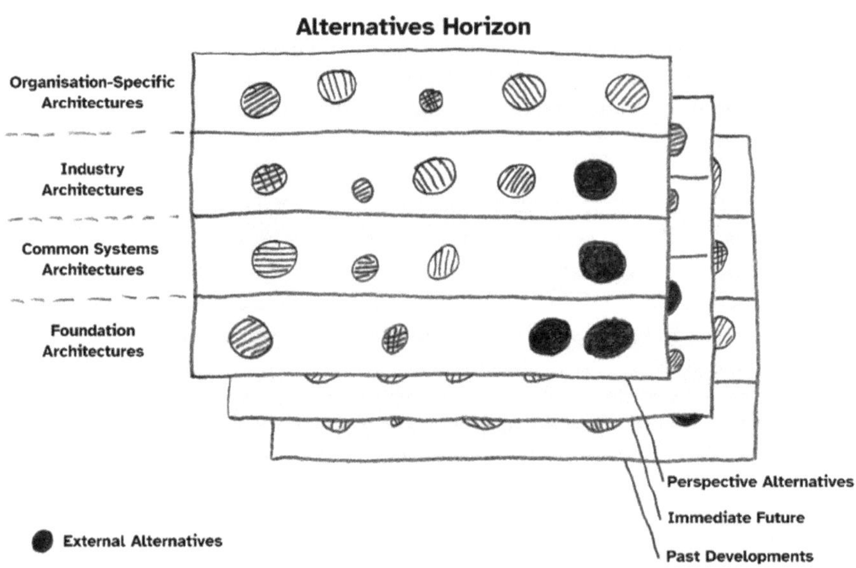


**Fig. 5.8** A basic structure for an alternative continuum

A use case summarises scenarios that should occur when a user attempts to achieve a specific business objective with the help of the service. It describes what can happen on the way to achieving the goal and does not include specific technical solutions. A user story is the description of a service's functionality from the user's perspective in the form of a simple narrative. An epic can be described as an overarching user story; it is the description of a requirement for a service at a high level of abstraction in everyday language.

Use cases, user stories, and epics are wonderful basic elements of alternatives. Their characteristic of not actively or implicitly specifying an actual technical solution is an important quality of alternatives. Alternatives that describe goals and paths without committing to solutions are easier to handle than alternatives with fixed examples of solutions. For orientation on what epics are and how they differ from traditional project business, we recommend the description of epics in the Scaled Agile Framework (Scaled Agile, Inc., 2023a, 2023b, 2023c).

Alternatives should focus on the desired outcomes. Requirement definitions should complement this definition and, in case of doubt, provide a more detailed consideration of the values. For example, we would like to have the same type of tool-supported processing of requests in facility management as currently functions in the IT organisation's service request management tool XYZ. Enclosed, you will find a list with 150 details from the tender for XYZ. An alternative based on this comparison should go from the general to the detailed and add what the most important values are, for example:

Every enquiry from an employee is processed thoroughly and answered promptly.

An enquiry from an employee must never be lost.

Our service requests are implemented within the timeframe defined in the catalogue.

We want to strengthen the trust our employees have in our facility organisation so that they don't do anything unauthorised in the future.

If this alternative is to be considered, it must be properly finalised. The existing service request tool only serves as a reference here. It is important to clarify which elements in the IT process represent which values and whether they are also required in facility management. For example, just like in IT, it could be important to send escalation and reminder messages via team management to strengthen confidence in seamless processes. However, the workflow itself can be made much simpler, as these are orders that are consistently processed by employees from the warehouse using Kanban cards.

Alternatives help to realise possible values. Similar values can be realised through several accepted alternatives. Depending on the team, level of knowledge, and existing or future technology, alternatives should be evaluated differently. They should be collected and further developed in the alternatives horizon. Depending on how the project progresses, some alternatives may become impractical and need to be replaced. Conversely, further alternatives may arise for capacity reasons and be included in a roadmap.

### 5.3.3 Opportunity Repository

While the Alternatives Horizon focuses on analysing and structuring business values, the "Opportunity Repository" deals with the challenge of innovation or the implementation of managed services. In the traditional tender, requirements and a budget also justify large investments in basic technologies, licences, and much more. Agile methods or frameworks rarely encounter such a challenge. As a rule, investments are decided as part of a product increment. Decisions on the basic technology may be made during product planning or the product roadmap. In some agile frameworks, this is even a component that is not managed in an agile way (Fig. 5.9).

However, we have tried to develop a concept that fully follows the idea of adaptive services and is adaptable at the same time. The organisations we have worked with use different trade-offs between hierarchical and adaptive approaches. Our methodology can map all of these requirements and has the advantage that these hybrid compromises could always be precisely localised in practice. It was always clear to the organisations in which areas Lean-Agile was used, in which areas the traditional management system was used and where our method still had potential for a fully adaptive approach.

The next step is to assess whether an additional adaptive element is the logical next development step. When analysing the first customer projects, which were only partially adaptive, we tried to think the concept through consistently. In doing so, we came across a challenge with current managed services that we had to solve.

In a managed service, a single increment can be very cost-intensive. Let's take a company with 10,000 IT users as an example. Software or a cloud service that covers the needs of all users is probably offered as a large licence package. This offer includes not only products that meet current needs, but also comprehensive

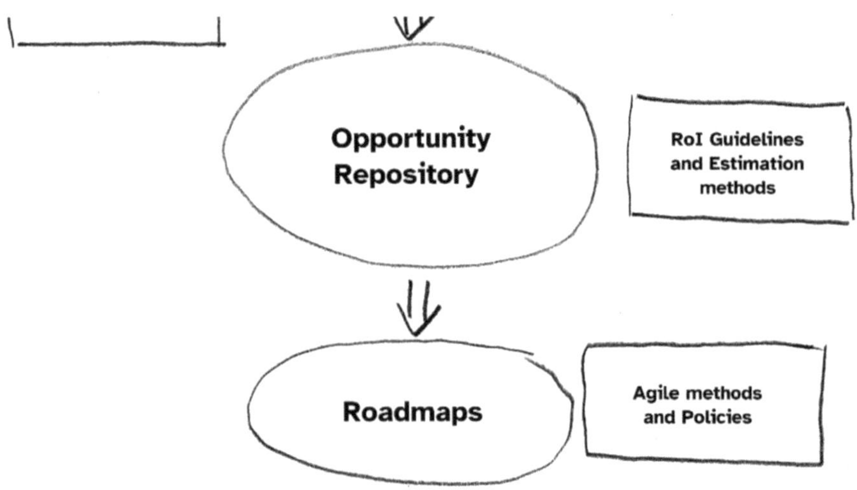


**Fig. 5.9** Opportunity repository

packages that the providers would like to sell. These include many functions that can be used in the future and are therefore offered as a reasonably priced bundle.

Gradual licensing as required with monthly extensions is probably much more expensive than an initial full package. Even such a gradual expansion would have to be planned in advance, as it may turn out after a few months of development that different basic software would be much more suitable. An adaptive concept should allow investment decisions to be made from time to time without restricting the scope for innovation too much. This is one of the most important findings from the "Opportunity Repository" section.

In addition to technology and licences, completely different cost blocks play a role when tendering for a service. One example of this is a service that stands between the platform and the application, such as a managed workplace. It can happen that increments are taken up by early adopters and other user groups also discover the increment for themselves. At a certain point in time, all users are on one of the adaptive workplaces that are now provided. Transformation costs, such as training and introduction costs for 10,000 users, must be taken into account as part of the overall project.

The overall solution should also include industrialised service elements, as it cannot be assumed that all user groups and elements will make a high value contribution. However, defining industrialised managed services too early and thoughtlessly could severely restrict the scope for potential value, which would result in the adaptive project failing before it has even begun.

The opposite approach of using fewer prefabricated parts and licence packages leads to a different problem situation. This results in increased effort for the creation of customised applications and services, which ties up resources and time. Industry-specific features have to be created individually in this approach, which is not considered appropriate. Using a smaller, open solution initially as a basis and incubator for value creation, only to switch to a large industry solution later, is also often too costly. Such bottom-up approaches are suitable when the focus is on exploring value, and when the organisation needs to learn what it wants and how to create value.

We need clear guidelines for our future roadmaps in order to maintain freedom, secure targets, and select components of appropriate complexity. Despite all the methods presented here, it is always good to make large investments as late as possible. The good news is that nowadays cloud services can often be used to develop innovations on a limited scale up to a certain level of maturity. A major investment decision, e.g. in a global licence model, can be postponed by 3 to 6 months with such approaches, when the first successes of the basic concept become apparent, and the potential can thus be secured.

Ideally, the opportunity repository is based on the potential business value and the scope of the managed service. It includes service and implementation options of target architectures, which are taken from the alternatives horizon and completed if necessary, at least to the extent that a value analysis can be carried out. The aim is to compile a potential business value of 150% to 200% for a roadmap of 6 months.

On the one hand, this makes it possible to work with ambitious targets, as is usual in an agile context, while on the other hand, sufficient freedom is retained in the creation of values. If it becomes clear during the development process that one development strand has a high potential, another must be put on hold, perhaps due to resource dependencies. If the roadmaps were filled only with ideas that have a potential of 100%, all ideas would have to be implemented and realise their full potential. However, such a planning approach does not seem very realistic and would be more akin to a waterfall approach.

The clustering and evaluation of opportunities according to value, dependencies, and costs also aims to obtain a certain level of basic funding for the service. All suitable and dependent alternatives are considered for a given managed service. These are ranked according to their potential value in a preliminary roadmap. This can be done with the help of agile estimation techniques, some of which are presented below.

However, it is not necessary to estimate an absolute value; it is initially sufficient to compare and rank two alternatives in terms of their value. These pairwise comparisons result in a semi-order (partial order), which is completely sufficient for our purposes to select the most valuable alternatives.

This and the following value assessment steps should be carried out with open eyes. The clusters should be formed in such a way that they result in independent and meaningful packages. However, some clusters may need to be regrouped or split to create a roadmap. The initial arrangement of the most valuable elements should ensure that important alternatives are evaluated first.

### Excursus Relative Estimation Versus Effort Estimation

The opportunity repository is the first stage in the process of evaluating alternatives in order to estimate their size. While we do not require a full cost or effort estimate, we have found that many organisations have their own established methods and doubt the reliability of external estimation practices. Some vendor-driven return-on-investment calculators are known to us. We understand the mistrust that stems from negative experiences. Unfortunately, there are a few market players who use their own calculators to calculate an unrealistic return on investment in order to encourage a purchase decision.

For us, this is the reason why we do not make a preferred specification here, such as SAFe suggests with Weighted Shortest Job First (WSJF) (Scaled Agile, Inc., 2023a, 2023b, 2023c). Basically, many methods are suitable for a final evaluation. The tools and processes that are defined in an organisation, for example in return of investment (RoI) guidelines, can also be used. The only problem that arises is the need for an estimate that is refined over time. An effort estimate only needs to be made very late in the iterations. For the opportunity repository, it is sufficient to categorise the alternatives into complexity categories.

Agile estimation methods are completely sufficient for our purposes and have the main advantage that they can evaluate many alternatives very quickly. Estimating relative values by many independent people is also much more reliable and easier for people than setting absolute values. By restructuring and decomposing alternatives, we very often need a new estimate. Relative values are completely sufficient until a roadmap is finalised, save a lot of time, and are more pleasant for those involved.

Furthermore, unlike effort or cost estimates, complexity estimates do not become obsolete. When specific effort measures are used, these estimates often have to be corrected by re-evaluation during the course of the project. Complexity, on the other hand, remains the same from the client's perspective and only needs to be adjusted if an alternative changes. A cost estimate can be calculated quite easily from the complexity.

We recommend introducing agile estimation methods so that only necessary assessments can be made quickly and effectively. A transition or reassessment using the methods proven in your organisation can take place at a later date. This can be done, for example, in preparation for the release of a roadmap. The use of established methods and approval channels strengthens confidence in a new approach at the beginning.

**Important** When applying agile estimation methods, a number of aspects are of crucial importance. Firstly, it is necessary to understand the context of the project, the team dynamics, and the available resources in order to create a sound basis for the application of agile estimation methods. This is essential to ensure the flexibility and adaptability of the estimation methods. Furthermore, it is crucial to know different estimation techniques and select the one that is most suitable. As agile estimation techniques are based on input from the entire team, it is essential to ensure that all team members are involved in the estimation process and that their perspectives are taken into account. Furthermore, it must be made clear to stakeholders that estimates are approximations and not guarantees. Estimates are subject to uncertainty and may change over the course of the project. Finally, a regular review of the estimates is necessary to optimise the estimation techniques. In addition, it is essential that teams are able to adjust their estimates as new information emerges or priorities change.

If you are starting with adaptive managed services on a small scale, you can use the Planning Poker used in Scrum programming teams, for example (McKenna, 2016). The Delphi method is suitable for estimating in larger groups of different participants (Beiderbeck et al., 2021). If you do not yet have an established method for prioritising sub-services, we recommend Weighted Shortest Job First (WSJF). This is a well-established quantified method for flow maximisation in Kanban.

WSJF prioritises according to Cost of Delay (CoD), i.e. according to the value that is lost by not implementing a potential order for a certain period of time. In our opinion, prioritisation by cost of delay has several advantages over return on investment: It reduces overproduction of, e.g., completed but not deployable modules without much further action. If the dependencies between the two increments are well understood, CoD reduces multitasking and the associated switching losses.

Furthermore, alternatives that can generate sales and profits relatively quickly are preferred. Compared to roadmaps, which favour larger alternatives with the same annual result, WSJF enables you to adapt at the time of release of the shorter alternative and to favour a newly emerging, more profitable alternative. CoD thus inherently increases the value potential of roadmaps.

As already explained, it can be crucial at the start of a project to orientate yourself on established standards and guidelines. For small projects learning about adaptive services, ranking and prioritising alternatives is of paramount importance. If WSJF is used to prioritise alternatives alongside a traditional business case approach with a RoI calculation, it is possible to switch to the more useful of the two methods at some point.

**Important** Brief instructions on how planning with WSJF can be applied in practice can be found on the Internet, e.g. in the Scaled Agile Framework. For more in-depth explanations, we recommend the chapter "Controlling Flow Under Uncertainty" from the book "Principles of Product Development Flow" by Donald Reinertsen (2009).

### 5.3.4 Service Roadmaps and Backlog

Roadmaps can now be composed from the opportunity repository. The opportunity repository has a similar function to a backlog, but the listed alternatives are at a more abstract level. They correspond to tactical projects in the classic environment. The alternatives are related to each other and must be selected, delimited, or minimised accordingly in order to be divided into the roadmaps.

In our environments, 6-month roadmaps have proven their worth. For the sake of simplicity, they are shown here as half-years. In practice, roadmaps are terminated as soon as sufficient added value has been achieved. They are often shorter than planned. Particularly when working with professional managed service providers, the value potential often lies in non-technical areas. Many of the technical areas can be taken out of the service factory and customised by the service provider.

It is recommended to plan three roadmaps at the same time. The current roadmap is filled with one or more specific projects. The next roadmap can be used to plan important additions to the service development. The roadmap after the next one serves as a memory for elements that are used to complete an investment, for example. Only the first roadmap is planned in detail and equipped with a backlog, as is common in Scrum, SAFe, and other iterative methods.

In many cases, an investment decision for a platform or service, including a licence model, can be made based on the value potential of the three roadmaps. It is advisable to have roadmaps approved by a committee. Initially, this can be a classic change advisory board or a management committee. However, the aim should always be to involve as many stakeholders as possible in an adaptive approach. In the next section, however, let us first turn to the challenge of making an investment decision. A characteristic conflict of objectives is the decision between a small, flexible service or a monolithic platform.

More flexible services can often be better adapted to alternatives, but require more complex integration into a service landscape and the customised creation of some basic functions. This type of service is also generally more manageable in the event of a slow transformation and offers licence models that can grow in line with the value gained or can be terminated if the value is not achieved.

Large monolithic services often offer a powerful range of functions that go far beyond the required properties. In order to achieve the desired outcome, individual elements need to be customised. Licence models and transformations aim to establish the platform or service on a broad basis. If individual elements prove not to be of value, it is generally not possible to decouple sub-areas.

Decisions regarding services, platforms, and providers must be included in the planning of the roadmaps. These decisions should be based on the specific roadmaps and the assessments in the opportunity repository. The focus should be on performance in the upcoming roadmaps. However, it is important not to hinder future development or overestimate the possible outputs.

In the case of small, flexible solutions, it should be checked whether alternatives from the opportunity repository can be utilised, or if there are combinable solutions for an overall concept. It is important to clarify whether these alternatives can be supported as things currently stand and what costs would be incurred if a move to a different technical basis became absolutely necessary after a few years of development. Do not include any projections of positive future developments of the solution in your evaluation, such as the expansion of this smart solution to other service areas in the coming years.

In the case of large monolithic solutions, it should be checked whether their functional scope can be supported by alternatives from the opportunity repository and at what cost this is possible. A detailed review in terms of detailed planning is not advisable, but it is a good investment to involve technical consultants who have experience with the implementation of such alternatives on the platform. Sampling may also be suitable, depending on the gap in the financing of known values. Particularly if there are major uncertainties between potential values and the specified scope of functions, you should check whether comprehensive contract or licence models can only be concluded at a later date. The presumed additional costs of a smaller contract scope or licence model may be well invested in order to avoid the risk of unfulfilled values.

Revolutionary investment decisions will not be the order of the day in the adaptive approach, but successful directional decisions are an important prerequisite for the degree of freedom of adaptive development opportunities. A solution that is too binding would jeopardise the development of future values, which would be a similar problem to the starting point of our analysis. Platform, providers, and tools could hinder further development if only the most necessary changes are implemented.

**Example** Imagine an enterprise that has almost doubled its business, number of employees, and factories over the last 10 years. Although the IT service setup never changed, they did their best to cover all aspects of past business development. In other words, a long list of opportunities waiting to be implemented has grown as a result of technical debt.

Now that the company is large enough to attract the attention of major IT service providers, several vendors of comprehensive product suites are sending their sales representatives to offer a wide range of functions and attractive package prices.

To avoid putting all their eggs in one basket, it is important not to assume that all the functions will fit all the alternatives and generate value. Our example company incorporates a dual vendor approach into the alternatives horizon. This generates a tree of operational alternatives assigned to a vendor.

The next stage is to develop a roadmap for one factory or business unit by switching to a comprehensive market solution. There is the option to extend the new services to more factories, but in nearly no case to all factories. Even after a successful campaign, the remaining factories will be the starting point for a different service setup that begins to explore new values.

After preparing decisions for platforms and service providers, the next step is to design roadmaps. In the initial phase of such an approach, only one service should initially be transformed, possibly including neighbouring services that are connected via interfaces and processes. Depending on the team size and development capacities, shorter roadmaps with fewer services should be transformed rather than many services at the same time, even at a higher level of maturity.

An important difference to the traditional approach is the integration in cross-functional teams, i.e. as many representatives as possible who provide, interact with, or make available this service must also be involved in the realisation of the roadmap. This goes far beyond the consultation and involvement of stakeholders in the planning phase. People who are actively involved in the provision of the service should also be included in the development.

When forming cross-functional teams, the existing job description should not play a major role, as it is much more important that people are confident enough to actively contribute. Scrum speaks here of the values of courage, openness, commitment, focus, and respect. In practice, the team members will primarily consist of the people who provide the relevant service today and in the future. Depending on the scope of the changes, these teams will be supplemented by specialists and consultants.

**Important** A significant principle is to always keep the information analysis as close as possible to the source of the information. This not only increases the amount of structured information. It also provides empirical knowledge and direct verifiability of working hypotheses with relevant data. Some traditional hierarchies tend to avoid such approaches. We would like to emphasise that this way of working facilitates the finding of new solutions and alternatives. However, the decision on the solution components or roadmap remains the responsibility of the hierarchy. Investing in a structured solution space is always worthwhile, as it helps to avoid fundamental errors.

An existing team can optimise its own service very well, but a change in the underlying technology should always be carried out with experts in the new technology. Otherwise, there is a risk that old design principles will be imposed on a new, completely different designed technology. This limits the performance of the new technology, creates completely new error situations, and is not future proof.

This new style of working in a cross-functional team will delight some employees and discourage others. This also applies to the employees of providers and other partners. In our experience, there are many volunteers for the first roadmaps, and you should only rely on them. There are usually many assumptions about a future agile way of working and if you rely on volunteers, you will get off to a positive start. The organisation can slowly learn from their experiences.

During the reorganisation of an existing service, various influences on the current service can occur. The quality of service can be limited during the term of the roadmap. In the simplest case, this can be due to the deployment of operational employees in the cross-functional team, who then have less time for the actual service in incident management and service request management. Remodelling work changes functions and performance. These changes are integrated into the service after each review.

In a classic approach, a new system or a new service provider would be set up in parallel and all users would be switched to a new system on a changeover day (change of control). In an adaptive approach, however, it can make sense to incorporate changes into an existing service, especially if efficiency increases primarily affect processes and organisations, but not primarily the technology.

The effects of a further development on the existing service must be taken into account in the release for the roadmap. A service is usually tested in the first iteration and then continued under the defined framework conditions. As soon as the desired increase in value has been achieved, the service should be brought back into the operational organisation. A "freeze phase" usually involves automation and full integration. Examples include processes such as knowledge management and technical systems such as monitoring.

A committee consisting of representatives of the company, stakeholders from the company, and the affected organisation, possibly together with specialist consultants who have experience in the desired area of change, should approve the next roadmap. It is recommended that this committee meets monthly to report on the developments of the current roadmap and to be involved in the planning of the next roadmap, including the development directions.

In addition to the consideration of technical aspects, which can be prepared by a change advisory board, all aspects of organisational change management and business value creation must also be approved by such a board. Especially at the beginning, it is important that these aspects are carefully weighed up and, if necessary, a balance is struck. In agile projects that are intended to create potential value, it is essential that degrees of freedom are retained. It is advisable to seek advice from an agile coach at the start of defining the boundary conditions in order to avoid a relapse into old working patterns due to overly strict framework conditions.

For example, after weighing up all the framework conditions, it may turn out that the expected project duration is too long if it is to be managed predominantly with internal resources. Don't simply decide to increase resources by using external resources only on an ad hoc basis. It is advisable to inspect such a planning specification intensively. When analysing the required framework conditions, values are supplemented or updated. Based on this, alternatives are identified with the help of the opportunity repository.

In our example, the desire for a shorter implementation time could stem from the fact that the expected return on investment is very high and every month saved is financially attractive. It may also be that the necessary adaptation of the technical systems must be ensured by a certain deadline due to upcoming legal changes. In such cases, the reorganisation of the roadmap can range from a simple restructuring of the minimum viable services to the complete outsourcing of sub-projects.

Including more external employees in a cross-functional team can make sense. This is particularly true if the organisation has experience of adaptive approaches and can manage several cross-functional teams on the same project. To ensure effective collaboration, the cross-functional teams should not exceed a size of 6 to 12 people. If a project is to be accelerated with more human resources, this means splitting it into several teams. Such teams must be given time to develop their own self-organisation, i.e. there must not be too much staff turnover, especially in the early stages. The organisation needs to establish and nurture its own culture. A compromise can be the integration of external employees from a long-standing service provider. In this case, low staff turnover and a positive cultural development can be expected.

**Excursus Backlog Refinement Versus Solution Focus**

In order to be able to include alternatives in a roadmap, they are first divided into manageable units. Refinement takes place regularly during the implementation phase. During the initial division into a roadmap, there may be projects that are so extensive that they have to be divided into several roadmaps. However, this will rarely be the case. If industrialised managed services are used as building blocks, a period of 6 months is sufficient in almost all cases. It is much more difficult to initially break down an epic into services with minimal value.

With agile working methods, the short iteration cycles eliminate the need for time-consuming analyses that occur with traditional approaches. A complex environment is analysed according to the sense–analyse–respond principle, and an overall architecture is developed. In comparison, an agile methodology uses the probe–sense–respond principle in a complex environment (→ Sect. 2.8). As described in the Agile Manifesto as the 11th principle: "The best architectures, requirements, and designs emerge from self-organising teams". (Beck et al., 2001).

However, our experience shows that it is difficult to break down a large epic into minimum viable services or increments that can be released at each review. In the traditional approach, various work packages with large dependencies are created over a period of months and the actual testing only begins when all modules are initially available. This is also not ideal in the traditional approach, as errors only become visible very late and are therefore usually very expensive. However, such a design can serve as a compromise in traditional programmes if limits are quickly found in the decomposition into work packages.

In an adaptive approach, it is neither acceptable nor a sensible compromise to implement large epics over several months and not take the release capability of each increment seriously. As in traditional projects, this leads to errors being discovered late. For example, if the stakeholders only realise months later in the review that their design idea will not achieve the hoped-for outcome because the functionality could not be tested in the previous iterations. Due to the higher effort and the justification of having overridden agile methods, this can also lead to a sunk-costs fallacy effect, which is actually avoided in the first place with agile methods.

**Example** The sunk-costs fallacy effect or escalating commitment bias describes a human behavioural pattern in which increasingly negative consequences of a project or an investment in general are ignored. The group sticks to its course without considering the obvious boundary conditions. This leads to irrational actions that are in line with previous decisions and actions, but in the situation represent a bad decision or pointless investment.

In addition to the above example of a project that will not achieve the outcome, a market development could also be ignored and lead to an escalating commitment. For example, if a manufacturer cancels a platform during several months of development of a software product. Instead of switching to an alternative platform and having lengthy discussions with the client, the product is simply developed further as the old platform still exists at the time of delivery. In this way, the work invested is not discarded and the project order is formally fulfilled. However, the result cannot be utilised, as the client is unlikely to find customers or has to migrate the product to a new platform as soon as it is completed.

Reducing dependencies and breaking them down into value-adding services, some of which build on one another, is almost impossible for inexperienced architects to achieve in large projects such as new business areas or extensive transformations. In practice, we know many organisations that fail at precisely this point. Established architects who are used to working classically in their area of expertise reject the decomposition of a large project into an agile backlog as impossible.

This is an attitude that we have a lot of sympathy for; it is a well-known phenomenon in the transformation of established methods to new approaches. The challenge is that an architectural problem or a technical aspect of the project can be solved with the old method and that this solution can be found quickly and without cognitive effort. The old method was developed over many years; when difficulties arose, they were eventually solved, and the solution was internalised as practical knowledge. The advantages of the new method seem to be a long way off, as there is still no experience and solutions for the difficulties that arise.

The impossibility of decomposition in the adaptive sense is usually due to entrenched solution strategies. Instead of thinking in alternatives, a solution idea is often already fixed, which is output-orientated in the classic sense and actually has few points on the development path where the outcome can be tested. The lack of involvement of all stakeholders also means that many aspects of the value stream are not seen by technically orientated architects, for example. In our experience, Managed Services have high value potential outside the "Information and Technology" dimension (see ITIL 4 model of the four dimensions).

On the other hand, in the spirit of co-creation, it is important to utilise and further develop the experience of your own experts. We therefore recommend filling initial roadmaps with small innovative alternatives. For example, possible efficiency increases in existing services, such as the avoidance of waste. Innovative new technologies, such as an automation tool, are also ideal. On the one hand, the permanent staff lack experience with the new platform, and on the other, external experts should be brought in who can contribute agile methods as well as automation expertise.

Frameworks such as Nexus or SAFe contain methods and examples for backlogs and overarching refinement; they are well suited as a guide to action or for building your own structure, which is why we recommend reading them (Scrum.org, 2024) (Scaled Agile, Inc., 2023a, 2023b, 2023c).

**Warning** To be clear, we believe that well-established agile frameworks on the market offer effective methods for certain areas. Trained agile coaches can provide valuable assistance in understanding and practically implementing these methods to underpin our adaptive approach. However, none of the existing frameworks will be able to cover all aspects of adaptive managed services, as many of the agile methods originate from software development. It requires a transformation to extend these to adaptive services. We hope to have outlined the most important service-related framework conditions and differences. If you encounter difficulties with the approach despite the assistance of agile coaches, please feel free to contact us.

The idea of solving the refinement problem through a combination of traditional and agile methods is unsuitable as a strategy; the organisation must learn to use alternatives to increase value. Leveraging value creation potential requires courage, openness, commitment, focus and respect, and the necessary tools must be learnt. This can be achieved in small steps and with good coaches. However, we would like to point out that there are tasks that, even after thorough examination, have no value potential and should simply be implemented.

Take, for example, an attractive new IT service that adds considerable value to your company. Part of the project is the relocation of the server farm to a new data centre, as the old data centre no longer meets the legal requirements. While the new service is developed adaptively, the data centre move can be carried out by an experienced transition team using classic project management. There is nothing wrong with traditional methods if they are used appropriately.

## 5.4 Orientation

If companies develop a practice from the above elements that enables them to establish a value orientation forecast of just over 1.5 years (3 roadmaps) using the Roadmap, Opportunities, Alternatives, and Current Inputs levels, this creates a stronger link to the business values and greater transparency at all levels. As discussed previously, the adaptive approach is well suited to making well-informed decisions based on relative values.

Even if a higher level of understanding is generated at every level, we recommend starting with small alternatives when introducing adaptive managed services. Ideas for increasing efficiency in established business processes are a possible first input that does not overburden the organisation. At the beginning, the number of people involved can also be reduced to one business area in order to better manage communication.

**Example** We found an organisation with an established continual service improvement process that only ever worked when a reduction in waste or an improvement could be implemented by a single delivery team. Improvements that required the involvement of more teams never materialised due to discussions over cost centres. Some of these improvement ideas were smart and had a short RoI.

When management wanted to pilot adaptive managed services, these smart improvement ideas were the perfect starting point. The scope was limited, the costs were reasonable, and two delivery teams formed the core of a cross-functional team.

We strongly advise against introducing adaptive methods from the top down. For example, do not initially deploy them in management staff functions. Such a strategy almost always means that the organisation's ability to learn is limited, which in turn means an increased willingness to persevere. Small successes that are well communicated help to strengthen the demand for adaptive services where most supporters can be found. If an organisation has found its perfect mix of adaptive and highly industrialised services after a few years and is constantly on the lookout for further value potential, it has achieved a great deal.

Your organisation should achieve a certain level of innovation and maintain the corresponding capacities via a service provider or with its own employees. In this way, you can develop a pipeline of innovation roadmaps and build up the necessary methods and skills organisationally. A number of Lean-Agile frameworks are available here, which can also handle very large teams and very extensive roadmaps.

Our method enables the effective use of industrialised managed services in a value-oriented manner, allowing them to be measured in terms of outcome. In our view, this is essential in almost all sectors, as the technical possibilities and changes in managed services are progressing ever faster. Those who do not utilise this in business development are wasting a lot of potential. Even well-done traditional tenders have a minimum term of 3 years, and there is no added value in the transition, only in the transformation. Adopting a purely IT-focused approach is a missed opportunity. In addition, adaptive services and Lean-Agile approaches help organisations to become more efficient and to better understand the potential of their own business.

## References


Ashby, W. R. (1956). *An introduction to cybernetics*. Chapman & Hall.

Beck, K., Beedle, M., van Bennekum, A., & Cockburn, A. (2001). Principles behind the Agile Manifesto. Retrieved July 7, 2025 from https://agilemanifesto.org/principles.html.

Beiderbeck, D., Frevel, N., von der Gracht, H. A., Schmidt, S. L., & Schweitzer M. V. (2021). Preparing, conducting, and analysing Delphi surveys: Cross-disciplinary practices, new directions, and advancements. Retrieved July 7, 2025 from https://www.sciencedirect.com/science/article/pii/S2215016121001941.

Laloux, F. (2014). *Reinventing organizations: A guide to creating organizations inspired by the next stage of human consciousness*. Nelson Parker.

McKenna, D. (2016). *The art of scrum*. Apress.

Niven, P. R., & Lamorte, B. (2016). *Objectives and key results: Driving focus, alignment, and engagement with OKRs*. Wiley.

Reinertsen, D. (2009). *The principles of product development flow: Second generation lean product development*. Celeritas Publishing.

Rogers, E. (2003). *Diffusion of innovations* (5th ed.). Simon and Schuster.

Scaled Agile, Inc (6 Sep 2023a). Epic—scaled agile framework. Retrieved July 7, 2025 from https://scaledagileframework.com/epic/.

Scaled Agile, Inc (9 Oct 2023b). ART and solution train backlogs. Retrieved July 7, 2025 from https://scaledagileframework.com/art-and-solution-train-backlogs/.

Scaled Agile, Inc (9 Oct 2023c). WSJF—scaled agile framework. Retrieved July 7, 2025 from https://scaledagileframework.com/wsjf/.

Scrum.org. (2024). Scaling scrum with nexus. Retrieved July 7, 2025 from https://www.scrum.org/resources/scaling-scrum.

The Open Group. (2022). TOGAF® Standard—introduction—enterprise continuum. Retrieved 7 July 7, 2025 from https://pubs.opengroup.org/togaf-standard/architecture-content/chap06.html.

# 6 Some Practical Illustrations of How This Method Works

At this juncture, we interact with customers and colleagues who either think our vision can be easily realised or who think the opposite. We can already reveal that neither extreme is the case. The challenges involved in implementing a new approach are manifold. The decision to adopt an agile approach is just one of the obstacles that must be overcome when it comes to adaptive service tendering. Others include a lack of knowledge and experience with adaptive methods, often contradictory objectives of the individual organisational units and functions involved, and the selection of a suitable partner for the implementation of such a project.

In addition to the organisational challenges and the lack of experience, however, there are others that we would like to examine in more detail here, namely the resistance of people and organisations to change. Such challenges can be intensified by prejudices, but they can also represent the typical hurdles of organisational change management. All these aspects are examined in this chapter. Following the chapter structure of this book, we start with the roles and functions of those involved in a traditional tender. Then we give tips on how to select a suitable candidate (partner) for the implementation of such a project. Finally, but crucially for the success of such a project, we discuss how to overcome resistance to change on the part of the client.

## 6.1 Personas and Stakeholders

As already mentioned, we will discuss the roles and functions listed in chap. 3 and possible conflicts with and between them. The conflicts listed here do not necessarily have to occur, but we would like to point out the risk so that you can deal with them appropriately and, above all, show understanding for the roles and functions involved in the project. You can only resolve conflicts efficiently if you know what caused them. Ideally, you want to resolve them together. You also want to involve project participants effectively. This way you can ensure the project's success.



G. Köhler et al., *Adaptive IT Service Tendering*, Management for Professionals,
https://doi.org/10.1007/978-3-658-49726-2_6

Conflicts can occur not only on the customer side, but also on the provider side. The stakeholders on both sides should therefore be taken into account. As in chap. 3, we start with the roles and functions on the customer side. In → section 6.1.8 we switch to the perspective of the provider, starting with a sales role.

### 6.1.1 The Management

Management traditionally thinks and acts in time-bound periods. Some periods are quarters. Others are years. In both cases, it is likely that management prefers something that can be planned. This means an end state that is described in detail. It should also be precisely calculated. This is especially the case with regard to the costs incurred. In the case of adaptive service tendering, the project must convince management that one cannot predict the result or status after 6 months, for example. In such a project, what can be successfully realised in the defined time is implemented. After implementation, you look at the remaining issues and decide how to proceed. This can and will slightly change the original project objective.

Management must therefore accept that it is not possible to estimate the total project duration, the exact project costs and the exact project result. At least not in the usual sense of output, i.e. which features and functions will be created in concrete terms. Even estimates of possible hardware or licence costs can be incorrect, as it is not known at the start of the project exactly when these costs will be incurred. This can lead to price fluctuations or other influences such as financing costs, etc. Alternatively, the required scope may change because, without experience, you realise during the project that you need more or less hardware or software than originally planned.

It is possible to estimate either a minimal increase in business value or a range within which business value will develop. Adaptive approaches encourage ambitious targets without restricting where this added value will develop. The people involved are typically the only fixed dimension, meaning an estimate of the core project team's costs over the project's lifetime is secure, as the team will mainly incur labour costs. These costs are usually subject to a certain degree of continuity in such a project. Therefore, it is possible to estimate the elements of a roadmap, their added value and the required resources, albeit in a different form than usual.

> **Important** In our experience, most organisations have established methods for recording, evaluating, and measuring values. As explained in → Sect. 5.3, these can usually also be transferred to adaptive methods. If you also have the option of using new methods, you will find these in the excursus of → Sect. 5.3.3.

The project objective should be agreed with the management, but at a more strategic level, e.g. cost savings, increasing the stability of an IT service or similar. A rough time schedule should also be negotiated. In addition to these two points of the agreement, an estimate of the project costs can also be agreed, but only for the costs of the project team. Costs incurred for project work carried out by the project team can then be estimated and planned accordingly. However, this applies only when they are actually incurred, analogous to the Scrum methodology.

Management involvement is crucial to the success of such a project. A management team that expects a common way of achieving results, where they describe and agree down to the smallest detail and calculate costs precisely, will not contribute to the success of an adaptive service tender, but rather prevent it. It may be necessary to educate management in order to create an understanding of the changed processes. If necessary, the special characteristics of adaptive service tendering should first be clarified as part of a smaller project and the above-mentioned understanding developed. This approach also makes sense for all other roles.

### 6.1.2 The Business Functions as Customers of the Services

With adaptive service tendering, users of the services should be more closely involved, as an incremental approach can be realised in the project. This means that the project process builds on previous stages. The business functions or departments can therefore be involved more or less intensively after each completed project phase, whereby the new and remaining project phases can be adapted and reorganised at any time where appropriate.

The area of responsibility of the business functions can range from coordination as a stakeholder with a product owner, through partial product ownership, to active collaboration in one of the cross-functional teams. Our experience shows that more intensive collaboration has a very positive effect when the business functions start to actively utilise early versions. As soon as a service with minimal added value is used by interested users and this leads to positive changes in their business area, demand arises.

If more and more functions are then added at the suggestion of these early adopters, it can even lead to a pull effect in which more and more business functions that have already utilised existing services want to join in. This is better than any project marketing, increases the visibility and attractiveness of the project and ensures interest and acceptance. If you involve the business functions more closely in the project, you will almost inevitably end up with a final state that optimally supports the business functions and departments at the time of delivery. This is in contrast to the planned support, which may have been conceived one or 2 years previously and not adapted and has now been overtaken by reality.

### 6.1.3 The IT Manager

The IT manager must constantly re-evaluate the individual work packages and subprojects as part of the adaptive service tender once one or more parts have been implemented. At first glance, this may seem like extra work, but it also gives them the opportunity to repeatedly adapt the upcoming work packages and sub-projects to the current situation, just like the business functions. Re-evaluation in an adaptive approach involves the values defined in the opportunities repository as described in → Sect. 5.3.3. This allows them to react flexibly to changing requirements and boundary conditions and thus achieve a more customised end result.

Unlike traditional approaches, they do not need to plan and agree on all work packages and sub-projects in detail at the start of the project. Depending on the stage of the project, a high-level plan in the form of a backlog is sufficient.

### 6.1.4 The Purchasing Department

Particular attention must be paid to purchasing, which, on the one hand, is deprived of the basis for selecting a suitable partner, as there are no comparable offers with regard to the expected project result. On the other hand, the purchasing department will often not be able to achieve its goal of reducing the costs for the product to be procured or the service to be procured, as no price reduction can be achieved from the first offer to the BAFO.

Adaptive service tenders will generally only involve individual hourly rates, in contrast to traditional projects, which often involve a total budget of several million euros. The project (team) should support the purchasing department in agreeing new targets with the management in order to obtain the necessary support and cooperation. A joint meeting with management is often sufficient if they have previously been convinced of the adaptive service tender.

It is possible to set a price for a roadmap. See → section 6.3 for details on different contract possibilities. Nevertheless, fixed or service-based pricing is not recommended if you are new to adaptive services. The risk of undermining the necessary freedom is too high. Some regulated industries require service-based pricing due to legal regulations or company policies. If this applies to you, seek advice from a trained Agile coach. Or perhaps you have contact with a company in your vertical that shares some experiences, which could be useful.

**Example** We had a situation with a customer where the purchasing department claimed that agile methodologies were not permitted due to legal regulations. This presented us with some challenges, most of which turned out to be easily addressable. The key to success in most cases was defining the adaptive framework as the way of working. The adaptive framework controlled all delivery commitments of a traditional transition project and service operation. The most challenging aspect was convincing and subsequently proving that all demands were assigned here.

The final stumbling block was a policy that triggered a new tendering process for a service when its price increased by more than 10%, we were told. This did not look like an issue as we were running an efficiency programme. Lower costs were to be expected. However, upon careful review of the policy, we discovered that it was not about a 10% increase; rather, it was about a 10% deviation. This meant that even an efficiency gain of more than 10% would cause a new tender.

We solved this issue by running some time-and-material projects to achieve the initial efficiency gains, followed by a tender for the new services. Still, this service needs to adhere to the 10% rule. Hopefully, this can be achieved by adding more utility for every percentage point of efficiency gained.

### 6.1.5 The Legal Department (Legal)

An interesting clash of interests occurs when uninformed agile supporters meet uninformed lawyers. In nearly all cases, both parties have had negative experiences with traditional tenders. These include overrun budgets, missing functions, poor quality and services that are not ready on the commencement day. Both parties want to resolve these issues, albeit by different means.

Agile supporters want to change the entire approach, developing value through iterations. This enables them to start early, avoid initial mistakes and control value. Lawyers, on the other hand, tend to work out the details and fix all parameters, milestones and scope so that no deviation is allowed. This restricts all movements from the provider that could have negative consequences.

A Lean-Agile approach recognises the value of deviations. If you want to limit results, time, and resources, an adaptive approach will be ineffective. Even in a traditional managed service tender, focusing on the wrong elements can significantly hinder any positive progress. A common mistake is to fix IT service management processes and procedures. Fixing such operational best practices in a contract means that the contract must be changed whenever the customer wants to improve these processes.

**Warning** We are aware that, at this point, some people may be thinking, "Who cares?" A contract is something that should be filed away and never looked at again. This means that customers expect the provider to change the way they work, despite the regulations in place.

Over a period of months, such actions can render large parts of these contractually stipulated instructions invalid. Consequently, the customer is working against their own legal counsel. In other words, to add details for protection that become impediments themselves makes no sense at all.

It is important to understand why lawyers need to protect their companies. The best approach is to include them in all training sessions and discussions on adaptive work. From our experience, most traditional contracts can be used as templates for adaptive services. The biggest change is replacing the service requirements with a visionary or simplified service scope.

We are not providing legal advice here, merely describing how we have dealt with challenges in such situations. As there are different interpretations of the law, it is up to each company's legal department to decide how to address these challenges.

The most frequently used solution is probably the conclusion of framework agreements in which the general cooperation between client and contractor is regulated. The subsequent project phases can then be commissioned on a time-and-material basis.

### 6.1.6 The Works Council

**Important** This role transformation is viewed from the perspective of the Netherlands, Austria and Germany. Here, the works council has an equal right of co-determination by law. Feel free to skip this section. Nevertheless, our roles are by example—perhaps you have a similar governance role in your organisation?

The works council faces similar or the same challenges as the legal department. In most cases, it will be dealing with the issue of temporary employment. In addition, the works council also has to make decisions or participate in discussions on smaller parts and not directly on the big picture, which can also have a positive effect on the understanding of these relationships.

In the past, some co-determination bodies have developed a very strong focus on specific functionalities. This may also have been the result of a less participatory information policy. In an adaptive approach, the focus should be directed one level higher again. Do the values and alternatives already contain elements that can be discussed and decided at an early stage? This saves work and frustration if the business users enthusiastically want to use a service after an iteration, but general objections only need to be clarified at this very late stage.

Even with the traditional approach, it is unpleasant if fundamental issues need to be clarified shortly before the main release. The difference between the adaptive approach and the development of a service in the waterfall model is the more frequent cycle in the adaptive approach, in which a new increment is presented to stakeholders, including the works council, at least once a month.

### 6.1.7 The Consulting Company

Consultancy firms can also support their clients in these projects. The challenges and conflicts mentioned here need to be resolved, as do the technical challenges that need to be overcome in the project. There are two areas of responsibility for consultants: Firstly, supporting the dynamisation of alternatives, i.e. the generation of roadmaps from the company's framework conditions and the methodology from → chap. 5.

The second area of responsibility is supporting the transfer to a new project organisation, i.e. primarily the application of Lean-Agile methods and organisational change for a sub-organisation. This also includes selecting the right IT service providers to operate and further develop the adaptive service.

The perspective and experience of outsiders can be extremely helpful, especially when preparing such a project, as the company itself probably has little or no experience with such an approach. The consulting company can also help to convince management of this new approach, in line with the colloquial biblical proverb: "In his own country the prophet is worthless".

Finding the right consultants for these areas on the market is quite difficult. Typically, the large consulting firms tend to have a general, not very deep range of expertise and the small boutique consulting firms can only cover partial areas. It is therefore advisable to start with small improvement projects and to bring in experts for the first few projects, who may well come from your own organisation or the provider organisation with whom you are already working successfully and trustingly.

### 6.1.8 Sales

Sales employees of providers are generally rewarded based on the number of contracts concluded. The amount of a sales employee's compensation that is performance-related varies greatly depending on the provider.

In contrast to classic waterfall projects, only a relatively low turnover can be planned for an adaptive service tender, as opposed to a managed service. Therefore, the remuneration of the sales employee will be comparatively low and will only materialise gradually over time if the provider fulfils the customer's requirements. A sales employee must consider future cooperation between the customer and provider, rather than trying to close contracts quickly with high sales turnover. Patience is required here, but this usually pays off, as the trust that can be established between the customer and provider is invaluable in service sales.

**Example** One of our partners transitioned to an agile organisation. We discussed the topic of performance related salary in the sales organisation in depth. All models covering projects and growing volume were dysfunctional. Nowadays, this partner has done away with performance-related pay. This has been replaced by a salary share based on business performance for every employee.

### 6.1.9 Pre-Sales

The spectrum of pre-sales consultants for managed services is very broad on the market today. It ranges from enterprise architects, who focus on the business value and develop suitable service concepts together with the customer, to service designers, whose main focus is on the integration of an existing industrialised IT service into the customer's existing IT landscape.

The transition to value-based adaptive services is probably not a profound one for enterprise architects or industry experts. Nevertheless, some ways of thinking are different in adaptive managed services. There is a difference in thinking in terms of values and visions when previously people thought predominantly in terms of monumental architectures. Above all, people tend to think in terms of specific example projects. This can be a completed major project from the past that seems to fit 80%. However, if you work with this reference in mind, the result cannot be adaptive. It becomes a copy of the large-scale project, i.e. people do not work on values across the board, but rather look for freedom in the details.

Pre-sales consultants who have sold ready-made IT services as a kind of product in the past will have some difficulty in making the transition. In the past, they have probably successfully tried to convince the customer that a particular service package they have put together somehow meets the customer's requirements. Even if not optimal, it was still suitable for the customer with minor compromises. At least that was the strategy and hope in consulting. This strategy is a hindrance with adaptive services, as it complicates the view of business value.

A combination of these areas of knowledge in pre-sales makes perfect sense in terms of cross-functional teams. Consultants who have advised on industrialised services in the past can help to find the right mix of innovative and industrialised services in adaptive managed services. This is very much in the spirit of the highly innovative services discussed in → chap. 5.

### 6.1.10 Transition and Transformation Team of the Provider

In a fully adaptive organisation, there would no longer be dedicated transition and transformation projects, as everything would be developed in an adaptive way. The focus of an organisational unit designed to support transformation would be on "change and adoption". This means promoting the use of the new possibilities during ongoing operations, providing support, building topic-specific specialist communities and establishing a feedback culture.

The future of transition and transformation mentioned above is rather abstract, as Adaptive Managed Services are developed by sub-organisations, at least in large organisations. This leaves room for the implementation of these projects analogue to the classic T&T approach, but in many small projects that are much less complex and therefore less prone to errors and easier to implement.

Note that cross-functional collaboration was involved in creating the project. Including people in the creative process greatly increases acceptance. Depending on the nature of the sub-organisation and the type of project, the focus will be on methods that are more geared towards the transition to new possibilities. Switching from the old to the new service, as is usual with classic managed services, will tend to be the exception with adaptive services.

**Important** The roles in this book are exemplary. In the previous section, we presented some examples of how roles change. As you can see, some roles evolve in terms of their views and scope, while others undergo a fundamental shift in their core function. You should not try to change this overnight, because there would be too much resistance. This is one of the reasons why we prefer to start small and transform the organisation from the bottom up. It's possible that, within your organisation, adaptive methods are just one of many tools in the toolkit. This means that people have an adaptive mode of operation in a traditional setting.

In any case, adaptive ways of working are a change of culture. This is true even if it is part time only. Our advice is to work with volunteers wherever possible in the initial projects and to prepare a communication plan. We hope you can use our example roles to define the changes and communication needs of each role.

## 6.2 Practical Everyday Procedure Model

The adaptive architecture model presented in → chap. 5 was deliberately designed without compromising an agile culture. The reason for this is that it makes it easier to assess whether only partial use in a customer project is suitable for supporting agile value development. It is also possible to assess the potential of a next project at any time to see whether it makes sense to go even further in the direction of Lean-Agile. Perhaps an organisation has found the right level of agility for itself, perhaps it still has an appetite for more.

The following pages outline a hybrid approach suitable for beginners that can be expanded to a large extent. Once an organisation has fully transitioned to a Lean-Agile operating model, the control and governance mechanisms presented here are transferred to this system. The time periods and processes selected are for illustration only. If a greater degree of customisation is required, we recommend consulting an agile coach for the first few projects. Such advice can help avoid beginner mistakes that could otherwise lead to serious reservations about the whole project.

**Important** Unfortunately, "coach" is not a protected job title, but "agile coach" has been an established term for years. It mainly refers to trainers and consultants for agile methods in software development.

As Lean-Agile has now also found its way into other areas of the company, there are agile coaches in fields other than software development. These consultants specialise in adapting Lean-Agile methods to processes, working methods, and organisations. You should therefore rely on agile coaches with such expertise.

### 6.2.1 Hybrid Agile Managed Services

This approach is based on IT operations procuring several managed services from an internal or external provider. The idea is to improve one or a few services at a time in order to increase their value. The operations team maintains a certain extra capacity to facilitate such increases. Depending on the level of technical debt or the need for innovation, we initially assume a range of 10–20%. Eliminating technical debt and maintaining innovation speed are necessary further developments for an organisation.

Technical debt can also accumulate over time in services that are typical of the industry. This is particularly likely if additional services or interfaces are added, or if original services are extended in a decentralised manner, without a central architecture instance. It can even reach the point where components that are no longer supported by the manufacturer must still be used because the resulting dependencies have not been resolved. This effect is common in IT organisations that are regularly denied the budget to eliminate such technical debt. It also occurs in IT organisations whose silos are funded to such an extent that central adjustments are dispensed with in favour of investing in the silo.

The need for innovation relates more to the core business or the central business areas. This includes not only products and services, but also all business processes from ordering to delivery. Here too, an innovation backlog, a lack of innovative strength or excessive internal regulations and dependencies may have led to a standstill. Increased external competition may also necessitate an increase in innovative strength. New business areas or start-ups are further examples of areas with a high pace of innovation.

If a company finds itself in the position of having to deal with a high technical debt or a massive need for innovation at short notice, adaptive methods can be an important element. In this presentation, we will first consider a situation with no particular scope or urgency. Although the following introduction can also be used in crisis situations, we recommend seeking the support of consultants in this case to increase speed and reduce novice errors.

Here, we assume a personnel capacity of 10% to 20%, which is to be deployed in the current roadmap for the transformation of services, increasing efficiency, replacing technologies or architecture alternatives. These employees come from Operations and usually make up the lion's share of cross-functional teams. Adaptive services are best started with small projects on existing services. Larger transformations are not described in this section, but can be implemented as an additional agile or traditional programme.

It is important that the team members have daily experience with the operation, the technologies, the users and the customers of the service. This experience and the personal network of contacts are essential. The employees must be fully involved, even if the legal framework conditions lead to additional work here. The capacities maintained in the company must actually be considered flexible; it is a matter of focussing on the services they provide together with the people.

If a service has been improved in one roadmap and the next roadmap focuses on a different service, the team typically changes. A fixed innovation team is not a viable option. Agile management and leadership can be left to the same product owners, Scrum Masters, etc., but cannot be consolidated by transferring large parts of the cross-functional team to the new roadmap.

**Important** DevOps would of course fit in perfectly with this approach, but commodity managed services in particular are typically provided by IT operations teams organised in a traditional manner. DevOps does not usually add much value here. If DevOps is already being used in certain, typically highly innovative parts of service delivery, some methods and organisational practices can certainly be adopted. We are primarily referring to a mode where operations teams are supported to innovate their service over a manageable period of time and then return to operations mode.

### 6.2.2 Defrosting, Value Enhancement, Freezing

The adaptive approach is only worthwhile if it is expected to generate profitable added value. Furthermore, we assume that a service has a high value contribution and that there are viable alternatives. This means that the service in question is planned for one of the upcoming roadmaps. We focus on an average case, as extremes involving very large or very small improvements would lead to special handling that might cause misunderstandings. Adaptive services do not require continuous large-scale improvement. Smaller improvements in the sense of continuous improvements can be established, as in traditional IT service management.

An industry-typical managed service should be optimised, automated and, if necessary, operated with established KPIs over time. This efficiency also goes hand in hand with a certain degree of familiarity or inflexibility, which is why the metaphor "frozen" is quite appropriate for industrialised services. However, changes to the outcome usually lead to more extensive changes to a service. This applies not only to technologies, but to all aspects of a managed service, organisation, knowledge, partnerships, licensing models, etc. It can therefore be assumed that a service must first be "defrosted" at the start of a roadmap.

A "defrosted" service goes into individualised operation for a certain period of time. During the upcoming conversion work, some automation must be switched off. The documentation and, for example, the solution scripts for the service desk change continuously. Some planned reductions in service quality may occur during the work. As part of the roadmap, the service will be transformed iteratively and transferred back to industrialised operation once a certain level of added value has been achieved. With optimum performance, documentation, support capability, automation, etc., this modernised service can now be "frozen" again.

The "defrosting—value enhancement—freezing phases" do not have to take place within a roadmap of 6 months. If a large increase in value is still expected towards the end of the roadmap, the state of individualised operation can still be carried over into the next roadmap. However, this should be the exception. In our experience, the 6-month period is rarely reached. Start with manageable, value-adding transformations in order to develop a feel for this rhythm. Do not optimise the selected service excessively. If significant added value has been developed, it is often worth finalising the roadmap and focusing on the next service.

**Important** When we talk about the reorganisation of a service and the associated disruptions, we have often heard the question of why the existing service should not be operated in parallel and then the new service put into operation smoothly on a switchover date. This method would be one option and is the standard version in the traditional transformation. Once the new service has been finalised, all users will be migrated to it on a given date.

In such a scenario, an adaptive approach would lack an important element. An adaptive approach is value-oriented, involving all stakeholders. When redesigning a widely used service, for example, this approach is particularly successful, as direct feedback can be obtained from many participants.

Of course, great importance is also attached to the quality and benefits of the existing service in an adaptive mode. For example, a new function may be hidden in the live system. Assuming it represents high added value, people will use it more and more.

In contrast to a service reorganisation, a service developed in parallel requires assigned users. Consequently, a service developed in parallel requires a transformation in the organisation. The existing service is deactivated and the users are migrated to the new service. The development itself can therefore only be accompanied by a small group of users. A traditional proof of concept with a few selected users is no longer sufficient, at the latest shortly before the end of the roadmap.

### 6.2.3 Evaluate and Release

Our methodology provides a solid foundation for making informed decisions regarding the anticipated increase in business value and other key company metrics. The definite implementation within a roadmap should be evaluated and approved by a committee. The same body that approves the roadmap and thus the change activities must also have the decision-making authority for evaluating the outcome. We refer to this as the Innovation Board below. Depending on the organisation, it may be preferable to use existing committees that already cover a similar scope. These committees or boards may already have an established name. Provided the scope, duration, and decisiveness are appropriate, keeping the original name is not an issue.

**Warning** One of the principles of Lean-Agile is to involve everyone. This does not mean that everyone should be a contributor to every committee. Rather, it means that everyone involved should be able to easily participate in the improvement and innovation process. In Lean-Agile organisations, committee membership is more diverse and fluctuates depending on the current focus. Be careful when choosing an existing committee; in traditional organisations, members are often chosen by position in the hierarchy. Ensure that business functions and users are represented in such committees.

It is crucial to manage not only the development of the technology and services, but also the resulting business value. As this may only be meaningfully measured months after completion of the service, it is important to establish a control level in this committee that keeps an eye on various aspects and their historical development and learns from them. These can be classic parameters of portfolio management or programme management. However, the focus of an innovation board should initially be on agile values, which lie in particular in the development of the organisation and responsibility for corporate values.

An innovation board should be made up of a broad cross-section of stakeholders. This should range from the management to the business functions and users through to the IT organisation, including the partners. A core of representatives should ensure the success of the innovation cycles over a longer period of time. Depending on the size of the organisation, additional representatives can be brought in for the roadmaps that are currently pending. It may also make sense to bring in experienced consultants who have already carried out similar innovation projects on a case-by-case basis.

The way in which the decision-making process takes place can be derived from the company's previous approach. If business, portfolio, and technology were largely separated or cascaded in the past, this separation must now be broken. The

Innovation Board must conduct the discussion cross-functionally. The actual decisions may also be organised hierarchically.

**Important** In the first instance, appoint a moderator to ensure that the discussion remains focused on the values and the desired outcome. Such an overarching innovation board typically consists of up to 20 people. There are a lot of stakeholders. The method is still unfamiliar. It is to be expected that the discussion will fall back into the old pattern of budget and output. This will happen without such moderation. Through such moderation, the key points of the discussion and the decision-making process can be mapped out in advance.

The release of interim results can be of a different nature. An important question here is the extent to which a new adaptive model co-operates with existing release processes, e.g. a Change Advisory Board (CAB). Today, enabling change should also be priority in traditional IT service management.

It is important to integrate existing processes and committees, but not to lose the freedom to develop innovations. In the "defrosting" of services for changes in a roadmap, defined standard changes or at least change models could be used to define frameworks in which a CAB only needs to be informed. The most important representatives for the service are represented on the release committee anyway.

If the service is not business critical, e.g. a sales information portal receiving new functionality in a technically secure area, informing a CAB during interactions is perfectly legitimate, a more formal release can possibly be made at freeze time. For changes that affect more critical services, one would try to establish new functionality in the background, as with DevOps, but if the releases affect or could affect core functionality, stricter approvals may be considered.

After a few roadmaps, when the organisation has gained experience with adaptive services, try to integrate existing bodies such as the CAB into the process. Representatives who normally inform and make decisions in the CAB can take on a similar role with stakeholders or even in the cross-functional team.

**Important** Some organisations have created structures in which committees meet once a month in a large group to decide on and approve certain points. Sometimes such structures are very firmly anchored in people's minds and the prevailing opinion is that such established structures have to be like this. This is not the case; the integration of control and governance into a Lean-Agile model is compatible with the standard IT service management frameworks. Be sure to involve these committees constructively and, if necessary, obtain an external perspective so that adaptive methods do not fail due to resistance from such committees.

### 6.2.4 Roadmap

Following successful approval, a 6-month roadmap is usually defined. An adaptive roadmap is not the same as traditional roadmap planning, which involves scheduling activities for individual months. Instead, the roadmap should be developed using iterative agile methods, such as Scrum. The selected alternatives should represent ambitious business values and be included as a backlog broken down by value creation.

An expert team and the operations team now form a cross-functional team and create exploratory values in iterations, e.g. 6 x 30 days. At the end of each iteration, a release-ready increment must be created, which is evaluated in a review. If there is still value potential, this period is extended by a further 6 months. If the potential decreases, the service is trimmed for efficiency in the last iteration at the latest, automated and converted back into a managed service. The cross-functional team will be dissolved once this freezing has been finalised.

With a little experience, the 6-month rhythm of the roadmaps can be maintained. A service that still has value potential beyond its last roadmap can be finalised in parallel with a roadmap for a new service. The basic cycle of 6 months is retained, but some innovation projects are completed in parallel with a new roadmap with a new team and a different service.

Depending on the organisation, alternatives such as a large backlog and roadmaps of different lengths can also be used. In the area of managed services, we usually talk about different technical and operational teams. These teams actually return to their operational processes once an innovation has been completed. There is no centralised agile development team. Therefore, different alternatives in a backlog cannot be freely distributed to existing cross-functional teams. For this reason, we do not recommend this approach unless it is already established in the organisation, e.g. through development teams (Fig. 6.1).

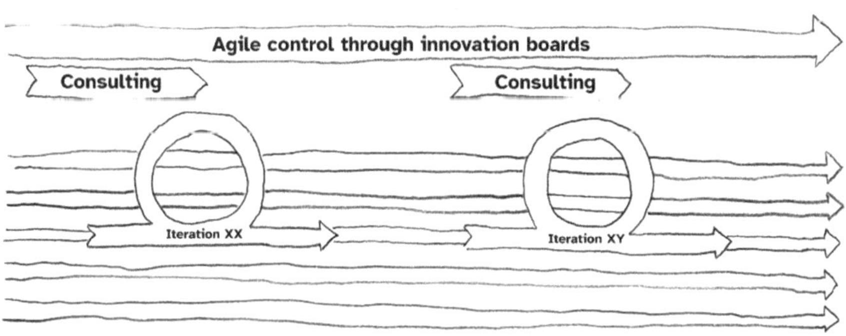


**Fig. 6.1** Agile control using innovation boards

**Important** Don't make the mistake of leaving parts of the business and operations team out of the cross-functional setup. A typical pitfall is the traditional separation between business users, the operations team and developers or integrators. Focusing on the most important values is only possible if almost all representatives who can measure the value of a service are also active participants. The roles in the cross-functional team must also be found through self-organisation. A typical mistake is that some organisations bring in existing roles or push specialist users into downstream tasks such as documentation or quality assurance. Use a tried-and-tested methodology such as Scrum or SAFe at the beginning. Only change these once you have fully mastered them and understood all aspects.

### 6.2.5 Splitting Tasks and Time

The idea of using specialist and operational teams for the further development of services or the creation of innovative services hardly seems possible in many organisations. The key people in particular seem to be indispensable; they are needed in day-to-day business. That is one part of the truth. An adaptive approach requires capacities. However, the additional work required by the adaptive approach is also demanded of employees in the traditional approach. However, the collaboration is no longer invested in the conceptualisation of innovations or further development of the service, but rather directly in development.

As described above, organisations should strive for a certain level of innovation capability and then invest this in their own employees or service providers. Many companies with historically grown organisations have created a structure in which employees have filled their roles with work, in most cases with meaningful work. These organisations tend to quickly integrate new capacities into the day-to-day business. In such a scenario, it is advisable to develop the organisation in parallel with adaptive services. This can be part of an alternative. Adaptive services involve people and social systems.

**Example** We helped a customer in a crisis situation. The current IT setup had historically evolved, resulting in numerous major incidents, stalled projects and a failure to innovate for years. Meanwhile, the core business was not even at the minimum industry standard.

IT was structured into business unit silos, with an umbrella organisation on top. When we analysed the current situation together with the customer, we found the most surprising fact. The number of IT personnel in a business unit correlated with the age of the business unit. Not in relation to the magnitude of the personnel or the intricacy of the IoT in the production; rather, it is a matter of its longevity.

When things became obvious, IT management became angry because the initial picture was: In a young business unit, 5 IT people did the work of 10, compared to an old business unit. However, a reality check showed that those 10 IT people performed valuable tasks. There were significant variations in the scope and quality of IT services and support across the different business units.

This customer was the kind of organisation where people found valuable work for themselves, and management was happy as long as no one complained. There is no control over whether this leads to an efficient, business-related setup.

Time should definitely be scheduled in the roadmap for a certain amount of time per week. This protects day-to-day business and makes sense when dealing with an existing provider. For example, let's assume that two days a week are used for cross-functional collaboration. On these two days, joint work takes place, such as the refinement of the backlog, but there should also be coordination of activities for the remaining three days.

Team members should also work on the roadmap on other days; this applies in particular to employees of a provider who may be able to provide more capacity. The separation into a defined cross-functional working time and a working time determined by the organisation helps to integrate agile working into existing organisations. If the path to an agile organisation is desired, the proportion of cross-functional work can be gradually increased.

In particular, labour law or organisational regulations such as authority to issue instructions, leave approvals, time management and training can be safeguarded by a part-time arrangement. These aspects must be very clearly regulated, especially when working with external employees. The development and coordination of tasks in a cross-functional team, on the one hand, and the execution of tasks in the respective company context, on the other, can be very well coordinated. A Kanban board can be used for tracking, where each party uses its own colour for marking, or of course a similar concept in a digital ticket system (Fig. 6.2).

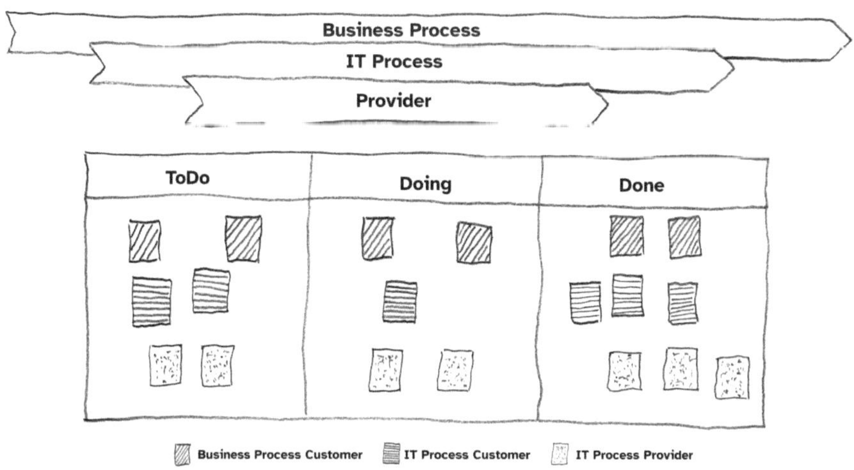


**Fig. 6.2** Colour-coded task assignments on a Kanban board

Every organisation has key employees who are go-to people, meaning they know how to handle all issues. These are prominent employees who can be relied upon to solve any problem. It is better not to send these key employees from the specialist or operational organisation to the cross-functional teams. These can be utilised much more effectively as stakeholders in the reviews. The decision to select good employees, but not key employees, for the agile teams reduces the risk of typical management override. In hierarchical organisations, it is common practice to reassign employees from cross-functional teams to work on other projects. Such external intervention undermines any level of self-organisation, including the simplest team decisions. This can lead to considerable disadvantages for an adaptive approach and should therefore be avoided at all costs.

## 6.3 Regulations for Cooperation

In the conventional managed service, the utility and warranty are defined once and set out in a service level agreement. In the traditional world, deviations from the norm tend to be avoided and contractually hedged as a potential risk. In an adaptive service, deviations are utilised positively in order to generate added value potential. This is a key distinction that needs to be examined.

**Important** Adaptive services change the culture of collaboration, which is why it is important to involve non-technical stakeholders such as the purchasing or legal department in training courses on agile methods. The parties involved can only develop an understanding of the necessary safety precautions versus the necessary freedoms if they have all been informed about agile working and its values in advance in a training course and exchange information about it.

Another difference lies in the most detailed definition possible, which in the traditional world often also includes the operational processes, the "how" of the service. This usually results from the customer organisation's desire to be particularly secure, as bad experiences have been made in the past with delivery gaps, unprofessional delivery or similar.

On the other hand, agile methods in software development were devised to counteract precisely these bad experiences with unusable software, massive delivery delays and the like. This is the second important distinction that needs to be actively changed in the rules of cooperation between service provider and customer.

All parties should always make a clear distinction between the positive aspects of the collaboration and the need to protect their own organisation. Both internal and external service providers strive to create value that helps the consumers of the service to improve in the provision of services, etc. However, a contract should also protect the organisations involved. It should regulate responsibilities, avoid cost increases, define compensation, etc. Representatives from both sides should discuss their respective goals, develop an understanding and work together to find good solutions for operations and contracts.

In the following, we would like to discuss some ideas on what the cornerstones of adaptive service contracts could be. These ideas come from the perspective of an agile organisation looking to create new value. They can use these ideas to discuss with their legal department a concept that works for them. It will become apparent that many basic concepts come from an existing IT organisation and its evolved culture. These concepts can evolve over time. We believe that it is neither necessary nor expedient to have a uniform concept for all organisations.

**Warning** Contracts typically become stiffer and more complicated at points where the legal department has had negative experiences in the past. Furthermore, knowledge of gaps and issues in managed service contracts is shared within the industry. This results in discussions and the integration of additional topics or details that lawyers would like to see in the contract.

This approach is perfectly understandable and supports the organisation's need for protection. Even in conventional managed services, those additions and details could go wrong when they are literally copied out of other contexts. This often means that operational functions lose the flexibility they need, or that paragraphs that do not fit tend to cause misunderstandings. Turning to adaptive managed services using historical wordings could amplify this harm.

We recommend outlining the main value chains of the new contract. Taking into account past negative experiences, take the legal text seriously and summarise cause and effect. Transform the scope and protection to fit the planned setup. Do the same with sample contracts from the industry and analyse whether the protection offered fits the purpose. Ask the legal department to shift their focus to agile contracts in the industry. In the beginning, a mix of conventional and agile contracts is a good knowledge pool.

**Example** A few years ago, it became popular to include clauses that protect intellectual property creation. The idea was that, whenever a customer and a provider developed something together, the IP rights would stay with the customer. The clauses presented by the lawyer were all encompassing, including the transfer of all rights to the customer. These legal constraints might be appropriate in a time-and-materials contract, where a provider develops a solution for a customer.

We asked the customer if he was aware that this clause meant a provider would no longer openly invest in existing IP for the service. For example, continual improvement identified a gap that could be filled with some clever scripts and automation. Fortunately, the provider had encountered a similar situation with another tenant and could reuse some of the scripts. This meant that the gap could be closed quickly and inexpensively by experienced engineers.

The IP clause initially presented would give the customer all the rights. The provider would no longer be permitted to use this solution for their previous tenant. All tools utilised would also be the IP of the customer. Clearly, this clause was not designed for managed services, where most tools are industry products.

We seized the opportunity to ensure that IP protection was adequate. The scope was expanded to encompass all the processes and tools that the customer required. We made sure that, in the event of a change of provider, the transfer would be smooth. However, this did not involve simply giving the customer all IP rights to whatever was developed.

Our focus was on ensuring the proper licensing of procedures, code, and tools. For instance, the provider offered to automate tasks free of charge, thereby enhancing efficiency. The contract included a clause that, whenever it ends, ensures that all knowledge, scripts, and the automation platform can be transferred to the customer at a reasonable cost. Furthermore, the customer had a pre-emptive right on all cooperatively developed code and documents.

### 6.3.1 Traditional Managed Service Contracts

The question of contractual protection quickly arose in the early days of our approach. Consequently, we conducted a survey of long-standing agile organisations and were surprised to find that most of them use traditional managed service contracts. While all respondents found the contracts to be unsatisfactory, they did acknowledge their overall fit for purpose.

The basic concepts of such a contract can work for agile services. Especially if the contract is reviewed at the end of each roadmap and the current benefits and guarantees of the updated service are set out in writing. In practice, we all too often see that contracts are hopelessly outdated and have also lost much of their protective function in the traditional sense. Adaptive services can perhaps also bring about a change in attitude here. It is a matter of cross-functional maintenance of an important protective function, instead of many stakeholders being happy not having to get the contract out of the drawer.

If a managed service contract is used, they pay attention to this:

- Do not include detailed operating models or technologies for services in the contract. While this also applies to conventional managed services, it is counterproductive to an adaptive approach. If such details are still required, they should be included in supplementary documents, which can be amended more easily during the contract period.
- SLA targets that are too specific can hinder innovation. If services are changed for the benefit of all, existing SLA targets may even prevent improvements. It is recommended to describe the intended purpose of the SLA targets in significant detail, or even in the form of a cascade. This allows low SLA targets to be cancelled by mutual agreement and replaced with better ones that fit the purpose.

The superior-level SLA in the cascade ensures compliance with contractual demands.

- Innovation clauses that focus only on cost reduction should be complemented by values with multiple dimensions, such as a balanced triangle of scope, quality, and cost. Another option would be to combine innovation clauses with value streams.
- Benchmark clauses must take into account changes in scope that occur during the lifetime of the service.

**Important** If there is a massive interest in including the service processes in the contract nonetheless, it can alternatively be suggested that the above practical day-to-day procedure model be integrated into the contract. This is the core of the new collaboration and contains many aspects to be protected, but does not define a rigid way of working.

**Warning** Stakeholders who are committed to providing the best possible service every day sometimes avoid discussing contract terms suggested by legal departments. At least, they tend to cut corners in the negotiation process. They avoid speaking about what could go wrong. Emotionally, they think that if something goes wrong, they will fix it and that they do not need a contract for this. This is an absolutely healthy attitude. In a trusting relationship, all players work together to resolve major and minor issues. That's not what contracts are used for.

We always try to convince those fine project management and operational people to work on a contract by explaining the function of the various elements of the contract. We also use examples of situations when we needed the contract to resolve issues. In all of those situations, it was better to agree on responsibilities before the contract was required. It's better to prepare for the rain while the sun is shining.

Some people still argue that there is no need to prepare for bad times because a good relationship will never break down, for example because a B2B relationship has existed for more than 20 years. It is brilliant to have such customers, who will happily support contract negotiations. However, beware that even strong business relationships can be broken by foolish people at short notice. Market disruptions, joint ventures or downsizing can also cause contracts and volumes to become a burden. That is why we need to prepare for such situations. The better they are understood at all levels, the easier those extraordinary situations can be handled.

In the following paragraphs, we will share some practical concepts relating to contracts. While we do not provide legal advice, we would like to share the basic structure of contracts suitable for adaptive IT services. We are confident that your legal department will understand the concepts and use them to design a contract for your adaptive setup.

### 6.3.2 Roadmap Wave Concept

Contracts often establish initial trust, particularly with new customers or service providers when you are inexperienced and require robust protection. An ideal approach here is to take a step-by-step, layered approach. For example, the services resulting from individual roadmaps are agreed in a compact contract that matches a framework agreement.

Such a concept:

- Is close to the existing contract concepts.
- Is conditional that the waves are designed in such a way that the value is defined and secured before the contract for the operating phase is signed.
- Is comparable to classic pre-sales projects, i.e. planned in advance and then a contract is concluded to match the scope.
- Includes the fact that the risk of value creation typically lies with the service provider.
- Has the disadvantage that if the service provider loses interest, the means of creating value no longer exists.
- Is a compromise between a classic 36-month full-scale operation and a genuine agile operation.
- Is not suitable for medium and large-scale transformations that have a longer planning horizon. However, short contract periods (waves) at the beginning can build trust and measure performance. Once trust has been established, subsequent waves can cover longer and longer periods.
- Particularly recommended for getting started with adaptive services, as it is based on familiar methods. Later on, it makes sense to switch to a more innovative contract model.

### 6.3.3 Time and Material

Agile collaboration comes from the world of programming projects and the basis of collaboration is often "time and material". The customer pays at the end of the month according to the time spent by the employees involved. Such a concept can only be applied to a service to a limited extent. However, such a construct can be suitable for setting up a new, innovative service, especially if the operating concept still needs to be developed.

Such a concept:

- Is based on standard professional services contracts, whereby ensuring the availability of resources should be dealt with in more detail. This is often not sufficient for a service operation and its management.
- Requires that platform and operational issues are dealt with separately. For example, the platform could be agreed as a separate service contract.

- Includes the fact that value creation is synchronised on behalf of the customer. This means that the risk of value creation typically lies with the customer. This works best when the values of the main business can be clearly described in IT values.
- Needs a solid relationship and only works if both sides benefit.
- Requires a high degree of transparency from both sides.
- Requires sophisticated IT and IT service management.

A well-known modification of "time-and materials" contracts, originating from agile programming projects, makes it easier to estimate time and resources. This involves evaluating the team's performance in relation to a certain scope, e.g. after 3 months. Based on the key figures, a rough concept is developed that includes the scope, the potential added value and the expected efficiency. The resources required for this are calculated accordingly so that the customer pays a fixed monthly fee.

If the value is not achieved in the estimated time, the supplier offers additional resources at a reduced price. If the value is achieved earlier than planned or is no longer required because the outcome cannot be achieved, both agree on additional alternatives for the utilisation of the team.

### 6.3.4 Hybrid Model

A combination of the concepts presented seems to us to be the most expedient option. If a service provider is commissioned for several managed services, a certain amount of development capacity can be added to this contract. The amount of this capacity depends on the innovation potential and technical responsibility and can be between 15% and 60%. In this way, the resources for an innovation roadmap are secured within a predefined framework.

Such a concept:

- Is a combination of a managed service contract and a predefined personnel service.
- Requires a certain number of robust services that are not easily affected by significant changes.
- Includes the necessary control and operation of frozen and innovative services.
- Has a conceptually secure, but also limited potential for value appreciation, so the scope and distribution should be updated regularly, approximately annually.
- Is suitable for most cost centre structures.
- Requires a solid relationship and a high degree of transparency on both sides.
- Requires continuous further development of IT management and IT service management.

### 6.3.5 Transformations

One of the most frequent responses to the above section is: "What if the company has to manage a major transformation at short notice?" This is something that traditional services and their contracts do not cover per se. Today's standard managed service contracts often address an increase in efficiency within the service, for example through internal improvements at the service provider. Depending on the service, these are often in the range of 3% to 8% per year. Adaptive models should realise a significantly higher value potential here, which should be at least 15% in the long term. Nevertheless, the adaptive model outlined in chap. 6 does not primarily focus on disruptive changes.

Significant changes to enhance the core business often necessitate transformation programmes that are intentionally planned and equipped with additional resources and funding. These usually have an impact on existing services. In principle, adaptive and traditional models can take a similar approach here. The planning and integration of these disruptive changes is likely to be simpler and more integrative with adaptive models, depending on how much experience the organisation has already gained with them or what level of maturity it has already reached with regard to the adaptive model.

Massive external changes that are unsolicited and have a significant impact on the customer's business in a short space of time usually need to be regulated by a pragmatic partnership agreement. In practice, this works very well in traditional models if the relationship is a win-win relationship. However, there are also business relationships in the traditional environment that are not designed for mutual value creation. In this case, problems are inevitable. Adaptive services only work anyway if the relationship is designed for a win-win situation.

**Example** One of our customers was facing a serious technical debt crisis. The products in operation were extremely outdated. Almost all the software and hardware were covered by extended maintenance contracts or had even exceeded them. The reason for this was organisational, that is to say, human issues. This customer operated within a highly regulated vertical sector. Once these issues became visible to the governance body, there was very little time to resolve them.

Nearly all of the customer's IT was being operated by him. Some time was lost due to management changes. The outdated technical architecture was so old that it was not possible to replace it with a modern version of the products in use. So, at one point, the favoured solution was to outsource all the faulty parts.

Then again, time was wasted finding consulting and support for a traditional tender. This became impossible because there was so little time left. Even an instant start to a traditional service transformation would not have been able to cover all the parts that were to be outsourced. We explained our view of the situation and suggested an adaptive approach. The Opportunity Repository's highest value was the impact on legal policies. Therefore, we were able to safeguard the timeline with the adaptive approach presented here.

In essence, our framework is not designed for large transformations, but, as with any set of methods, it can be adapted for large transformational projects.

## 6.4 Choosing a Provider

As previously mentioned, the adaptive service tender lacks a comparable range of services and desired results based on requirements, making it difficult to make a sound decision. However, experience shows that the ability to make a clear and comprehensible decision does not necessarily mean that it is a good one. The value of future states depends on more than requirements and delivery promises.

Therefore, you must choose a partner who can provide the expected services in line with the functional and non-functional requirements. In our experience, there are several ways to achieve this. We will discuss two of these options in more detail below. Trust and the nature of the partnership between client and contractor are crucial to the success of a project in the service sector. Without trust, it is extremely difficult to carry out projects successfully in the service sector that also satisfy everyone involved. Successful projects in the service sector always involve a win-win situation for everyone involved. As soon as these two foundations—trust and a win-win situation—are absent, cooperation will always be difficult.

**Important** The idea that both sides must trust each other does not mean that this is an inherent assumption. Trust must be earned and maintained by both parties throughout the collaboration! The topic of trust will also play a role in the following chapter, "Penalisation of Services".

### 6.4.1 The RFI

An RFI is one way to confirm or demonstrate the provider's performance and innovative ability. This can then be underpinned by references from other customers. However, you need to keep your own expectations in mind when it comes to references. In most cases, references from other customers of the provider will not really be comparable. This may be because, for example, the requirements and possibly also the expectations of other customers of the provider differ from your own. One customer wants a very favourable price, another a very high quality or the customer has very high requirements in terms of the complexity of the service he wants to obtain from a provider.

The same service can be designed and provided in very different ways as a result of all of this. In most cases, a reference therefore only provides a statement as to whether the provider has general experience in providing the service, but not as to whether the performance of this service will also meet the requirements of the requesting customer. This is where a discussion with the provider's customers comes in handy. In these discussions, you should be clear about your own basic expectations. Asking whether the agreed SLAs will always be met is not very helpful if the service does not correspond exactly to what you would like to receive. We think it makes more sense to ask about flexibility and the way in which the customer and provider work together. It is also very important that the provider regularly provides information about possible innovations and offers these.

**Example** One of our customers, whom we will call A, was very unhappy with an IT service management application from a well-established vendor. The redesigned application came with a lot of bugs. The customer's organisation encountered serious issues when transferring to the new platform. Whenever they asked their appointed partner about a bug and its resolution timeframe, they received a vague answer after weeks of silence. This caused huge frustration and an urge to change the software platform.

When they met another customer from the same industry—let's call him Customer B—they could not understand his frustration. Customer A was trying to circumvent a specific bug. When Customer B heard this, they replied, "Oh, you should simply wait. This bug will be fixed in an emergency release next month. We told the vendor we needed it urgently".

The reason was simply that B was receiving direct support from the vendor due to a specific beta software module that he was using. Customer A was obliged to contact the vendor through a local partner. A simple difference in a technical parameter turned customer A into an unhappy client, whereas customer B was a good reference. There were bugs, but they were under control and the relationship was good.

### 6.4.2 Dual-Provider Strategy

An alternative option would be to commence with two providers and then determine, within the initial weeks of the collaboration, which provider you would prefer to continue working with.

In most cases, you will also need a foundation on which to base your decision, which you can then use to justify your choice of provider, or your decision not to work with the other provider. This foundation should also be documented for future reference. This is especially important with regard to legal requirements and to exclude personal advantages. This selection process is particularly impractical for public clients.

## 6.5 Organisational Change Management

Why is Organisational Change Management so important that it is explicitly mentioned here again?

Because it has a major impact on the success or failure of a project. It does not matter whether it is an agile project or a traditional waterfall project, e.g. according to PRINCE2. In Chap. 2, we already referred to the principle of "culture eats strategy for breakfast", which is attributed to the economist Peter Drucker. With good organisational change management, a project can prevent its strategy (however good it may be) from being "eaten", i.e. from failing because of the culture.

**Important** History from the perspective of the employee
As an example, we would like to cite a very big change from our own past. It involved outsourcing part of a large insurance company's IT to an IT service provider. Of course, nobody in the client's team was enthusiastic about being outsourced, to put it mildly. The project manager of the IT service provider we were to switch to went through with his plan and proved to be a know-it-all when it came to clarifying issues.

For example, those of us affected could not understand why we were no longer allowed to help our closest colleagues if they had not first opened a corresponding ticket on the hotline. Why our way of working, which we had developed over the years, absolutely had to be changed. The transformation gave the impression that almost all of the working methods of the past were wrong. After these explanations, you can imagine that the motivation to change was practically non-existent.

But it got even worse! The employees formed groups and developed strategies as to why the new working methods might not work. All new ways of working were generally dismissed as "rubbish". The way in which the employees facing the change were treated was so inadequate that they tended to sabotage rather than co-operate. This example is certainly an extreme, but it shows that not all changes are implemented in a professional and humane manner.

When introducing new processes and procedures, it is important to pick up the stakeholders, involve them and, above all, motivate them to change their previously learned and sometimes trained behaviour.

Organisational Change Management as it is called in ITIL 4 is also known as Adoption and Change, simply Change Management or also Change and Adoption.

There is currently (as of 2025) no official and standardised definition of organisational change management. However, many people are aware that changes need to be accompanied. Until now, this type of change management has typically been included under Change Management. However, this harbours the risk that it is not carried out due to time constraints or that project participants understand this to mean change management in accordance with ITIL, for example, and do not support the employees affected by the upcoming change, but merely manage this change.

**Important** It should also be noted that organisational change management cannot be implemented without associated costs. Considerable expenses are sometimes incurred, but in our experience, these are well worth the investment. Furthermore, when it comes to organisational change management, it is also important to decide together with the project team where to start. In some cases, it can be hugely advantageous to start with the pockets of resistance within your own company. In other words, start with those who you know will not welcome change. However, sometimes it is beneficial to start with those who welcome change. It is important to consider this and weigh up both approaches. Our tried-and-tested tip: "Know your stakeholders".

The purpose of the Organisational Change Management according to ITIL 4 is:

> The purpose of the organizational change management practice is to ensure that changes in an organization are smoothly and successfully implemented, and that lasting benefits are achieved by managing the human aspects of the changes. (Axelos 2019).

So what is it all about?

The aim is to encourage those affected to embrace the change, overcome their resistance, and (ideally) look forward to it.

Most people do not want change and resist it. There is a small proportion of people who welcome change even without need. But in our experience, this is by far the smaller proportion of people.

ITIL 4 describes the purpose rather than the methodology to be used. We have had very good experience and success with ADKAR in our projects. ADKAR is a methodology from Prosci Inc. (Prosci Inc. 2024) and is used to accompany changes and ensure their successful implementation and introduction, in addition to the technical aspects. We do not want to explain the methodology in detail here, but merely outline what we believe it is based on.

**Important** If you require support with implementing organisational change management, we recommend contacting the relevant consultants before the start of your projects to arrange them to accompany your work.

How can the change process be supported and implemented? (Fig. 6.3 & Table 6.1)

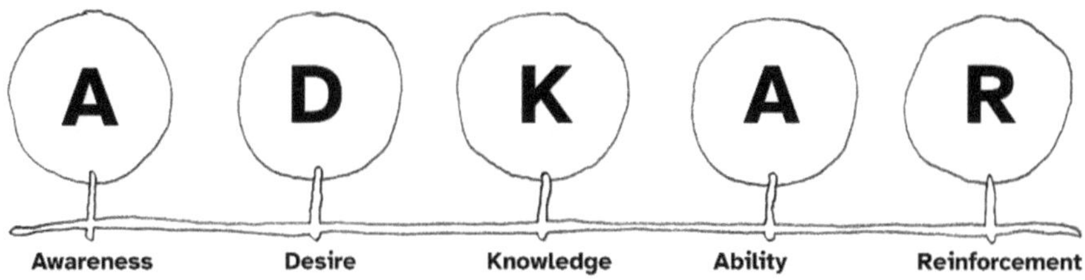


**Fig. 6.3** ADKAR

**Table 6.1** ADKAR

| Awareness | Desire | Knowledge | Ability | Reinforcement |
|---|---|---|---|---|
| Create awareness | Stimulate the desire for change | Imparting knowledge | Expand skills | Reinforce change |
| Clarify intention, initial situation and roles<br>Why is change needed?<br>Who is affected and when and to what extent?<br>What effects does the change (not) have? | Creating shared motivation<br>How can I get involved?<br>How does the change help the organisation?<br>What's in it for me personally?<br>Identify success patterns and fields of action | Communicate knowledge on how the change can be implemented<br>Training and education<br>Share and multiply information<br>Agree realistic goals | Enable affected persons to follow the changes<br>Methodological support for the implementation of the selected measures<br>Application of new communication and collaboration patterns | Continue to anchor change positively and support sustainable change<br>Retrospectives and getting better together<br>Celebrate successes |

**Awareness**

Create awareness. The affected stakeholders must develop an awareness of why a change is necessary. It should be explained who is affected by the change and to what extent, and what impact it will have on them.

In our case, the cross-functional team therefore not only needs to think about how the project is to be implemented technically, but also which stakeholders are affected by a change and how. We also recommend thinking about the type of communication from the project to the stakeholders and from the stakeholders to the project. In some cases, it will be sufficient to inform the stakeholders by email, in others regular meetings will be necessary, possibly also physically on site with the affected parties.

**Important** We recommend the use of change agents. In other words, dedicated employees who are fully informed about the project, its progress, the next steps and why some things will or cannot be implemented. The change agents can then take this information to the stakeholders, obtain their feelings and advice and reflect it back to the project. In this way, those affected become part of the project and this alone reduces resistance to change.

**Desire**
Stimulate the desire for change. The cross-functional team and the entire project are responsible for identifying and monitoring the benefits for the stakeholders. This must be done throughout the project, although the deployed change agents will also ensure this. The positive aspects may differ from stakeholder to stakeholder. This must be taken into account, as it is important to consider all the relevant factors.

**Knowledge**
Share knowledge. The project team needs to consider what knowledge the stakeholders require in order to support and implement the change without encountering major obstacles. What training courses need to be set up and made available to stakeholders at the beginning and in the future to help them implement the change? Attention should also be paid to the effort required to acquire the knowledge, how much time stakeholders need for this, and whether they have sufficient capacity.

**Ability**
Alongside providing knowledge, the project must ensure that the stakeholders are able to implement the selected measures and that this approach is methodologically sound.

**Reinforcement**
At the end of the change, or at the end of the project, the organisational change management is not yet complete.

Change requires time to adapt personal working methods to the change. The change must also be positively anchored afterwards, e.g. by communicating the achievement of objectives through the project. But celebrating successes also helps stakeholders to accept the change in the long term.

**The Team**
As mentioned above, appointing change agents has proven extremely useful in projects involving organisational change management. These agents are responsible for informing stakeholders about the project's progress and supporting them during the transition. At the same time, they are the focal point for stakeholders' requests for changes to the project if something is not running optimally and the planned procedure needs to be amended.

**Important** We firmly believe that every organisation should use change agents. The project should agree with the change agents what the project expects from them, the tasks they should take on in detail, and how much time they have available for these tasks in addition to their daily work. From our experience, there are change agents who provide optimal support to stakeholders, but there are also those who merely pass on information. In the latter case, you should avoid using change agents and perhaps set up a website on the company intranet, which you should do anyway.

## 6.6 Penalisation

When it comes to adaptive service tendering, we often talk about trust, which is a particularly important foundation for cooperation between customers and providers. If there is mutual trust, there is no need for a penalty scheme for non-compliance with previously defined service quality. Or is it?

In this context, it is necessary to take a look at the working methods and structures of many of these providers. A provider will try to convert a service into a standard that it can offer to many customers in the same way in order to utilise synergies and make the service more cost-effective. On the one hand, this can improve the provider's margin situation. On the other hand, standardisation generally offers a more favourable price and therefore a competitive advantage.

One aim of adaptive service tendering is to customise the services for a customer as precisely as possible to their needs. For example, it may be that a service is provided on a dedicated basis for a customer with equally dedicated resources (hardware, software, and also employees of the provider). As long as this is the case, a penalty regulation may not make sense. It could even destroy the trust that has been built up.

However, if the provider converts this dedicated service into a standard, which both sides should endeavour to do, the situation looks different again. In a standard, a customer has to assert itself against other customers of the provider. Like every market player, a provider will focus its attention on where it can expect the greatest benefit, or where the greatest risk or potential catastrophe currently resides.

**Important** A customer should carefully consider which service or which part of a service is subject to a penalty. In our experience, penalty agreements between the provider and customer make perfect sense. However, they should only cover genuine operational risks for the customer and only contain an appropriate level of penalties. It is also important for the customer when considering a penalty that a provider usually takes its risks into account in its costs. So, if the provider sees a risk in the penalty, it will take this into account in its costs. Ergo: The higher the penalty, the more expensive the service usually is. Furthermore, in the event of a critical deviation from the service to be provided, direct dialogue should always be sought first in order to reach a win-win solution.

**Important** Minimum quantities

Percentage values are often used when formulating service level targets. At the service desk, 80% of calls should be answered within 30 seconds. The availability of an application is 99.9% during the operating time. It is not uncommon for a percentage value to be specified for services that are processed in very small numbers. For example, 95% of all major incidents (MI) must have reached the support unit responsible for the respective subject area within 15 min.

Major incidents, i.e. disruptions with a significant impact on business operations, should only occur once or twice a month anyway. An SLA target of 95% major incidents makes no sense, as a one-off deviation in the measured month can no longer be made up due to the low number of units. To make up for a single missed MI, 20 major incidents would be necessary in one month (19/20 = 0.95).

It must be possible to catch up on missed SLA targets, otherwise resourceful service providers will save resources for the rest of the month, which can no longer be made up. Otherwise, internal IT departments quickly become demotivated. This can be achieved, for example, by taking a cumulative view of the last 6 months, i.e. all transactions, calls, or tickets from the last 6 months are analysed. It is even better to take the business purpose as the objective and align the SLA target with it (key result).

For example, an outage lasting more than 10 min costs the company € 50,000 per minute of production downtime. The isolated major incidents in recent months have shown that the solution teams did not react quickly enough, and the repair itself was then sufficiently fast. A weekly alarm exercise could therefore be introduced, focussing on this key result in the reviews. A corresponding service level target for key parameters of these alarm exercises would then also make sense.

## 6.7 Is Everything Available for Implementation?

After creating many individual elements with a set of Lean-Agile pieces for our work with customers, we were able to use these as a piecework approach to add value. However, some customers felt the need for a well-founded methodology. This is how our model emerged from everyday business life. It can be adapted to a wide variety of needs and organisations. In particular, it maps the tension well between an organisation's classic methods and its need to adopt adaptive methods that have yet to prove themselves.

Based on the traditional roles, we have outlined the most important changes and challenges. These can serve as the basis for a communication plan in your organisation. Although the roles will not be reflected 1:1 in your organisation and partner landscape, we are convinced that our outline can provide assistance. Start by planning the communication of your project as a plan for your organisation. Our roles and examples are a good assistant for further elaboration (Fig. 6.4).

The process model presented should definitely be tried out in small projects without major deviations. It should be suitable for classically organised organisations and form a basis for learning the cultural aspects of Lean-Agile. It is also worth sticking to the time periods we have specified, e.g. 6 months, for a roadmap. Introducing a new method and gaining initial experience in using it presents

| | 1:1 | Update | Jour Fixe | Newsletter | Review | Event | Planning | Town Hall | Individual |
|---|---|---|---|---|---|---|---|---|---|
| **Division Management** | **Leon Hudson** | **Weekly** | | | | | X | X | X |
| **Team A** | **Mollie Gallagher** | **Daily** | X | X | X | | X | X | |
| **Team B** | **Mollie Gallagher** | **Daily** | X | X | X | | X | X | |
| **Team C** | **Mollie Gallagher** | **Weekly** | | X | | | X | X | |
| **Marketing** | **Lucy Reeves** | **Monthly** | | X | X | X | | X | |
| **Works Council** | **Leon Hudson** | **Monthly** | X | X | X | X | | X | X |
| **User Group A** | **Lucy Reeves** | **Weekly** | | X | X | X | X | X | |
| **User Group B** | **Lucy Reeves** | **Weekly** | | X | X | X | X | X | |

**Fig. 6.4** Example communication plan

organisations with certain challenges at the beginning. It is important to find out which procedures prove successful and which adjustments need to be made.

Nevertheless, we hope that our presentation is structured and comprehensive enough for the organisation itself to learn how to deal with adaptive services. To accompany this, we recommend training project staff in Lean-Agile methods as they are available on the market. Here they can acquire knowledge about organisational change, cultural change and how to deal with certain detailed issues. A good approach is to divide the employees between different courses and providers. Broad training in different methods and directions makes more sense than a complete team that has taken part in a "Scrum Master" course, for example.

The advice to try out our process model without any deviations is aimed in particular at organisations that already use a specific agile framework. Although these have a comprehensive claim, they contain agile software development methods at their core. At least we are not aware of any framework that is suitable for Adaptive Managed Services in this way. If your company insists on the support of a specific framework, transfer the idea presented here to carry out the project using the methodology presented here and report into the company framework on a monthly basis, for example. In this way, all requirements are met and the project team can better learn and work out the differences.

The sections on organisational change management should help to understand the conflicting objectives of some of the organisational units and functions involved. The two approaches to partner selection presented here also offer a concrete aid or strategy for finding one or more suitable partners for the tender or the adaptive process of service transition and transformation.

The resistance of those involved to change their way of working or their position is certainly the biggest challenge. To ensure that everyone pulls in the same direction, a great deal of educational and persuasive work must be carried out at an early stage. In addition, a continuous flow of information about the upcoming steps and the associated changes is necessary. At the same time, training courses need to be organised in order to acquire new skills and understand the changing contexts. Finally, stakeholders with an affinity for change should be appointed as change agents to support the process at a collegial level.

## References

AXELOS Limited. (2019). *ITIL foundation: ITIL* (4th ed.). TSO.

Prosci Inc. (2024, May 22). *The Prosci* ADKAR® Model | Prosci. Retrieved 7 Jul 2025 from The Prosci ADKAR Model: https://www.prosci.com/methodology/adkar

# 7 Summary—Conclusion—Outlook

We have summarised the essence of our experience with the new generation of IT tenders. A book or a method you learn theoretically can only be the first step towards application. Many things sound easier than they are in practice; some of our lessons may sound overwhelming, but they can be learnt step by step. The biggest challenge, however, is implementation. Most companies will have to deal with a faster pace of business change and with more and more technology.

This book is intended to provide support for this industry transformation in particular. On the one hand, it is an assurance that adaptive methods can also bring innovation and value orientation to managed service tenders; on the other hand, individual methods can be looked up and tried out at any time. You have to develop the transformation for your business and your IT organisation yourself. Our methods are building blocks that you can integrate into your business, starting with a handful of methods and, depending on your development and needs, expanding to a full system. In our experience, the degree of innovation and the speed can be customised. This is demonstrated by the following customer stories.

At the beginning of the development of our approach, we openly advertised and talked about the fact that we had some experience, but that the entire approach had not yet been tried and tested. A conservative client was very interested in the outcome approach and in the management of values that cannot be expressed 1:1 in euros. The company wanted to become more attractive to employees, i.e. also offer a better user experience. However, no one was able to convincingly demonstrate the added value of investing in certain technologies and how greater attractiveness for employees can be measured in euros.

An adaptive approach solved two of the problems. The improvement in attractiveness could be measured and controlled with each step. This applies both to the evaluation of alternatives for the next roadmap and the increments created during implementation. A translation of the relative values could guarantee the increase in value and ensure long-term measurability in figures. However, agile approaches did not fit into the existing organisation. Agility was not seen as added value or a


G. Köhler et al., *Adaptive IT Service Tendering*, Management for Professionals,
https://doi.org/10.1007/978-3-658-49726-2_7

desirable development goal, but agile project methods were accepted. They were seen as a kind of toolbox that could deliver the above-mentioned benefits and posed no threat to the organisation.

We offered to run the agile development completely as a service provider and to utilise the existing structures and committees. A kind of parallel operation in which the agile part was very autonomous but had to report to the traditional part. Interested project managers or other stakeholders could learn in this protected environment if they wished. However, there were no plans to introduce agile methods into the company. If project participants were trained accordingly, this was an additional benefit, but not a requirement. The client liked this type of parallelism, as the existing organisation was not strongly influenced. The client's requirements not to disrupt the organisation were initially too strong.

His first idea was not to involve any employees, if possible, as the service provider should know the improvements from other customer environments. So, the first challenge was to convince the customer to involve all levels in order to get permission to include employees in cross-functional teams. For this customer, the main issue was limiting the number of employees involved. The involvement of end users, key users, etc. was also not clear in this form at the beginning. However, the typical fears of becoming too transparent or losing control were not present with this customer. As a result of this intensive clarification phase and the many discussions that were held, there was a lively demand over time to get involved in the project. As a result, we had to deal with very motivated participants over the course of the project.

Synchronisation with the existing project organisation took place on a monthly basis in accordance with the iteration duration. All necessary conventional project documentation was created by the agile team at least once a month as additional work. The agile project managed itself visually, i.e. all important elements were always visible to all participants on digital whiteboards. In addition to a Kanban board and the backlog for managing activities, things such as impediments and important metrics were also publicly visible, similar to a burn-down chart. This meant that some typical project elements such as action trackers could be dispensed with (Fig. 7.1).

After a certain learning phase, there were also some conflicts. These were mostly due to the project organisation's demand to adhere more closely to the tried-and-tested waterfall models. The good agreement with the management at the beginning to approve this agile project with all the boundary conditions soon led to an agreement. The motivation of those involved in the project and the focus on the values gave the impression of having a particularly fast project that ultimately achieved its goals.

The next example is a customer from the public sector who had had very good experience with agile methods and was therefore interested in our approach. After an initial assessment, our ideas did not fit in with the usual procurement procedures. As experienced lean methodologists, we kept asking "why" questions until we were able to enter into a joint development process. Interestingly, there were so many

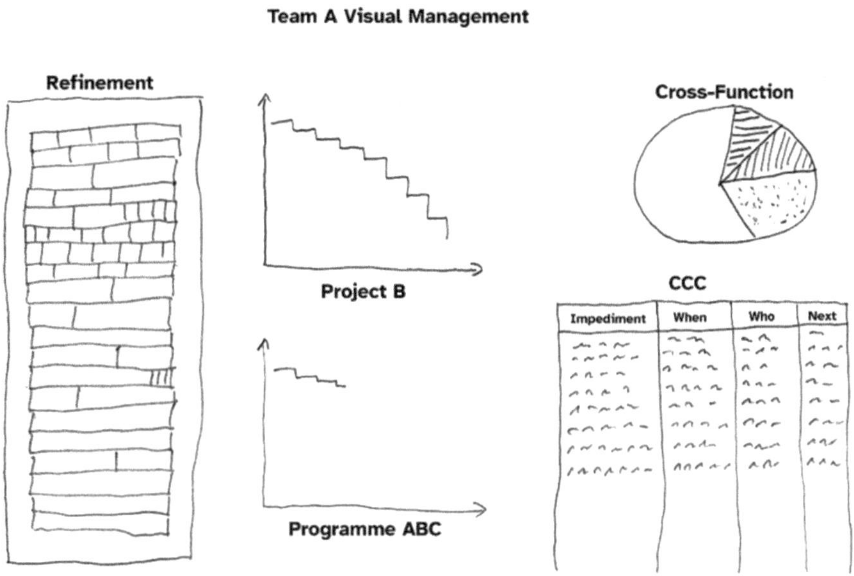


**Fig. 7.1** Teamboard manage visual

opponents here who kept coming up with new reasons against adaptive collaboration that after just under a year we were very sure we had found a good concept.

The result was a combination of different types of contracts. At the centre of this was a part-time employee assignment in order to be able to work together on adaptive roadmaps. In cross-functional phases, many use cases can be included in the backlog, which are also processed separately according to service content in role-separated phases. In Germany the maximum transfer duration of 18 months must also be observed here, but it fits well with 6-month roadmaps.

The actual managed services could be commissioned in the concept in the conventional way. A user-centred description of the services is important here. This description should contain as few specific operating procedures as possible. A defined operational organisation and processes can be used as examples. Major innovation changes and projects can be handled via the third component, e.g. consultancy contracts or service independent contracts covering IT projects.

The last example is about failure. The customer, an internal IT department, had accumulated a huge technical debt. With an outdated infrastructure, dozens of self-built technology stacks and interfaces, modern developments were almost unthinkable. In addition, the maintenance of this historically grown system cost huge sums of money. Users therefore had an expensive, outdated service and were no longer prepared to accept this.

Adaptive Services were the perfect solution to solve this highly complex problem step by step. In the first iterations, easily definable parts were modernised in order to achieve initial success and inspire users. This enthusiasm made waves, and the fact that key users and end users were now able to actively participate was a particularly welcome innovation. This was now clearly demanded as standard by the client's committees.

The previous system relied heavily on the hierarchy, in which the management level defined the right solutions and considered the involvement of business users to be tedious preparatory work. The IT management was obviously surprised by this new type of user involvement and strongly defended the previous structures. Arguments against the involvement of users supposed problems in governance and IT service management, but also a considerable amount of extra work in communication and a lack of expertise on the user side.

All counter-arguments could be countered by the two previous successful adaptive projects. However, the challenge was that the next project had to be more extensive, as many technical dependencies had to be taken into account. Some of the technologies were so outdated that they were no longer supported by the manufacturer and therefore had to be replaced in one step. Due to the framework conditions and the constantly changing requirements, there were repeated delays, which meant that the start of the project was a long way off. Over time, the collaboration was increasingly questioned by both sides and eventually abandoned.

## 7.1 Lessons Learnt

The good news from our own experience and from coaching adaptive ways of working is that it works and companies are adopting their part of the culture and methods. In particular, adaptive methods work when they are needed. This is often the case in situations where complex environments come under pressure. This can certainly have a positive impact on business because the necessary speed of innovation in the core business is increasing. But there is also massive pressure to save money, especially if previous savings based on the principle of "same for less" have brought IT to the edge of quality and costs.

Adaptive methods primarily address people and their collaboration. In most cases, this means massive potential for innovation and efficiency. Where and to what extent this type of collaboration is used in a company ranges from a project to a service area, the IT organisation to the entire company. These are all valid and stable approaches that can be combined with other structural philosophies of organisations.

At this point, we encounter many preconceptions that do not align with our experience. This is highly relevant to the application of our methods, as such prejudices cause us to focus on sources of potential danger that are of secondary importance in real projects.

- The start-up bias: Adaptive managed services and approaches are only for disorganised small companies, such as start-ups.
- The self-organisation means relaxation bias suggests that self-organisation means the team can literally do what they want, such as having beach parties instead of working hard.

However, in both cases, the opposite is true: the introduction of adaptive methods requires stable, resilient structures and a high degree of discipline.

**Important** In the context of Lean-Agile, self-organisation involves certain stages of converting data into information, information into know-how, and know-how into decisions. The low stages of self-organisation do not differ much from traditional hierarchical systems, despite the fact that data and information are used to solve problems and decisions are prepared by people who hold this information.

The control of adaptive methods is focussed on the type of collaboration and its further development. However, there is no magical component in adaptive methods that replaces control. If you break down the individual elements and actions of these methods and compare them with the atomic actions of classic projects and organisations, you will find all the control aspects of traditional project management or leadership. They are just distributed differently in adaptive methods. This is an important aspect of discipline that the team must create together. If control is distributed to teams, they must develop working methods to fulfil these requirements.

Our methods can serve as a template here, but the individual characteristics must be developed by the team itself. A typical challenge here is that the characteristics of the methods must first be developed. The advantages and disadvantages of the new working methods must be understood and adapted to the team's own working environment. A cardinal mistake is that agile methods are often scaled back in practice shortly after training and development, without the meaning or cultural aspect behind them being understood. Let's take Scrum as an example, where a development team has not understood the "Daily Scrum" meetings, and mistakenly runs them as a kind of project meeting and turns the daily meeting into a weekly meeting.

**Important** For this reason, Agile Coaches like to refer to Shu-Ha-Ri when implementing their programmes. This categorisation of gaining knowledge into three phases is highly recommended, but whether you relate it to a Japanese martial arts concept is up to you. The three phases are:

"Shu"—Learn the rules, follow them strictly and copy the master. Use the methods exactly as they were trained or as they are written in the book. If the meaning of an action is not clear in the long term, always consult the "master", i.e. an agile coach. Maybe this certain action really makes no sense in your environment, maybe it is not understood correctly, but it is most likely that the transfer to the working environment is incomplete.

"Ha"—The rules and execution have been internalised and can be recalled. The background to the methods should now be inspected. The underlying principles and modes of action should be researched and made aware of. In this phase, it is worth paying particular attention to effectiveness and spreading the new working methods to all possible areas. New methods do not necessarily have to replace all existing processes, but a homogeneous working environment should be created without media disruptions. Efficiency measures can be started in this phase. These must fully preserve the methods.

"Ri"—The team is at the trainer's level of knowledge and can explain and train itself. Only now should the methods be refined, further developed and changed using their own creative impulses. If the new methods still contain actions that do not bring any added value, these can now be omitted to minimise waste. However, this should very rarely be the case. However, it can happen that methods do not fit into the work context. In this case, it is necessary to analyse the original context for values and see whether these values can be transformed into your own environment. This is neither easy to recognise nor easy to implement, otherwise it would have been done in the first or second phase. An agile coach or someone from the original context can provide support here.

## 7.2 Social Systems

As previously mentioned, we are familiar with the various ways in which Lean-Agile working methods can be integrated into organisations. There are probably enough examples in your environment of conservative, hierarchical medium-sized companies whose software development department has been working 100% agile for years and takes advantage of all the necessary freedoms. Nevertheless, there are always challenges within an organisation when it comes to converting existing systems to Lean-Agile. This may be due to serious cultural differences or simply a misunderstanding in which a member of management pulls a team member from a cross-functional team for something completely different as part of an escalation, without considering the negative consequences for a self-organised team.

It is beyond the scope of this book to go into detail about organisational change management. However, we would like to report on which approaches have worked well in practice and which ones require more staying power. You yourself know best how to assess the political situation in your organisation and how best to communicate it. We can only encourage you to communicate as transparently and clearly as possible. It is better to discuss red lines from the beginning than to cross them unnoticed at some point and have to iron out the communicative damage.

Our experience shows that much more is possible than you might think. We have realised that demonstrating methods that directly contribute to business value and make this value development controllable through an iterative approach arouses great interest among conservative managers. Due to the high value proposition, intensive discussions about the consequences of Lean-Agile working can be held openly in parts of the organisation with mutual wishes and limits. Although these discussions should primarily begin within the organisations, the experience of the providers of adaptive services will make a valuable contribution.

It is always advisable to start small. Ideally, an area in which a major improvement can be achieved should be carefully sought. This could be increasing the efficiency of an existing service. Such an improvement does not usually have to be put out to tender, but existing or potential service providers can be brought into the team. They can help with advice or, even better, with experience from existing adaptive services. In such a constellation, they create a training ground in which their own organisation can learn, future service providers can demonstrate their capabilities and tangible value can be created by increasing efficiency.

A small team should first develop a broad horizon of alternatives and analyse a manageable and valuable opportunity. The reverse approach, which starts from management and involves large parts of the organisation, requires a lot of perseverance. Don't expect adaptive ways of working to run smoothly from day one. The change in working methods and project communication will not be fully understood at first, which can cause avoidable fears and resistance.

Make use of the experience of the service providers involved; this should essentially serve the learning of the organisation or a department. It is advisable to have your own employees manage such initial small projects with high priority. These employees must be open to new methods, but should also be able to communicate the wishes of the organisation in day-to-day business and manage communication. This is important in order to be able to decide how the new methods can be integrated into the organisation once the first project has been completed.

Start by creating demand to attract committed employees for the first cross-functional teams. For example, several opportunities can be analysed and, as in a marketplace, the most committed department wins the deal. The first iterations require strong attention and support from specialists, both in terms of content and the new working methods. Appoint supporters from management as mentors and ensure that these mentors engage in an active learning process. Even if they support the new ways of working, it takes insight and discussion to understand the new culture.

Critical voices can be involved to a certain extent as stakeholders who discuss the progress of each review and decide on approval. This gives them an active role with a steering function and means they can no longer simply comment from the sidelines. In addition, critical feedback provides a good breeding ground for further development. Critics who are known as procrastinators or blockers are less suitable as stakeholders in one of the first projects.

It will take some time to find a sustainable organisational and working structure that works better than in the past. This applies at least to the work areas outside the development teams. Lean-Agile is now so well established in software development that it can be trained and implemented with little adaptation. Such standardisation does not yet exist in the areas we are addressing. We ourselves had to do a lot of transfer work by relying on Lean-Agile consultants, trainers, and coaches who work outside of software development.

Advice from the service provider's experts can usually accelerate the development and learning process. Being allowed to make your own experiences and mistakes deepens understanding and ensures better integration into the core business, but costs time and requires perseverance. This area of tension should be actively utilised, depending on what the environment allows: A successful company that sees adaptive methods as the next booster for its business success certainly has time to learn from mistakes. A company that needs to emerge from a crisis quickly, e.g. through more innovative competition, should favour the consulting approach.

Extremes should be avoided. For example, you should not rely entirely on staff from your own organisation who learn from mistakes, nor should you use a swarm of consultants who set up structures in a fast-track process that only prove to be uncomfortable much later.

In the right mix, consultation is important at the beginning to equip the first versions of your new methods with all the necessary features. Typically, there are three levels of difficulty when adapting new methods. There will be methods that can be applied one-to-one in a different working framework. Then there are methods that require a highly visible and obvious transfer. These can easily be created and developed over time until they have reached their full value.

The third category comprises methods whose values are of great benefit, but which cannot be easily transferred to the world of work. Developing them is a challenging task that requires time and mutual knowledge. An ideal combination could be an internal software development team that has been using Lean-Agile methods for years. Through mutual exchange, the Adaptive Managed Services team can learn from the established culture and its values, while the Scrum Masters from software development understand the subject matter, goals, and challenges of managed services. Together, new methods can now be developed that fit Managed Services and transfer values from agile software development.

Few companies will offer such an opportunity to develop the transformation of methods. If this is purchased as a consulting service, a longer period of time for understanding and development must be expected. An intensive consultancy phase should be planned at the start of the project, with less consultancy required as the methods are developed and adapted. Coaching for the further development of the team and the methods should be planned for later phases.

In our experience, the first versions of new working methods are developed with a lot of dedication and energy. It usually turns out that these first versions work rather poorly and offer great potential for improvement. In most cases, the second version can also be improved. An agile coach should be brought in for the third version at the latest, as this is where feedback can maintain momentum. This can be a point of disappointment, especially for employees who have entered into the design of the new methods with a great deal of confidence and vigour. Feedback from an experienced agile coach that you are on the right track or that small corrections are necessary ensures the commitment of the entire team.

**Example** It's been more than 7 years since we started our first Lean experiences and 7 years since we started adding an Agile culture. I love remembering times when we doubled our outcome with the same number of people. I remember a particular phone call from a team member. She told me that she had used some leftover resources to go the extra mile. She was successful.

I also recall situations where I was frustrated because our ideas did not work. We thought we were so clever and understood how things worked. But we failed several times. However, there was always someone in the team who encouraged us to get back up, redesign, and try again.

## 7.3 Is It Worth Investing in Adaptive Methods?

For our own portfolio planning, we have been following the analyses of the major market research companies for several years to see how companies react to Adaptive Managed Services. Notably, the periods during which technologies and methodologies are in the public spotlight. We have noticed that demand is stable and that sustainable applicability is becoming established. We have also received similar feedback from companies with which we are in direct contact.

We believe that Adaptive Managed Services will help many companies to remain at the forefront of their ecosystem. This is not only about innovation in the core business and a closer integration of IT and business values, but also about challenges such as the shortage of skilled labour, necessary savings or values within the company.

We initially underestimated the potential of companies using Adaptive Managed Services. In our environment, the potential is currently conservatively estimated at a quarter of all companies. As this is a recent development, we are hoping for strong growth, but we do not believe it is appropriate to make a long-term forecast about its development.

Over the last two decades, we have also observed a kind of rubber band model in the IT industry when it comes to the acceptance and successful utilisation of new technologies and working methods. There are companies that are very hesitant to adopt new legal requirements, methods, or technologies. These are then usually unable to realise their full benefits. On the other hand, some companies adopt new developments very quickly and, after overcoming initial difficulties, gradually exploit them to their advantage.

However, this does not appear to be a linear effect, whereby all organisations achieve high efficiency gains after a certain delay. Rather, it works more like expanding markers on a rubber band. Imagine companies with hesitant acceptance on one side of a spectrum and companies with high technical acceptance on the other.

Between these two extremes are companies that are only partially realising this potential.

Change over time is like pulling on a rubber band. Innovative companies that constantly challenge their IT and other functions widen their gap much more than companies at the other end of the rubber band. Basically, evolution is positive, but not linear. This means that Adaptive Managed Services will be so versatile and innovative that they will also appeal to companies for which IT is not the main focus.

The greatest interest in adaptive services can be expected where a high level of added value can be generated. These are managed services in business environments with high differentiation potential. IT's share of value creation can be increased through an aggressive shift from individual to industrialised services. In addition to reducing costs by increasing efficiency, this creates scope for new innovations. This opens up opportunities for adaptive managed services to become an innovation driver for IT providers in the future. In any case, providers whose strategy is focussed on services with high efficiency or innovation should rely on adaptive services.

When discussing the idea of using adaptive methods, many of our dialogue partners focus on IT services that are very close to the core business in their current service architecture, such as production control systems, logistics systems or process automation systems. At first glance, technical IT services or supporting systems such as managed workplaces, virtualisation systems, databases, or networks do not promise any major added value from adaptive methods.

We do not see such a clear gradation in the applicability and benefits of adaptive services. From a technical perspective, platform services typically offer less efficiency potential than application services that are closer to the process. However, disruptive changes to business processes, including IT services, often extend across several layers. Horizontal services such as IT service management, IT security and centralised monitoring should not be forgotten, as their innovation cycles impact a company's entire service portfolio.

The greatest and unexpected efficiency improvements through Adaptive Managed Services are achieved by organisations and their service provider ecosystem from the point at which cross-functional collaboration is captured at all levels and the value streams are gradually understood across all areas. As a rule, the first step is to increase the efficiency of individual IT services, then to break down and optimise the needs of individual service consumers. Only when the remaining alternatives have little value potential do most organisations start to think big and find unexpected potential together (Fig. 7.2).

The effects of adaptive managed services are not yet foreseeable. However, development trends can be recognised. Especially in hybrid use, it is an advantage if sub-services become more finely granular. In technological terms, this means modularisation to microservices. It would have far-reaching effects on licence models and would have a significant impact on the management of services for IT service management. A new role will emerge for tender consultants and a market for service providers who focus entirely on the role of controlling and accelerating innovation.

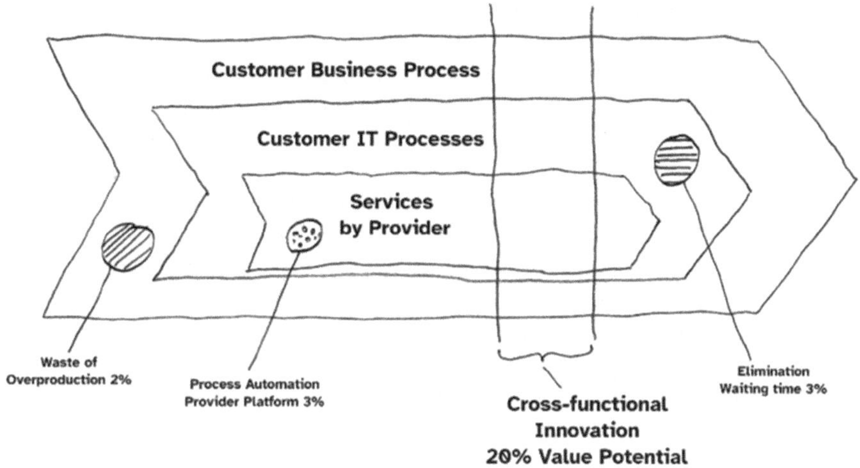


**Fig. 7.2** Improvement in the business process

If we restrict ourselves to a purely technological perspective, many aspects of such a service landscape can already be observed today in some start-ups and their rather experimental service architectures. These are generally not suitable for industrial use as they lack industrial suitability and security. We look to the future with hope and excitement to see whether these gaps will be closed by adaptive services.

**Example** One customer was very keen to learn about adaptive managed services. The head of IT had heard about it and was fascinated. In all the initial questions, his desire was to ensure that transformation to an adaptive managed service was a "silver bullet" that would solve all his issues. However, we found out that his IT department was at a very poor level of maturity and, in certain areas, unprofessional. For example, they were running a 24/7 service with just two employees. Whenever this critical service was down, the two employees were contacted by mobile phone to return to work.

We discussed the fact that the first huge transformation would be to get the IT back on track, i.e. to implement suitable architectures and structures for the business needs. This would involve introducing basic IT service management for incidents, problems and changes, and proper reporting. We estimated that it would take 2 years to turn the current situation into a professional IT setup. The head of IT was disappointed; 2 years and an investment to achieve "the same" was not what he had wished for. "I thought adaptive services were a silver bullet", and yes, they can be. However, turning such a problematic IT department into a professional, innovative, adaptive organisation overnight requires three wishes and a fairy.

## 7.4 Get Started and Learn

Whether classic Managed Services or Adaptive Managed Services: We have learnt a lot, especially in comparing the two worlds. For this reason alone, it is worth reading this book. Even in the most adverse environment, e.g. if your organisation rejects modern variants of IT service development, some of the ideas and values of adaptive services can be incorporated into traditional project management.

We have realised that adaptive services have huge potential, and we have witnessed the impact they can have on innovation and engagement among all stakeholders. Nevertheless, traditional approaches and services remain relevant in certain situations. Combining both approaches takes the organisation further. Individual projects can learn a lot by comparing the two approaches. In turn, the experiences of these projects can inform good decisions for the organisation's further development. Either way, your experience will increase exponentially.

In conclusion, Adaptive Services provide an important basis for the discussion on IT Business Integration. From experience, we know many organisations that still see the value of their IT as a support function that implements requirements and is otherwise a cost factor. Adaptive methods are a good way of slowly creating a changed awareness here, e.g. by cooperating with management representatives in cross-functional teams. The same applies here: Start with a small, valuable alternative to promote cooperation. Do not convince with theory or references from market competitors. Learning by doing is more successful and sustainable.

With this in mind, we hope that you too will embark on an exciting journey of discovery with adaptive services. We look forward to hearing your insights and stories and wish you every success!

Gerhard Köhler, Werner Roth and Achim Schmidtmann

# 8 Glossary

The following pages offer explanations of terms used in this book and in the context of IT tenders. Some of these terms have a broader meaning that extends beyond the context of IT tenders. To make sure this glossary is a useful tool for work, we have not said in most cases that some words may have different meanings outside the IT environment (Table 8.1).

**Table 8.1** Glossary

| Term | Short | Explanation |
|---|---|---|
| Active directory | AD | Is a directory service from Microsoft that was introduced with Windows 2000. As a directory service, the AD is the central source of information in a network. It provides information about users, passwords, access authorisations and restrictions as well as objects connected to the network. |
| AI bias or AI distortion | | The term "AI bias" refers to the occurrence of biased results due to human prejudices that distort the original training data or the AI algorithm. This can lead to distorted results and potentially harmful outcomes. |
| Alternative | | In our adaptive method, alternatives are all kinds of valuable architectural elements. This can be an epic or a use case, but an alternative encompasses much more. These can be design ideas or collections of requirements. If they are relevant, they must be revised in the further process → Section 5.3 |
| Application programming Interface | API | API is the generic term for a programming interface that software makes available to a service application, for example, so that it can work together with other programmes or exchange information. |

(continued)


G. Köhler et al., *Adaptive IT Service Tendering*, Management for Professionals,
https://doi.org/10.1007/978-3-658-49726-2_8

**Table 8.1** (continued)

| Term | Short | Explanation |
|---|---|---|
| Artefact | | In the original sense, an object produced by humans. The term appears primarily in the context of Scrum, where the product backlog, the sprint backlog and an increment are referred to as artefacts → Section 2.4.8. TOGAF also uses the term artefacts for objects that are created in the architecture → Section 2.3. |
| Audit | | An IT audit is a review of the control mechanisms within the IT service organisation by an internal audit or external certification. In most cases, the audit is carried out on the basis of a company policy, legal regulations or an industry standard. The audit determines whether the IT systems protect assets, ensure data security and run processes efficiently. |
| Augmented reality | AR | Is the computer-aided extension of perception in a virtual world. This extension can appeal to several human senses. In practice, however, the most common form is the extension of the visual representation, e.g. by superimposing 3D objects in a 2D environment. |
| Backend (frontend) | | Backend is the part of a system that is close to the system or programme, i.e. the more functional part of a system. The front end is the part that is close to the user or is operated directly by the user. |
| BANI | | BANI is a framework that enables organisations to make the actions and effects of increasingly unstable markets more tangible. The individual letters have the following meaning:<br>• *Brittle*: Established systems that still appear robust but are already vulnerable and dilapidated<br>• *Anxious*: The fear of not making the right decisions<br>• *Non-linear*: Lack of causality, action and reaction are detached from each other<br>• *Incomprehensible*: Events or decisions are incomprehensible due to complexity or information overload |
| Benchmark clauses | | Many managed services contracts contain a benchmark clause. The aim of such a benchmark is to determine standard market prices for parts or all of the service on an annual basis, for example. The aim is to determine whether the current prices for the service tendered for a period of several years may have fallen (or risen) more than expected. In the event of major deviations, the contracted service provider should make appropriate price adjustments or the services can be outsourced elsewhere. Providers of market research results and analyses of developments in IT often serve as a neutral source for market price benchmarks. |

(continued)

**Table 8.1** (continued)

| Term | Short | Explanation |
|---|---|---|
| Big data | | Big data refers to the huge amounts of data in a company that provide information for the company with the help of analysis software, for example data from social networks, sensor data from industrial companies' machinery, transaction data and much more. |
| Blockchain | | The blockchain is a distributed database that can be continuously expanded with data records in individual blocks. Each transaction is managed transparently and decentralised. This means that a blockchain is not located on a central server, but on many distributed computers. Blockchains secure transactions in this way and are therefore difficult to manipulate. Cryptocurrencies such as bitcoin rely on this technology. |
| Bottom-up | | Top-down and bottom-up are two opposing approaches to communication, processes, or planning. A top-down approach starts from a superordinate, general level and arrives at the individual elements. A bottom-up approach starts from specific individual elements and ends with an overall view. Both approaches tend to attach too much prominence to their starting point. |
| Boutique consulting | | In recent years, the prefix "boutique" has become established for small, specialised management consultancies. These companies commonly employ fewer than 100 consultants who are very well versed in certain topics and sectors. If the expertise of these firms is precisely matched to the task at hand, the work results are generally of a high quality. Boutique consultancies are usually unable to meet a broad range of challenges. |
| Bring your own device | BYOD | The term BYOD is used when companies integrate their employees' private mobile devices (computers, laptops, mobile phones) into the company network and allow employees to do their work with their private devices. This is usually done by technically separating business and private domains. |
| Brownfield approach | | See Greenfield approach |
| BSI | | The BSI (Bundesamt für Sicherheit in der Informationstechnik), or the Federal Office for Information Security, is Germany's national authority for cyber security. Founded in 1991, it is the country's competence centre for information security. |
| Burn-down chart | | Is a graphical visualisation of the task packages still to be completed depending on the remaining time. Burn-down charts have become very popular in agile software development. Here, the remaining work until the end of a sprint is visualised. Forecasts about the sprint backlog can be validated by changing such a progress chart over time → chap. 7. |

(continued)

**Table 8.1** (continued)

| Term | Short | Explanation |
|---|---|---|
| Business continuity management | BCM | Ensures preventive measures to increase the resilience of business processes. This also includes plans to be able to react quickly and purposefully in the event of a crisis. BCM is the basis for IT service continuity management. |
| Business process outsourcing | BPO | BPO refers to the outsourcing of business processes. In most cases, a supporting function of the core business, including IT technology, is outsourced to a service provider. Examples include accounting, logistics, and HR processes. |
| Capability Centre | | See delivery Centre |
| Change advisory board | CAB | Decision-making board within the IT organisation for the coordination of changes. All those responsible who are affected by upcoming change requests are invited to a CAB. Change requests are communicated in the CAB and, depending on the type, submitted for approval and implementation. |
| Chatbot | | Chatbots each have a text input and output that they can use to communicate in natural language. From a technical perspective, chatbots in IT service management are more of a further development of search algorithms. Many chatbots even manage without AI (artificial intelligence) in their core function. |
| Chief technology officer | CTO | A CTO is responsible for the technical development and research of a company. Depending on the size of the company and the industry, the functions of head of IT, chief information officer and chief technology officer are sometimes performed by one person.In less technology-intensive companies, the CTO develops, optimises, and updates the company's technical equipment. He is the link between the latest market developments and the management's current requirements for the technical infrastructure. |
| Claim management | | Also known as claiming, claim management is an attempt to fend off unjustified requests and enforce justified ones. In projects, this usually relates to failure to co-operate, deadlines, dates, and deviations from expected results. But also cost changes, additional requirements and unfulfilled delivery scopes. Claim management tends to have a negative reputation, but it can also be useful for the equalisation of minor contractual deviations in a spirit of partnership. |
| Completely automated public Turing test to tell computers and humans apart | CAPTCHA | Captchas are used to prevent automated attacks on registration forms, contact forms or similar resources. Captchas help to differentiate between humans and robots. |

(continued)

**Table 8.1** (continued)

| Term | Short | Explanation |
|---|---|---|
| Configuration item | CI | A service component that must be managed in order to provide an IT service. Examples of CIs are network components, hardware, software components or technical services. |
| Configuration management Data Base | CMDB | A database in which configuration items are stored throughout their entire life cycle. The CMDB also manages the relationships between configuration data records. A higher-level configuration management system (CMS) is a logical data model that can contain several CMDBs. |
| Configuration management system | CMS | See configuration management Data Base |
| Control | | "A control" often refers to a control component, activity, or operational part of a governance process. For example, "problem control" is the control of activities for analysing problems and documenting workarounds and known errors. |
| Cookie | | A cookie is text information that is stored on your computer by a visited website via the browser. Cookies store certain information, such as the contents of a shopping basket when visiting a shopping site. However, they are also frequently used to store the behaviour of a visitor to a website so that it can subsequently be analysed. |
| Current mode of operation | CMO | In outsourcing projects, the term refers to the established service as it is provided at the time of the tender. This includes the current operation, its technology, processes, and workflows. The term CMO is usually used when the current operation is also to be transformed by the new provider. For the planning of the transition and transformation, there is then the sequence CMO, CMO+, and FMO. One example is the change of provider and the switch to a new technology platform. CMO is the current operating mode of the previous provider. Current mode of operation "plus" (CMO+) is the takeover of the current mode of operation, as it is, by the new provider. Future mode of operation (FMO) is the operation converted to the new technology platform. |
| Dedicated service | | See shared service |
| Delivery Centre | | An IT service provider's delivery centre is a specialised facility (physical location) that is responsible for providing and managing IT services for customers. It pools technical resources and expertise to ensure efficient and standardised service processes. They are sometimes called "capability Centres" to emphasise the range of competencies that can be covered. For example, a customer may receive two different services via two different capability centres, as they specialise in certain services. |

(continued)

**Table 8.1** (continued)

| Term | Short | Explanation |
|---|---|---|
| Design thinking | | The design thinking approach aims to solve problems and develop new ideas. The aim is to develop solutions that are convincing from the user's perspective and at the same time market- and product-orientated.Design thinking is a recognised framework of methods that is often associated with agile practices. Various institutes and schools offer training programmes in design thinking. |
| DevOps | | DevOps refers to a methodology in the area of software development and IT operations. DevOps is not a uniform methodology, but rather a type of organisational culture that aims to eliminate the separation between the two areas. As a collection of practices and tools, DevOps integrates and automates the work of software development (dev) and IT operations (ops) to optimise and accelerate the system development lifecycle. Several elements of DevOps originate from the agile way of working. |
| Due diligence | DD | As part of due diligence for IT tenders, the service provider assesses the strengths and weaknesses of the subject matter of the contract and the associated risks. This assessment can relate to the employees to be taken over, the IT assets to be taken over and, above all, the efficiency of the current service provision. Due diligence is typically carried out before a binding offer is made → Section 4.7 |
| Early adopter | | The term "early adopter" was originally introduced by Everett Rogers in his diffusion theory and has since become a generally recognised term. Rogers defines five user types for the question of the adoption of technological innovations, which differ according to how quickly they adopt an innovation. Early adopters are the user group that adopts an innovation second fastest after innovators. |
| Enterprise architecture | | Is located at the management level and creates a holistic view of the importance of information technology in the company. Based on the corporate or IT vision at a strategic abstraction level, it describes how information technology supports the company's business activities. |
| Enterprise resource planning system | ERP system | Is an IT system consisting of many application modules that is used to support resource planning in the entire company. A central task of ERP in manufacturing companies is material requirements planning for an efficient production process. In addition to materials, ERP also includes the needs-based planning of capital, personnel, resources, operating resources, etc. |
| Epic | | These are summaries of the features of the service or product function, described as tasks and brief explanations of how the user experiences the value. Just like user stories, epics are written from the perspective of the end user and use their language and expression. Epics are usually more specific than common alternatives and must contain the value contribution in a measurable way. |

(continued)

**Table 8.1** (continued)

| Term | Short | Explanation |
|---|---|---|
| eXperience level agreements | XLA | XLAs are a variant of service level targets and attempt to measure the benefit of an IT service via customer satisfaction. This can be the end-user satisfaction with the service desk or the personal IT environment in the form of a school grade, as established in the industry. But it can also be more innovative metrics, such as the evaluation of a technical service for the business value of the environment by key users. |
| Feature | | Certain attributes, functionalities, or characteristics of a service. In traditional tenders, these are usually queried via requirements, in an agile environment, e.g. via user stories; in our adaptive approach, features can be included in alternative architectures. |
| First-generation outsourcing | | See outsourcing |
| Framework | | A framework is usually a collection of methods and tools in a specific context. Frameworks often offer a broad selection so that the most suitable method for a problem or the method favoured by those involved can be selected. |
| Frontend | | See backend |
| Full IT outsourcing | Full ITO | The term full IT outsourcing is used in tenders that aim to outsource the entire IT operation to a service provider. Depending on the terminology used, central IT service management functions may also remain within the organisation in the case of full IT outsourcing. The outsourcing of business processes is not usually part of full IT outsourcing → business process outsourcing (BPO). |
| Full-service provider | | This usually describes big IT service companies that offer a wide range of services. In particular, these providers operate complete IT environments for their customers. They may rely on partners for individual services or business applications. |
| Future mode of operation | FMO | In the context of outsourcing projects, FMO typically refers to the moment when the new provider takes over operations and implements changes to technology, processes, and the range of services. In most cases, the service is transferred from the existing provider. The service is then usually reorganised during the transformation process or later during operation. In the case of comprehensive outsourcing involving several transformation phases, these are sometimes numbered CMO, FMO_1, FMO_2, and so on (see also CMO). |
| Generic | | An artefact is a representative of an entire category, a particular set or a genus. We have tried to conceptualise the roles, processes, or artefacts in this book generically so that they can be applied to as many companies and situations as possible without foregrounding their specific characteristics. |

(continued)

**Table 8.1** (continued)

| Term | Short | Explanation |
|---|---|---|
| Governance | | Refers to the control and regulation system for managing, organising, and monitoring a company's IT. This includes the procedural and structural organisational framework. The term "governance" is used inconsistently in the industry, particularly with regard to its scope and distinction from operational processes. |
| Greenfield approach | | This is a solution approach in which IT services can be designed as if there were no existing services and processes. If IT services have to be planned and implemented within the context of existing services, this is referred to as a Brownfield approach. A Greenfield approach can be used to determine the potential of a new start. Some people say that Greenfield approaches no longer exist, as every organisation has some IT. In our experience, however, they do exist and can certainly be used in practice—For example, in the merger of two equally strong companies. |
| Hybrid cloud | | The hybrid cloud is a mixture of private cloud and public cloud. It is intended to combine the advantages of both cloud variants. A private cloud is a dedicated service that is set up specifically for a company. Corresponding security requirements or a specific data centre location can be implemented in a private cloud. A public cloud, on the other hand, is a shared service that accommodates several companies whose technical resources and data are shared and are only separated from each other by a multi-client capable management tool. |
| Impediment | | The term was coined in the Scrum methodology and refers to an obstacle or disruptive element in agile projects. An impediment restricts the cross-functional team in its work and can jeopardise the achievement of the defined goals. Impediments are therefore actively dealt with. |
| Incident | | In the context of IT service management, an incident is an unplanned interruption to a service or a reduction in the quality of a service. The aim of the incident management process is to eliminate the interruption as quickly as possible and restore the service.<br>A major incident (MI) is an incident that leads to significant operational disruptions. A major incident requires a response that goes beyond the routine incident management process. A special process with shorter deadlines and higher priority is used for serious incidents. This enables a faster resolution process for incidents with a significant impact on business operations. |
| Increment | | Is an actual development step on the way to the desired service. Each increment builds on all previous increments. The team ensures that all increments together are functional and ready for release. At least one increment must be created per sprint. → Section 2.4.8 |

(continued)

**Table 8.1** (continued)

| Term | Short | Explanation |
|---|---|---|
| Industrialised service | | The provision of certain managed services, the processes and interfaces involved and the services included, is not generally standardised. However, a number of best practices have emerged, meaning that many managed services are provided in a very similar way by various large IT service providers. We refer to such comparable managed services as "industrialised services", which can usually be transferred from one provider to another quickly and smoothly. |
| In-flight project | | These are projects that are firmly planned and approved within the organisation, particularly ongoing projects that have not yet been completed. Comprehensive information about these projects is highly relevant for the transition or transformation of IT services, as they represent a significant investment of time, resources, and labour for an organisation. Delays in an ongoing project could overload or divert resources needed for T&T. |
| Information security management system | ISMS | Defines and controls the measures that an organisation must take to protect the confidentiality, availability and integrity of its assets from threats and vulnerabilities. At the heart of this is information risk management, which involves assessing the risks an organisation faces in managing and protecting its assets and communicating these risks to all relevant stakeholders. |
| Information technology infrastructure library | ITIL | ITIL is a framework designed for IT organisations. Specialising in IT service management (ITSM), it provides guidelines on how to manage and control an IT organisation. It provides independent practices, processes, procedures, tasks, and checklists that can be used by any organisation, regardless of technology. ITIL has been used as the basis for professional IT operations since the early 1990s. Version 4 is currently available at (PeopleCert. 2025). |
| Insourcing | | This is a term that describes the opposite of outsourcing. It refers to the retaking of managed services by the company's own organisation. If this does not involve taking over staff and technology, insourcing essentially involves the outsourcing provider taking back all services at the end of the contract. |
| ISO 9001 | | Is a standard for systematic quality management in companies and is applicable to any organisation, regardless of type, size, products, and services. The requirements of ISO 9001 are intended to ensure that suitable processes are in place within the organisation in order to provide products and services of sufficient quality. Quality management should be subject to a continuous improvement process. |

(continued)

**Table 8.1** (continued)

| Term | Short | Explanation |
|---|---|---|
| ISO standard | ISO | Are international standards with the aim of ensuring service quality and safety and creating a framework for requirements. They define conditions for the provision of services and for the associated management systems and processes of companies. |
| ISO/IEC 20000 | | Is the international standard for IT service management. The standard was first published in 2000 and is updated on an ongoing basis. This standard supports common IT service management frameworks and related methods. ISO/IEC 20000 specifies and describes the necessary processes, including the minimum requirements, for providing and managing IT services in a defined quality. |
| ISO/IEC 27001 | | Is an international standard for information security management designed to help organisations improve the security of their data and information systems. The standard was first published in 2005 and is updated on an ongoing basis. The standard describes the requirements for the introduction, implementation, maintenance, and continuous improvement of an information security management system (ISMS). |
| IT service management | ITSM | ITSM refers to the activities with which an organisation plans, develops, provides, operates, and controls information technology (IT) services for its end users and customers. The ISO/IEC 20000 standard specifies minimum requirements for IT service management processes. |
| Iteration | | In adaptive services, a process is repeated to obtain a sequence of intermediate results that approximate a defined value proposition. Each repetition of the process is a single iteration, and the results of each iteration (increments) form the starting point for the next iteration. |
| Kanban | | The Kanban method is a production process control system based exclusively on the actual usage of materials at the point of provision and consumption. The use of Kanban can lead to a decrease in local stocks of primary products in and near production. These products are then used in products in the next integration stage.<br>The objective of the Kanban method is to control the value chain in a cost-effective manner at each stage of a multi-stage integration chain.<br>In the traditional Kanban system, Kanban cards serve as the primary control element and information carrier. These cards contain all the relevant production, storage, purchasing, and transport data from source to sink. |

(continued)

**Table 8.1** (continued)

| Term | Short | Explanation |
|---|---|---|
| Key performance indicators | KPI | Is a performance indicator used to measure the success of an organisation or specific activities such as projects, products, services, etc. KPIs are key performance indicators designed to provide an analytical basis for review and decision-making. More rarely, other metrics are also referred to as performance indicators. |
| Key results | KR | In OKRs, key results measure the achievement of objectives. A key result is usually a tangible representation of what needs to be done to achieve the objective, including a challenging yet achievable target. |
| Key user | | An end user is the main contact person in their department for the IT solutions used there. Key users provide support at the interface with IT, e.g. when reporting errors, searching for the causes of problems, acting as multipliers for training courses, advising on future developments, and much more. Key user concepts are not standardised across the industry. They have many advantages, e.g. faster resolution of incidents due to a technical language translator. However, there are also many disadvantages, e.g. key users tend to become the go-to people for all IT issues, which consumes a lot of their working time. Consequently, many companies change their area of application over time. |
| Lean-agile | | It is an umbrella term for the methods, ways of thinking and beliefs of lean management and agile frameworks. Although agile methods often utilise lean methods specifically, a lean management culture is also compatible with an agile culture in many respects. Lean-agile can be seen as a combination of both cultures. |
| Local area network | LAN | A LAN is a spatially limited network. It comprises at least two peripheral devices. It can be wired or wireless. A wireless LAN is referred to as a WLAN. |
| Longlist | | In tenders, a longlist is a comprehensive list of IT service providers invited to tender. As the process progresses, more and more providers are eliminated from this list until only a few remain, at which point it becomes a shortlist. As a rule of thumb, the initial RFI phase of a managed service should involve a maximum of 12 candidates. No more than six providers should take part in the actual competition. The shortlist typically consists of two providers with whom concrete negotiations are held, and depending on the process, one provider in a waiting position. |

(continued)

**Table 8.1** (continued)

| Term | Short | Explanation |
|---|---|---|
| Machine learning | ML | Machine learning (ML) deals with statistical algorithms that learn from data and can apply what they have learnt as a mathematical model to new data. In this way, tasks can be carried out without instructions drawn up by humans. ML can therefore process areas that are too complex for conventional analyses. Applications from the field of predictive analytics in business environments generally utilise ML technologies. ML is a sub-area of artificial intelligence. |
| Maintenance | | In IT, maintenance includes hardware and software products. It includes all measures to maintain the functionality of the components. As a rule, this also includes adaptation to changed environments, interfaces, or legal requirements. For components in an IT service, maintenance should be part of the service provided by the provider. If a service is split between the customer and provider, the maintenance contracts for the components are very important. It is essential that the contract clearly defines ownership and entitlement. A service is only operated by a provider on hardware that is covered by a maintenance contract. |
| Major incident | MI | See incident |
| Managed service | | Managed services are specific IT services that can be separated from other IT services, such as the provision of a helpdesk for a company. |
| Managed service provider | MSP | An MSP is an IT service provider that generally provides managed services for corporate customers. |
| Managed workplace | | Managed workplace services include components, maintenance, and services relating to the digital workplace. These range from the basic supply of end-user devices, such as smartphones, tablets, and PCs, with operating systems and firmware, to user-related services, such as email, office packages, collaboration software and storage space, and all integrations in office environments, such as support for telephones, printers, and meeting rooms, among many other things. |
| Method | | A method is a systematic approach to achieving a specific goal. It can be described in the form of more or less binding guidelines, rules, procedures, tools, and practices. In contrast, a methodology comprises the totality of all methods in a specific field. In practice, the terms method, methodology, and framework are not strictly separated from each other. → Section 2.6 |

(continued)

**Table 8.1** (continued)

| Term | Short | Explanation |
|---|---|---|
| Minimum viable service | | Based on the term minimum viable product (MVP) from agile software development, a minimum viable service is an early basic version of a service that fulfils certain minimum requirements for use. In particular, this service can be actively used from this point onwards and trialled in business use. In addition to further iterations, this active customer feedback enables the expansion and improvement → Section 5.2 |
| Monolithic architecture | | We speak of monolithic software and service architectures when the components of the application or service are firmly linked and mutually dependent on each other. This usually also means the complete provision of all modules and resources for a system. Monolithic architecture has been the consistent model for designing software programmes for a long time. In contrast, modern approaches are evolutionary and iterative, and include microservices architecture. |
| MoSCoW method | | The MoSCoW method can be used to prioritise the importance of fulfilling the various requirements. The acronym MoSCoW is made up of the first letters of the four priority classes: M—must have, S—should have, C—could have, W—won't have (this time). |
| Multiprotocol label switching | MPLS | Is a high-performance technology for building scalable and reliable enterprise wide area networks (WAN). MPLS assigns a short path label to each data packet. These labels determine the packet's path through the network, enabling faster and more efficient data delivery. MPLS also supports traffic prioritisation, which is crucial for real-time applications such as VoIP and video conferencing. |
| Natural language processing | NLP | NLP is essentially concerned with the support and processing of human language by computers. This involves analysing natural language data sets in order to capture the content of documents, including the contextual nuances of language. Key aspects of machine language processing are the understanding of natural communication, speech recognition and the generation of natural language. |
| Nearshore | | The term refers to the relocation of a service to a neighbouring country. This means that the operating team or project management is provided by personnel from countries that are geographically close. From a German perspective, this usually refers to relocation to EU countries, as economic, linguistic, or safety-related aspects are easier to regulate here. |
| NoCode | | The idea is that expert users without in-depth programming knowledge can create or modify an application for their own purposes. This is typically achieved through a graphical user interface that enables components to be added or modified according to a modular principle. |

(continued)

**Table 8.1** (continued)

| Term | Short | Explanation |
|---|---|---|
| North star | | In lean philosophy, the term "north star" represents a company's overarching goal, towards which its objectives are aligned. The north star provides employees with important guidance. This serves to counteract the temptation of managers to constantly change goals. This ensures a consistent goal orientation across all processes. |
| Objective | | In the OKR, an objective is an overarching qualitative goal that is clearly derived from the vision or the mid-term goals. It contributes to the vision and should provide a strong incentive to achieve this goal within a given timeframe. An example of an objective could be: "We want to become number 3 in the world in terms of sales". |
| Offshore | | Offshoring is the relocation of services abroad, usually to countries with significantly lower labour costs than in Europe. This means that operations are carried out by staff from countries several hours away by plane. From a German perspective, this usually means relocating to Asian countries. In individual cases, these can also be south American or African countries. Whether, for example, a French-speaking service desk in Morocco is considered offshore or still nearshore is not clearly defined. |
| Onshore | | The term is used in contrast to nearshore and offshore to define that a service is provided from the same country or even in close proximity (a few minutes by car). Typical reasons for onshore are a high quality of the local language, legal framework conditions or a more complex transformation of a service, e.g. the separation of services from an established IT system. |
| Operating system | OS | An operating system (OS) manages the hardware and software components of a computer and provides essential functions for integrating these components. |
| Opportunity costs | | When deciding between several alternatives that are mutually exclusive, opportunity costs are the lost profit or benefit compared to the best alternative. In the context of IT services, opportunity costs are usually compared with maintaining the status quo. An example is a low-cost IT service that is currently provided internally but limits the number of paying customers due to resource constraints. The better alternative would be an external IT service, which would not have such a bottleneck but would be more expensive. The lost profit can be interpreted as opportunity costs. |
| Outcome | | It is defined as an actual result for a stakeholder that is facilitated by one or more outputs. The benefit of the result is directly related to the change brought about by the output. The value created must be measurable in direct relation to the use of the output. Example: With the help of a new ice cream van (output) and new ingredients (output), 25% more ice cream portions were sold today (outcome). → Section 2.13 |

(continued)

**Table 8.1** (continued)

| Term | Short | Explanation |
|---|---|---|
| Output | | Is defined as the tangible or intangible result of an activity. The output is often the final, quantifiable result that is achieved upon successful completion of the project. It is usually a specific, quantifiable product or service that is formally accepted → Section 2.13. |
| Outsourcing | | It is the transfer of entire business processes or functions to an external service provider. In outsourcing, the customer pays for the benefits, but the specific costs and risks are borne by the service provider. The service provider is usually responsible for managing and developing operations.<br>First-generation outsourcing occurs when a customer has previously provided the relevant services within its own organisation and is now about to outsource these services for the first time. |
| Outtasking | | Is a sub-category of outsourcing. As the name suggests, it actually involves the client transferring individual tasks to a service provider. The client retains control over results and assignments. Extensive outtasking contracts can be justified by the fact that the client wishes to retain strong control over the execution processes. |
| Patch | | A patch is a collection of changes to an IT service. These are usually minor changes to the underlying software or configuration data. The term patch is most commonly used for updates that fix bugs or close security gaps. A patch can also contain functional updates. |
| Penalty | | This is a sum of money agreed by the two parties as compensation for any damages that may have occurred. It is part of the service level agreement set out between them. These lump sums are defined in the contract and are payable if a certain service level is not met, regardless of the actual amount of damage incurred. |
| Personal data | | Are defined in the general data protection regulation (GDPR). This is any data that can identify a natural person. This includes surname and first name, but a static IP address can also be considered personal data if it is only used by one person. |
| PRINCE2 | | PRINCE2 is a structured method for successful project management that is used worldwide in companies in various industries. It is based on seven core processes and is characterised by flexibility, efficiency, transparency, and control. → Section 2.4.3 |
| Private cloud | | See hybrid cloud |

(continued)

**Table 8.1** (continued)

| Term | Short | Explanation |
|---|---|---|
| Programme | | Is a framework under which several projects are summarised and managed. In outsourcing, for example, the transition of individual IT services could each be carried out as a project with its own project manager; these projects are then managed as a programme by the service provider and client. |
| Project | | A project is a one-off, carefully planned endeavour in which different people work together for a limited period of time to achieve a specific goal. A project can involve team members from different parts of an organisation, partner organisations and possibly external consultants. A project has a specific scope, budget, resources, and time frame. Agile projects always have at least one flexible dimension in order to develop values with a certain degree of freedom. Several projects on one topic can be part of a larger programme management. There are commercially available project management methods and the DIN 69901 series of standards. |
| Proof of concept | PoC | Is a milestone in a project or generally a feasibility analysis that checks the central requirements or values of a project. The PoC is usually accompanied by the development of a prototype with the desired main functionality. In the case of software or service projects, the PoC can also be used to test the interaction, e.g. the connection to selected interfaces or related process flows. In contrast to agile methods, which work with increments that build on each other, in classic project management prototypes can be developed separately and discarded after the PoC. |
| Provider | | This is a common term for a service provider, supplier, or vendor. In our context, it refers to an IT service provider offering everything from managed services to complete outsourcing. |
| Public cloud | | See hybrid cloud |
| Purpose | | The corporate purpose, sometimes referred to as the corporate philosophy, describes why a company exists and what it wants to achieve. It goes beyond mere profit maximisation to encompass the company's values, beliefs, and goals. For most companies, it is also an overarching mission for the world. The corporate purpose answers the 'why' and 'what for' questions about the company. |

(continued)

**Table 8.1** (continued)

| Term | Short | Explanation |
|---|---|---|
| RACI matrix | | A RACI matrix is a model that describes in tabular form the involvement of various roles in the fulfilment of tasks or results. In IT tenders, RACI matrices are usually used to describe the roles and responsibilities for operations. They describe, for example, where and how the client is involved. RACI is an acronym derived from the four key responsibilities: Responsible, accountable, consulted and informed. In IT service management, for example, the process owner is accountable for the results of the process, while the process manager is responsible for its implementation and improvement (detailed → section 4.7.3). |
| Request for information | RFI | This is a non-binding enquiry from clients to suppliers as to whether they are basically able to cover an outlined requirement under defined conditions (detailed → section 2.1) |
| Request for proposal | RFP | A call for tenders is a document that is usually created in the course of a tendering procedure. In this procedure, a public authority or company invites potential service providers to submit a bid for the procurement of an IT service. The RfP is the most important document in this procedure (detailed → section 2.1) |
| Request for quotation | RFQ | Based on a detailed description of the requirements, the client obtains a bill of quantities with a price that is as precise as possible but generally non-binding (detailed → section 2.1) |
| Requirements specification | | The requirements specification, also known as the customer requirements specification or requirements catalogue, describes the client's complete requirements for a contractor's deliveries and services.<br>The requirements in a specification sheet should be as general as possible and as specific as necessary. This gives contractors the opportunity to develop adequate solutions (e.g. software) without being restricted by overly detailed requirements. |
| Retention costs | | In the area of managed services, this refers to costs that are still incurred for a service even if this service is no longer provided or is only provided to a reduced extent. A service provider incurs costs because a service contract with a customer expires, but the staff are still involved in the reassignment of the service for some time. Costs may also be incurred for staff reductions if the service provider is unable to conclude new contracts for this service area. Retention costs can also include costs for office space, vehicles, software licences, hardware, etc. that are still payable for a certain period of time. |

(continued)

**Table 8.1** (continued)

| Term | Short | Explanation |
|---|---|---|
| Return on investment | RoI | This is a measure of a company's earning power, on the one hand, but above all for the valuation of individual investments, on the other. The return on investment is calculated from the capital employed and the profit share calculated over the useful life. In particular, the amortisation period is taken into account. The calculation is clear in principle, but the parameters and rules differ from company to company. In addition, there is room for interpretation in the case of services, which are assessed inconsistently. |
| Roadmap | | We use the term roadmap as a visual overview of how potential values can develop. The roadmaps in our method fill in backlogs, for example, or provide a development direction. In our method, they do not contain any planning of specific steps or activities → Section 5.1. |
| Robotic process automation | RPA | RPA is usually automation at a human–machine interface using a software algorithm. The operator's input is taken over or supported by a software robot at a point belonging to a user interface. This can lower the barrier to the use of automation in products that would otherwise not offer application programming interfaces (APIs) for this purpose. The technology of these RPA agents may or may not be AI-based. Automations that use APIs or scripting extensions of applications are not labelled with the term "robot". |
| Service capability | | Includes the ability of an IT service to be operated in such a way that the required service levels can be met. Service capability includes the ability to install, configure, monitor, and uninstall a service or an associated software product. Being able to identify errors during operation, analyse the causes of problems or carry out maintenance work. |
| Service commencement date | SCD | This is the switchover date at the end of a transition or transformation project, from which the new provider assumes full responsibility for a managed service. Depending on the service and situation, the new provider may be authorised to provide parts of the service before this date or, less frequently, the old provider may continue to provide support after the SCD. In addition to the term service commencement date, the term go live date is also used. |
| Service integration and management | SIAM | SIAM is a holistic process for integrating IT service providers, which forms a bracket around the individual providers in order to manage a closed, business-oriented IT organisation. The aim is the seamless integration of interdependent services from different internal and external service providers to create consistent services in order to fulfil the specialist business requirements. |

(continued)

**Table 8.1** (continued)

| Term | Short | Explanation |
|---|---|---|
| Service level agreement | SLA | An SLA is essentially a complete service contract between a service provider and a customer. In it, key features of the service such as scope of service, quality, availability, obligations, and duties to co-operate are agreed. Colloquially, the term SLA is also only used for the core element, the service level targets, of such an agreement. These describe the scope of services in KPIs and their measurement. |
| Service level target | | See service level agreement |
| Service portfolio management | | Systematic management of IT investments, projects and activities of companies and service providers. This includes the continuous development of all services operated by the internal or external service provider. The aim is to provide the right mix of services with an appropriate investment volume in order to achieve the desired business results. |
| Service request | SR | Is a formal enquiry from a user for something that is to be provided. A service request is typically triggered by a user who needs new hardware, new software on their PC, user rights for an IT system or a reset password, for example. Service requests are usually provided via a user portal. |
| Shadow IT | | Shadow IT refers to information systems that are operated without the knowledge of the responsible IT department. Shadow IT often arises out of frustration with bureaucracy, long waiting times or high internal costs. Naturally, the rules of proper IT operations are disregarded, which often leads to data protection problems, security problems, compliance conflicts, etc. in the past, people often talked about the server under the desk, but today it is more likely to be the decentralised cloud systems purchased with the company credit card. |
| Shared service | | Refers to the way in which a service provider delivers a managed service. In contrast to a dedicated service, where employees and systems are used exclusively for one customer, with a shared service the resources are divided between the customers. The type of division is very important: There are scenarios in which, for example, one team is responsible for three customers from different sectors. However, there are also highly industrialised services in which employees carry out individual activities for a large number of customers in a time split. |

(continued)

**Table 8.1** (continued)

| Term | Short | Explanation |
|---|---|---|
| Shift-left | | The principle of shifting the processing of tasks to the beginning of a process chain wherever possible. In service management, shift-left is primarily known from the service desk. Here, for example, the aim is to resolve faults during a user's call using solution scripts or automated processes instead of recording them and having them resolved by teams of technicians. Shift-left can even go so far that human intervention is no longer necessary, e.g. for a password reset in the self-service portal. However, shift-left is also an important optimisation principle for more specialised technical functions, as it helps to save on personnel costs. |
| Shortlist | | See longlist |
| Silo | | The term "silo" is used in the corporate world to describe a situation in which departments or teams within an organisation are isolated from each other and have little or no exchange of information and knowledge. Silos can be functional, hierarchical, or geographical. |
| Software-defined wide area network | SD-WAN | Is a modern approach to managing wide area networks (WANs) that uses software-based technologies. It allows organisations to securely connect users to applications by intelligently directing traffic across multiple connection types, such as MPLS, broadband, and wireless communication, based on real-time network conditions and business policies. |
| Stakeholder | | Stakeholder is a common term for entitled parties and refers to persons or groups who have a legitimate interest in the course or outcome of a change, the introduction of a service, a process or a project. Typical stakeholders of a company are, for example, employees, the works council, customers, suppliers, and so on. |
| Sunk-costs fallacy | | A common behaviour based on cognitive bias is sticking with a project in which a lot of time and effort has already been invested, even if the upcoming expenses are too high in relation to the expected result. |
| System specification | | The system or functional specification describes the contractor's approach to fulfilling the client's requirements in detail. This includes both the realisation method and the means to be used. The client defines all the requirements for the product to be developed or produced in advance in the specifications. The contractor implements the solutions described in the specifications after they have been accepted by the client. |

(continued)

**Table 8.1** (continued)

| Term | Short | Explanation |
|---|---|---|
| Technical debt | | In IT, 'technical debt' is a common metaphor for the potential consequences of the poor implementation of software. IT specialists use this term to emphasise to managers and other stakeholders in software projects that delaying improvements to technical quality slows down development. Technical debt can also arise from the ageing of hardware elements and interfaces. → Section 6.2. |
| Temporary employment | | Refers to work arrangements that have a set end date. These arrangements often involve fixed-term contracts, project-based work or seasonal labour. The employer's rights and obligations generally lie with the hirer. The employer's right to issue instructions and the duty of care are transferred to the hirer, who can arrange the specific workplace and working methods and must also ensure safety in the workplace and equal access to company social facilities. |
| Top-down | | See bottom-up |
| Trace files | | A trace file is a log file that records detailed information about the execution of a programme or system. It is more detailed than the log file. It is used to diagnose errors, analyse performance and track the behaviour of the software. |
| Transformation | T&T | In contrast to a transition, a transformation usually involves major changes compared to the current state. For example, the transition from an internally developed service to an industrialised managed service from a provider is usually a transformation, as processes, interfaces, communication channels, etc. are changed. A transformation can be designed before a service is taken over or as a planned changeover during the term of the contract. The generic term "transition and transformation" (T&T) is often used. |
| Transition | | In the context of managed services, this typically refers to a transition project involving the changeover of services from one provider to another. Essentially, it is a specialised IT project for which the new provider should have a number of standardised methods, particularly for industrialised services. Depending on the scope, the transition period begins three to twelve months before the changeover from the old to the new provider. Unlike a transformation, in a transition the service and all processes are essentially taken over as they are. |
| Use case | | A use case describes a summary of all potential scenarios that can occur when an actor attempts to achieve a specific business goal with the help of the system under consideration. It describes the content-related events that can occur when attempting to achieve the goal and abstracts from specific technical solutions. The result of the use case can be a success or a failure/cancellation. |

(continued)

**Table 8.1** (continued)

| Term | Short | Explanation |
|---|---|---|
| User story | | Are the smallest elements that describe a value for a user. They explain the functions or features of a service from the end user's point of view in their language and expression. Often in the form "as a business traveller, I would like to receive an electronic pre-invoice to check that all details are correct". |
| Variety | | In information theory, this refers to the expansion of a system's range of actions and modes of communication. For instance, a team of specialists can analyse a specific problem area from different perspectives. An additional technician can either contribute the same knowledge or cover additional areas. In the latter case, the team's variety increases. |
| Vendor management | | Also known in ITIL as supplier management. These are procedures that ensure the selection of the right IT service providers for certain services and products. In existing relationships, this practice ensures that all suppliers fulfil their contractual obligations. |
| VUCA | | VUCA is a framework within which organisations can interpret the challenges and opportunities of an increasingly complex multilateral world. The letters have the following meaning:<br>• Volatility refers to the rapid and unpredictable nature of change<br>• Uncertainty refers to the unpredictability of events<br>• Complexity stands for interlocking factors that make causal relationships unclear<br>• Ambiguity refers to unclear realities and the danger of misunderstandings |
| Waterfall model | | Is a process model that divides development activities into linear, successive phases. Each phase focuses on a particular specialisation of the task and depends on the results of the previous phase. One phase ends and its result establishes the next cascade, like stairs in a waterfall. Almost all waterfall models provide for a return to previous phases and thus a new start, but not an iteration that builds on existing results. |
| Workaround | | Is a diversion that avoids a technical system's known faulty behaviour. It is an auxiliary procedure that does not solve the actual problem, but instead works around its symptoms, requiring additional effort. A workaround is usually a temporary solution until the actual cause of the problem has been resolved. |
| Workplace | | See managed workplace |
| XLA | | See eXperience level agreements |

# Reference

PeopleCert. (2025). https://www.peoplecert.org/Frameworks-Professionals/ITIL-framework. Retrieved 7 Jul 2025 from https://www.peoplecert.org/Frameworks-Professionals/ITIL-framework

MIX
Papier aus verantwortungsvollen Quellen
Paper from responsible sources
FSC® C105338

If you have any concerns about our products,
you can contact us on
**ProductSafety@springernature.com**

In case Publisher is established outside the EU,
the EU authorized representative is:
**Springer Nature Customer Service Center GmbH**
**Europaplatz 3, 69115 Heidelberg, Germany**

Printed by Libri Plureos GmbH
in Hamburg, Germany